MISCELLANEA
NEOTESTAMENTICA

VOLUMEN ALTERUM

SUPPLEMENTS TO
NOVUM TESTAMENTUM

VOLUME XLVIII

LEIDEN
E. J. BRILL
1978

MISCELLANEA NEOTESTAMENTICA

STUDIA
AD NOVUM TESTAMENTUM PRAESERTIM PERTINENTIA
A SOCIIS SODALICII BATAVI
C. N.
STUDIOSORUM NOVI TESTAMENTI CONVENTUS
ANNO MCMLXXVI
QUINTUM LUSTRUM FELICITER COMPLENTIS
SUSCEPTA

EDENDA CURAVERUNT

T. BAARDA • A. F. J. KLIJN • W. C. VAN UNNIK

VOLUMEN ALTERUM

LEIDEN
E. J. BRILL
1978

ISBN 90 04 05686 6

PRINTED IN BELGIUM

CONTENTS

LIST OF ABBREVIATIONS

ACR	*Australian Catholic Record*
AIHI	Archives internationales d'histoire des idées
Akten IKBS	*Akten des ... Internationalen Byzantinisten-Kongresses*
AnBib	*Analecta Biblica*
ANTT	Arbeiten zur neutestamentlichen Textforschung
AThANT	Abhandlungen zur Theologie des Alten und Neuen Testaments
BBB	Bonner biblische Beiträge
BEThL	Bibliotheca ephemeridum theologicarum Lovaniensium
Bib	*Biblica*
BIH	Bibliographisches Institut Hochschultaschenbücher
BJRL	*Bulletin of the John Rylands Library*
BNTC	Black's New Testament Commentaries
BSt(F)	Biblische Studien (Freiburg)
Bijdr	*Bijdragen, Tijdschrift voor Philosophie en Theologie*
BZ	*Biblische Zeitschrift*
CBG	*Collationes Brugenses et Gandavenses*
CB.NT	*Coniectanea biblica, New Testament Series*
CBQ	*Catholic Biblical Quarterly*
CChr	Corpus Christianorum
CChr.SL	Corpus Christianorum. Series Latina
CHaer	Corpus Haereseologicum
CNT(K)	Commentaar op het Nieuwe Testament (Kampen)
Conc	*Concilium*
COT	Commentaar op het Oude Testament
CSCO	Corpus Scriptorum Christianorum Orientalium
CSEL	Corpus Scriptorum Ecclesiasticorum Latinorum
CSHB	Corpus Scriptorum Historiae Byzantinae
CUFr	Collection des Universités de France
EHPhR	*Études d'histoire et de philosophie religieuses*
Eranos	*Eranos, Acta Philologicae Suecana*
ET	*Expository Times*
ÉtB	Études bibliques
EThL	*Ephemerides theologicae Lovanienses*
EvTh	*Evangelische Theologie*
Exp	*The Expositor*
FGNK	Forschungen zur Geschichte des neutestamentlichen Kanons
FThSt	Freiburger Theologische Studien
FTS	Frankfurter Theologische Studien
GNT	The Greek New Testament
GThT	*Gereformeerd Theologisch Tijdschrift*
HNT	Handbuch zum Neuen Testament
HTC	Herder's Theologischer Kommentar zum Neuen Testament
ICC	The International Critical Commentary

IDB	Interpreter's Dictionary of the Bible
JA	*Journal Asiatique*
JBL	*Journal of Biblical Literature*
JBW	*Jahrbücher der biblischen Wissenschaft*
JJS	*Journal of Jewish Studies*
JMUEOS	*Journal of the Manchester University Egyptian and Oriental Society*
JRAS	*Journal of the Royal Asiatic Society of Great Britain and Ireland*
JThS	*Journal of Theological Studies*
Kairos	*Kairos. Zeitschrift für Religionswissenschaft und Theologie*
KatBl	*Katechetische Blätter*
KBANT	Kommentare und Beiträge zum Alten und Neuen Testament
KEK	Kritisch-exegetischer Kommentar über das Neue Testament
KeTh	*Kerk en Theologie*
KNT	Kommentar zum Neuen Testament
LeDiv	*Lectio Divina*
LV(B)	*Lumière et Vie (Brugge)*
MBPF	Münchener Beiträge zur Papyrusforschung und antiken Rechtsgeschichte
MGWJ	*Monatsschrift für Geschichte und Wissenschaft des Judentums*
MSSNTS	Monograph Series. Society for New Testament Studies
Muséon	*Le Muséon*
NBG	Nederlandsch Bijbelgenootschap
NedThT	*Nederlands(ch) Theologisch Tijdschrift*
NGWG.PH	Nachrichten von der Gesellschaft der Wissenschaften zu Göttingen, Philologisch-Historische Klasse
NHS	Nag Hammadi Studies
NJKA	*Neue Jahrbücher für das klassische Altertum (etc.)*
NLC	New London Commentary on the New Testament
NT	*Novum Testamentum*
NTA	Neutestamentliche Abhandlungen
NTS	*New Testament Studies*
NT.S	Supplements to Novum Testamentum
OrChr	*Oriens Christianus*
OrChrA	Orientalia christiana analecta
ParPass	*La Parola del Passato*
PBA	Proceedings of the British Academy
PCB	Peake's Commentary on the Bible
PG	Patrologia Graeca
Pharus	*Pharus, katholische Monatsschrift für Orientierung in die gesammten Pädagogik*
PL	Patrologia Latina
PLB	Papyrologica Lugduno-Batava
PO	Patrologia Orientalis
PUD	Publications de l'Université de Dyon
RAC	Reallexikon für Antike und Christentum
RB	*Revue Biblique*
RE	Realencyklopädie für protestantische Theologie und Kirche
RevSR	*Revue des sciences religieuses*

RSR	*Recherches de science religieuse*
RThPh	*Revue de théologie et de philosophie*
SC	Sources chrétiennes
SCP	Scriptores Christiani Primaevi
Scrip	*Scripture, Quarterly of the Catholic Biblical Association*
SGKA	Studien zur Geschichte und Kultur des Altertums
SPAW.PH	Sitzungsberichte der Preussischen Akademie der Wissenschaften Berlin, Philosophisch-historische Klasse
StANT	Studien zum Alten und Neuen Testament
StC	*Studia Catholica*
StT	Studi e Testi
StUNT	Studien zur Umwelt des Neuen Testaments
ThLBl	*Theologisches Literaturblatt*
ThLZ	*Theologische Literaturzeitung*
ThQ	*Theologische Quartalschrift*
ThR	*Theologische Rundschau*
ThStKr	*Theologische Studien und Kritiken*
ThWNT	*Theologisches Wörterbuch zum Neuen Testament*
ThZ	*Theologische Zeitschrift (Basel)*
TTh	*Tijdschrift voor Theologie*
TU	Texte und Untersuchungen zur Geschichte der altchristlichen Literatur
UMS.HS	University of Michigan Studies, Humanistic Series
UnSa	*Unam Sanctam*
VAKMF	Veröffentlichungen der Alexander Kohut Memorial Foundation
VD	*Verbum Domini*
VigChr	*Vigiliae Christianae*
VoxTh	*Vox Theologica*
VT	*Vetus Testamentum*
WI	*Welt des Islams*
WThJ	*Westminster Theological Journal*
ZÄS	*Zeitschrift für ägyptische Sprache und Altertumskunde*
ZNW	*Zeitschrift für die neutestamentliche Wissenschaft (und die Kunde der älteren Kirche)*
ZPE	*Zeitschrift für Papyrologie und Epigraphik*
ZThK	*Zeitschrift für Theologie und Kirche*

THE YEAR OF THE DEATH OF HEROD THE GREAT
(Τελευτήσαντος δὲ τοῦ Ἡρῴδου ..., Matthew ii 19)

J. VAN BRUGGEN

1. *The importance of the subject*

The year of the death of Herod the Great is not only of importance for the chronology of this king and his successors. It appears from the New Testament that the Lord Jesus was born *before* Herod had died (Matthew ii 1; Luke i 5), and that, after Herod's death, He returned from Egypt to which His parents had fled with Him because of Herod's threat (Matthew ii 13, 19). Since we have little data available to determine the date of the Saviour's birth, it is important for the chronology of the New Testament to fix the date of Herod's death as accurately as possible. This is even more significant because another datum that could be used here, namely, the enrollment by or in the time of Quirinius of Palestine's population (Luke ii 1-3), is particularly difficult to date due to various problems surrounding this census and the life of Quirinius. It is preferable to approach the chronology of Jesus' birth from a less vague starting point than this enrollment, so that the date of Herod's death becomes the key for this chronology.

2. *The necessity of this discussion*

Under the influence of the monumental work of SCHÜRER, the communis opinio in the first half of the twentieth century was that Herod the Great died a few days after 1 Nisan 4 a.n.[1] Simplified, the argumentation for this date amounts to the following: Josephus says that Herod died 37 years after he was appointed king in Rome and 34 years after he recaptured Jerusalem from Antigonus. The senate appointed Herod to be king in 40 a.n. and he recaptured Jerusalem in 37 a.n. Because Josephus, according to SCHÜRER,[2] counts the years of

---

[1] E. SCHÜRER, *Geschichte des jüdischen Volkes im Zeitalter Jesu Christi* I, Leipzig ⁴1901, 415 n. 167.

[2] E. SCHÜRER, *o.c.*, 415 n. 167. SCHÜRER presumes that the usage of Josephus' counting corresponds with what the Mishna writes in *Rosh-Ha-Shana* 1, 1: "There are four new year's days: Nisan the 1st is the new year for kings and feasts..." SCHÜRER, however, does not cite what follows, from which it appears that the Mishna *also* knows of a new year's day for kings on 1 Tishri. Probably with this, non-Jewish kings are thought of. Did Josephus, if he already knew and followed the rule of the Mishna,

the reigns of Israel's kings from 1 Nisan, the year in which Herod died
must have been 1 Nisan 4 a.n. — 1 Nisan 3 a.n. Now he died shortly
before a passover feast, which means that his death occurred in the
beginning of Nisan 4 a.n. This concurs with the fact that, shortly
before his death, a lunar eclipse took place (March 12/3, 4 a.n.).

The only unsatisfactory aspect of this argumentation is that Josephus counts the few days which the dying Herod must have lived in
the month Nisan 4 a.n. as the 34th or 37th year of his reign. However,
if one postulates that he died a year later, then the datum of the lunar
eclipse is missing. Not until January 9, 1 a.n. does another eclipse
take place. In itself, the time period between January 9th and the
next passover feast would agree very well with the events which
preceded Herod's death. However, even if one assumes that Josephus
follows the "accession-year-method"[3] in counting Herod's years of
reigning, one still does not come to 1 Nisan 2 a.n. — 1 Nisan 1 a.n.
(Herod then could have died *before* 1 Nisan), but to 1 Nisan 3 a.n. — 1
Nisan 2 a.n. Nevertheless, in 1966, W. E. FILMER still proposed to use
the "accession-year-method" but at the same time to assume that
Herod was not appointed king in 40 a.n., but in 39 a.n., and that he
recaptured Jerusalem only in 36 a.n. (not in 37 a.n.). By placing the
beginning of Herod's kingship a year later and at the same time
applying the "accession-year-method", FILMER bridges the gap between
4 a.n. and 1 a.n. and defends the postulation that Herod died in the
first months of 1 a.n.[4]

FILMER's thesis was challenged by T. D. BARNES in 1968.[5] He states
that placing the date in 1 a.n. leads to unsolvable confusion in the
chronology of Herod's successors, while it is also impossible that
the process concerning Herod's testament in Rome would have taken
place in the year 1 a.n. On the other hand, BARNES senses the
unsatisfactory aspects of placing the date of Herod's death a few days
after 1 Nisan. He thinks that there will be more room for the
development of the events between Herod's death and the next passover

---

consider the kings from the house of Herod as kings *from* Israel or as kings *over*
Israel? This is relevant for the counting of the years.

[3] By "accession-year-method" is meant the counting of the years of reigning, of
which the first full calendar year of a king counts as his first year. The preceding
part of a calendar year, between the day of accession to the throne and the next new
year's day, is not counted. As "accession-year", it is excluded from the counting.

[4] W. E. FILMER, The Chronology of the Reign of Herod the Great, *JThS* (NS)
17 (1966), 283-298.

[5] T. D. BARNES, The Date of Herod's Death, *JThS* (NS) 19 (1968), 204-209.

feast if one proceeds from an earlier lunar eclips (September 15, 5 a.n.) and sets Herod's death on 7 Kislev (December 5 a.n.).[6] Josephus' remark that the passover feast was near should, then, not be taken to be too precise.[7]

The discussion FILMER-BARNES, even if it turns out in favour of setting the date of Herod's death before the passover feast of 4 a.n., still has as consequence' that SCHÜRER's generally accepted argumentation leaves some questions. The correction which BARNES proposes is certainly not sufficiently developed. Immediately the question arises how BARNES can yet do justice to a 34 or 37-year reign of Herod, if he would have died already in December 5 a.n.

There is reason to discuss the date of Herod's death again, paying special attention to the problem of the (required) few days in Nisan 4 a.n.

3. *Method of discussion*

To determine the year of Herod's death approximately, one can proceed in two ways. It is possible to start with the beginning of his reign and take the duration of that reign, but it is also possible to calculate backward from the end of the reigns of his three successors and the duration of their respective reigns. For two reasons, the latter is recommended. Firstly, it is then possible to calculate backward along three separate lines to the year in which Herod was to have been succeeded : this strengthens the thrust of the argument. Secondly, it may be assumed that the duration of the reigns of Herod's successors has been described by Josephus at least as accurately as the reign of Herod himself, since the time of these successors was nearer to Josephus' own time : data are less likely to be vague during that time.

When it comes to determining a more precise date, the matter of the lunar eclipse and the total duration of Herod's reign can be further investigated.

A general methodical problem is how Josephus calculated the years of the rulers over Israel. Following SCHÜRER, we generally proceed from the idea that Josephus counted from 1 Nisan. However, since, in the

---

[6] According to a list of days of fasting, originating from the 1st century p.n., named *Megillat Ta'anit*, there was also a fast on 7 Kislev and 2 Shebat. No reasons for fasting, however, are given for these data. Later rabbinical tradition saw in this the days of the deaths of hated, and therefore, not mentioned kings from the latest history, namely, Herod and Alexander Jannaeus, respectively. When BARNES sets the date of Herod's death on 7 Kislev, he bases it on this later tradition.

[7] T. D. BARNES, *o.c.*, 209.

case just mentioned, this results in an unsatisfactory situation concerning Herod's last days, which, according to SCHÜRER and others, still must have fallen in Nisan, we shall also apply, each time again, the counting from 1 Tishri as working-hypothesis beside the counting from 1 Nisan, in order to discover to what results this leads. At the end of our investigation we can judge each individually to determine if one of the two countings ad hoc is preferable and if this is of significance for Josephus' counting in general.

4. *The first year of Herod's successors*

4.1. *Archelaus*

Josephus' father, Matthias, was born in the 10th year of Archelaus.[8] Archelaus, therefore, reigned *at least* 10 years, but elsewhere, it appears also that he was ethnarch *not longer* than 10 years, for in his 10th year he was called to account before Caesar due to complaints brought in and was, therefore, deposed and banished.[9] His sentence was pronounced in the summer, for, when Archelaus' steward in Rome, whose name was also Archelaus, receives Caesar's command to bring his master from Judaea, he hurries to Palestine *by sea*, upon which both return to Rome with great haste.[10] Certain events, therefore, occur during the shipping season. However, a difficulty is that Josephus mentions nine years of reigning for Archelaus in *Bellum* instead of ten.[11] Since, in two other places, he speaks about the tenth year, it is recommended to proceed from there for the time being.

Archelaus' banishment occurred in the year 6 p.n., according to the interpretation of Dio Cassius 55,27,6,[12] followed by most scholars. In this place, Dio mentions Archelaus' banishment after a remark about Achaea and it is not impossible that he here combines a few similar decisions regarding the provinces, so that there is only virtual

---

[8] Josephus, *Vita* 5.

[9] Josephus, *Antiquitates* 17, 342, 345-348.

[10] Josephus, *Antiquitates* 17, 344.

[11] Josephus, *Bellum Judaicum* 2, 111. Both in the *Antiquitates* and *Bellum*, Josephus tells about the dream which Archelaus had before the bearer of bad news arrived from Rome. He dreamt that a number of ears of corn were devoured by oxen. Diviners took this to denote that the end of his reign was approaching. The number of ears of corn corresponds with the number of years of reigning until that day. In *BJ* 2, 112 it says *nine* ears of corn and in the parallel passage, *Ant.* 17, 345, *ten* ears of corn. Therefore, in one of the two stories, Josephus has adapted the dream to correspond with the number of years of reigning cited by him.

[12] E. SCHÜRER, *o.c.*, 453 n. 13. T. D. BARNES, *o.c.*, 205. H. W. HOEHNER, *Herod Antipas* (MSSNTS 17), Cambridge 1972, 301.

simultaneity. With some hesitation, we can proceed from 6 a.n. for the time being.

Since the banishment took place in the summer, it comes *after* 1 Nisan and *before* 1 Tishri. Proceeding from 6 a.n. and 10 years of reigning means that Archelaus began his reign between 1 Nisan 4 a.n. and 1 Nisan 3 a.n. or between 1 Tishri 5 a.n. and 1 Tishri 4 a.n. However, if the banishment took place a year later, then the beginning of the reign must also be a year later. This is not entirely impossible on the basis of Dio's writing.

The problem of the 9 *or* 10 years of reigning cannot be solved if one follows the Nisan-counting, but if one maintains the Tishri-counting, it is possible to count the 10 years from the factual beginning of Archelaus' reign, immediately after Herod's death, while then the 9 years are counted from the moment when Archelaus formally began to reign after Caesar Augustus had made a decision concerning Herod's testaments. This decision, namely, was not made before 1 Tishri 4 a.n. because Caesar awaited reports from Syria concerning the developments in Palestine.[13]

4.2. *Antipas*

The year in which Antipas was deposed is not 39 p.n., as many think, but 40 p.n. It was in *that* year that he was banished shortly after August 31st.[14] There is still a coin from Antipas' 43rd year of reigning.[15] From that it appears that he reigned at least 43 years.

If we follow the Nisan-counting, a coin from the 43rd year can originate no later than in the year 1 Nisan 40 p.n. — 1 Nisan 41 p.n. because Antipas was deposed in that year. At the latest, then, he began to reign in 1 Nisan 4 a.n. — 1 Nisan 3 a.n.

If one follows the Tishri-counting, then a coin from the 43rd year can originate no later than in the year 1 Tishri 39 p.n. — 1 Tishri

---

[13] For a description of this process, compare H. W. HOEHNER, *o.c.*, 19-39.

[14] It is my intention to give the arguments for the dating of Antipas' departure in 40 p.n. in a following publication.

[15] For this coin, see H. W. HOEHNER, *o.c.*, 262, n. 4. Also discussed here is a coin which would originate in the 44th year of reigning. However, there is much controversy regarding this coin. If it indeed must be seen as a coin from the 44th year, it is possible, with the Tishri-counting, that it concerns a coin here which was minted with a view to the 44th year of Antipas' reign which was about to come. The supply for the 44th year, however, was no longer necessary, because Antipas was deposed just at the eve of his 44th year.

40 p.n. At the latest, then, Antipas began to reign in 1 Tishri 5 a.n. —
1 Tishri 4 a.n.

4.3. *Philip*

According to Josephus, Philip died in the 20th year of Tiberius,
after having reigned 37 years.[16] If Tiberius' years are counted according
to factual years of reigning, then August 19, 33 p.n. — August 18,
34 p.n. is his 20th year. If one counts according to the Julian calendar,
then the year 33 p.n. is the 20th year.

The date of Philip's death, then, falls within the years 1 Nisan
32 p.n. — 1 Nisan 35 p.n. or 1 Tishri 32 p.n. — 1 Tishri 34 p.n.
This means that he began to reign in the years 1 Nisan 5 a.n. — 1 Nisan
2 a.n. or 1 Tishri 5 a.n. — 1 Tishri 3 a.n.

4.4. *Herod's successors*

The year in which Herod's successors came to power can be shown
approximately by a summary of the data.

The last time periods mentioned were : (Philip) 1 Nisan 3 a.n. — 1
Nisan 2 a.n. or 1 Tishri 4 a.n. — 1 Tishri 3 a.n. For Antipas, however,
these time periods are ruled out. This means that the last years possible
are 1 Nisan 4 a.n. — 1 Nisan 3 a.n. or 1 Tishri 5 a.n. — 1 Tishri
4 a.n.

An earlier time period for Archelaus is not entirely ruled out,
although it is very unlikely. An earlier year is possible for Antipas.
However, for Philip, a time period *before* 1 Nisan 5 a.n. — 1 Nisan
4 a.n. or *before* 1 Tishri 5 a.n. — 1 Tishri 4 a.n. is impossible. This
means that Herod's successors came to power in the period bounded
by 1 Nisan 5 a.n. — 1 Nisan 3 a.n. A more precise date cannot be
determined until other data have been considered.

5. *The end of Herod's life*

Josephus gives an accurate report about the events at the end of
Herod's life. Of this we give a brief review in which the points important
for the chronology are included.

After Herod had discovered the conspiracy of his son and successor-
designate, Antipater, he imprisoned him and sent ambassadors to Rome
to ask permission from Caesar to execute Antipater.[17] After the
ambassadors have departed, the people hear more and more that

---

[16] Josephus, *Ant.* 18, 106.
[17] Josephus, *Ant.* 17, 146.

Herod is seriously ill, and that his condition is deteriorating. When the rumour is spread that Herod is dead, Matthias with a group of fanatical supporters ventured an attack on the eagle above the temple gate.[18] When this group is arrested, the leaders of the people at Jericho dissociate themselves from their action.[19] Nevertheless, Herod deposes the highpriest, also called Matthias, and burns the rebel Matthias and his followers alive.[20] In the night that followed, there was a lunar eclipse![21] At that time, the messengers had not yet returned from Rome. Herod goes beyond the river Jordan yet to seek a cure by taking warm baths. Upon his return to Jericho, he devises the plan to have the leaders of the Jewish people, who were gathered there, killed on the day of his own death, thus ensuring himself of lamentation.[22] It is then that the messengers return from Rome, however.[23] Very shortly thereafter, Antipater is killed.[24] Herod again alters his testament. Five days after Antipater, Herod dies.[25] After seven days of mourning, Archelaus addresses the people.[26] Soon afterwards, unrest grows. In the meantime, the passover feast, at which disturbances occur, has come near.[27]

Schematically, the events can be arranged in three series:

a) Departure of the messengers to Rome.
b) Herod's illness. Revolt. The death of Matthias and his followers. Lunar eclipse.
c) Return of the messengers. A week later Herod died. Still a week later, Archelaus addresses the people. Then the passover feast is near.

The journey of the messengers to Rome cannot have taken more than a number of months. The time between a) and c) can hardly have been more than half a year. Since the burning of Matthias and his followers took place in the course of this period, there is less than half a year between the eclipse and the passover feast. This means that the eclipse of September 15, 5 a.n. is too far removed from the

---

[18] Josephus, *Ant.* 17, 148ff.; *BJ* 1, 648ff.
[19] Josephus, *Ant.* 17, 161-164.
[20] Josephus, *Ant.* 17, 164, 167.
[21] Josephus, *Ant.* 17, 167.
[22] Josephus, *Ant.* 17, 171, 174; *BJ* 1, 657-660.
[23] Josephus, *Ant.* 17, 182ff.; *BJ* 1, 661.
[24] Josephus, *Ant.* 17, 187; *BJ* 1, 663.
[25] Josephus, *Ant.* 17, 190-191.
[26] Josephus, *Ant.* 17, 200; *BJ* 2,1.
[27] Josephus, *Ant.* 17, 213ff.; *BJ* 2, 10.

next passover feast. It also means that the eclipse of March 12/3 4 a.n. cannot be combined with the passover feast of 3 a.n. : if *this* eclipse is meant, then the passover feast of 4 a.n. must be meant.

Is the period between eclipse and passover feast sufficient? In 4 a.n. the passover feast fell on April 11. There are 30 days between eclipse and passover feast. Herod died at least 10 days before the passover feast. The messengers returned from Rome no more than 7 days before his death. The events between the eclipse and their return could easily have taken place within 10 days. From the fact that the people still mourn for Matthias and his fellow-martyrs towards the passover feast, and press for revenge for their execution, it appears that their death is still fresh in the minds of the people.[28]

6. *The duration of Herod's reign*

Herod reigned after his appointment by the senate 37 years and after the recapturing of Jerusalem 34 years.[29] These events cannot be dated earlier than 40 a.n.[30] and 37 a.n.[31] respectively, but that means that Herod, according to the Nisan-counting, must still have lived in the period 1 Nisan 4 a.n. — 1 Nisan 3 a.n. It appeared to be impossible, however, to place Herod's death *later* than 2 or 3 Nisan 4 a.n. It is even very well possible that he died just *before* 1 Nisan. It is very questionable whether the days 1 and 2 Nisan, if Herod indeed was still living then, are counted as a new year of reigning because even Herod's last *weeks* were no more than a prolonged dying process. The last deeds of his reign which are mentioned occurred a few days before his death : before 1 Nisan.

Although the Nisan-counting here does not lead to absolute insuperable difficulties, there is reason to look into the consequences of a Tishri-counting.

The whole problem of dating Herod's last days falls away if 1 Tishri 5 a.n. — 1 Tishri 4 a.n. counts as the 37th or 34th year of reigning.

This is only possible if both the recapturing of Jerusalem and the appointment by the senate occurred before 1 Tishri of the year in question. Herod laid siege to Jerusalem in 37 a.n. immediately after the winter.[32] The total duration of the siege was 5 months,[33] of

---

[28] Josephus, *Ant.* 17, 206ff.; *BJ* 2, 5ff.

[29] Josephus, *Ant.* 17, 191; *BJ* 1, 665.

[30] Josephus, *Ant.* 14, 389 mentions the consular year of Calvinus and Pollio.

[31] Josephus, *Ant.* 14, 487 mentions the consular year of Agrippa and Gallus. For Dio Cassius' dating of Jerusalem's fall, see Appendix 1.

[32] Josephus, *Ant.* 14, 465.

[33] Josephus, *BJ* 1, 351.

which the last three were in cooperation with the Roman troops under the leadership of Sosius.[34] If the siege began in February or March, then it ended in June, July or August.[35] This means that the year in which Jerusalem was reçaptured by Herod can also be described as the year 1 Tishri 38 a.n. — 1 Tishri 37 a.n. (instead of 1 Nisan 37 a.n. — 1 Nisan 36 a.n.).

Does this also apply to Herod's appointment by the senate in Rome in 40 a.n.? From a number of data it can be inferred that this appointment took place in the time of storms, not in the shipping season. SCHÜRER, therefore, places it in the *late autumn* of the year 40 a.n.[36] This would mean that it must be dated *after* 1 Tishri of this year, so that the method of calculation suggested above would not be applicable. SCHÜRER, however, must at the same time assume that Josephus makes an erroneous statement about the time of Herod's appointment as king. Josephus, namely, does not only say that he became king during the consulate of Gnaeus Domitius Calvinus and Gaius Asinius Pollio (40 a.n.), but also says that his appointment took

[34] Josephus, *Ant.* 14, 487, cf. 14, 473, 487-488. When the "third month" is mentioned in 14, 487, this refers to the third month of the siege by the *Romans*. Not Herod's, but Sosius' siege is cited here. It is also his soldiers who plunder the city after capturing it, and Josephus compares Sosius himself with Pompeius who, years earlier, had captured Jerusalem on the same day. See the following note.

[35] Sosius' recapturing of Jerusalem in June, July or August corresponds with Josephus' information that Pompeius had captured the city on the same day (*Ant.* 14, 488). Pompeius, namely, laid siege in the spring (*Ant.* 14, 53) and maintained the siege three months (*BJ* 1, 149; *Ant.* 14, 66). Pompeius' capturing of Jerusalem, therefore, also occurred in the summer. Since Josephus still places it in the 179th Olympiad which ended June 30, 63 a.n., the capture would even have to be placed before the end of June (*Ant.* 14, 66). If Herod laid siege to Jerusalem at the beginning of February 37 a.n. and if the five months were not complete, then its capture in 37 a.n. is also possible in June of that year. It is more difficult to explain how Josephus can say that the capture in 37 a.n. was exactly 27 years later than that by Pompeius. The latter is dated under the consuls, Antonius and Cicero (*Ant.* 14, 66). That is in 63 a.n. The interval amounts to 26 years. Probably, Josephus did not mean the interval here, but counted the years, including the year in which Pompeius captured the city. The day on which Jerusalem fell was a day of fasting, both in 63 a.n. and 37 a.n. (*Ant.* 14, 66, 487). Probably we can think here of a fast in the fourth month, Tammuz, in remembrance of Nebuchadnezzar's invasion of Jerusalem (Jeremiah xxxix 2; lii 6; cf. Jos. *Ant.* 10, 135) on 9 Tammuz. From Zechariah viii 19 it appears that days of fasting were known in the 4th, 5th, 7th, and 10th months. In Babylonian Jewry, 17 Tammuz was a day of fasting in remembrance of Nebuchadnezzar *and* a later desecration of the temple (*RE*³ VII, 16). A day of fasting in Tammuz would correspond with a capture by Pompeius and Sosius, resp., in June. A. SCHALIT, *König Herodes. Der Mann und sein Werk*, Berlin 1969, 761-764, assumes that the fall of Jerusalem, both in 63 a.n. and 37 a.n., occurred on a day of fasting which was proclaimed because of the siege. The dates, then, are not the same, but both times, the capture took place precisely on a day of fasting. Josephus' manner of formulation, however, makes us think of a fasting on a set date.

[36] E. SCHÜRER, *o.c.*, 355, n. 3.

place in the 184th Olympiad.[37] The fourth and last year of this
184th Olympiad ended on June 30, 40 p.n. There is reason to pay
special attention yet to the exact beginning of Herod's reign, before
a final conclusion is drawn.[38]

7. *The exact date of Herod's appointment as king*

The year of Herod's appointment as king by the senate in Rome
is certain. It is the year 40 a.n. In order to determine the exact date
within that year, one could discuss the entire chronology of Antonius'
travels in that time, the attacks of the Parthians in Syria-Palestine,
and Herod's flight to Rome. This, however, would go beyond the
framework of our subject. For the subject in discussion (Herod's year
of death), Josephus' own dating *suffices*, for when he writes that Herod
reigned 37 years after his appointment in Rome, he offers a calculated
number of years for this occasion. As a rule, Josephus counts Herod's
years from the time that King (!) Antigonus was killed by him. With
Herod's death, the *first* thing mentioned, then, is that since that time,
he reigned 34 years.[39] For the sake of completeness, Josephus then
also calculates how many years he reigned after his appointment by
the Romans. To ascertain Josephus' method of calculating in the
foregoing, we only have to note the manner in which he himself
indicates Herod's beginning elsewhere. To judge the *historical accuracy*
of his calculations, also data other than Josephus' must be discussed.
However, even if his calculations would be historically inaccurate,
that does not take away the fact that we must, when interpreting his
data, start from his *own* judgment of the time of the beginning of
Herod's reign. Therefore, we limit ourselves to the latter, because this
is decisive for our subject. We will not take into consideration here the
historical accuracy of Josephus' information about the exact date of
Herod's appointment.

The first datum of Josephus has already been mentioned. He dates
Herod's appointment in 40 a.n. before the end of the 184th Olympiad,
and so, before June 30.[40]

---

[37] Josephus, *Ant.* 14, 389.

[38] Since the decree of Herod's appointment as king was ceremoniously deposited
in the Capitol (Josephus, *Ant.* 14, 388), and since there is a good chance that Josephus
later was able to see the text of this decree in Rome, it remains a puzzle why Josephus
would make an error at exactly this point of the dating.

[39] Josephus, *Ant.* 17, 191; *BJ* 1, 665.

[40] Josephus, *Ant.* 14, 389.

The second datum is the fact that Herod sailed from Egypt to Rome in a time of storms, in which the sea is perilous.[41] He arrives in Italy, then, after surviving very stormy weather.[42] For SCHÜRER, this is a reason to think that it is late autumn, but the fact that Herod sets sail again 7 days later conflicts with this.[43] Apparently, it was not difficult to find a ship, then, prepared to undertake the journey. Josephus also does not mention problems on the journey any more, but merely writes that he was heading for Ptolemais.[44] This gives the impression that Herod arrived at the end of the winter season and departed again immediately at the beginning of the shipping season. The fact that Herod, upon his arrival in Palestine, immediately engages in various campaigns before the winter quarters would have to be occupied, agrees with this, then, too.[45] This points to an arrival in spring and not in early winter. Decisive evidence, however, we find in a passage in which Josephus mentions that Herod embarked in Alexandria towards mid-winter.[46] Since his journey was not without difficulties, he could only have reached Rome towards the end of the winter. *This* is how Josephus conceived it. This corresponds with the dating in the *first* half year of 40 a.n. and not with a dating in the autumn of that year.

The third datum, which confirms the first two, lies in Josephus' information that Herod besieged Jerusalem in the year 37 a.n. immediately after the winter was over. Then Josephus notes that, at the same time, the third year of his appointment as king by the senate in Rome also came to a close.[47] In this passage, Josephus, therefore, goes out from an appointment towards the end of the winter.

In short, we may conclude that from Josephus' various data, it

---

[41] Josephus, *Ant.* 14, 376.

[42] Josephus, *Ant.* 14, 377, 380; *BJ* 1, 280.

[43] Josephus, *Ant.* 14, 387.

[44] Josephus, *Ant.* 14, 394; *BJ* 1, 290.

[45] Josephus, *Ant.* 14, 394-405. Not until 14, 406 (cf. 14, 411, 414, 418) does the winter play a role. The same applies to Josephus, *BJ* 1, 297ff. with respect to 1, 290-296.

[46] Josephus, *BJ* 1, 279 καὶ μήτε τὴν ἀκμὴν τοῦ χειμῶνος ὑποδείσας μήτε τοὺς κατὰ τὴν Ἰταλίαν θορύβους ἐπὶ Ῥώμης ἔπλει). Cf. 1, 281 (διὰ χειμῶνος). Not only the typification of the winter time, but also the reference to the tumults in Italy make us think of the first months of 40 a.n. O. MICHEL and O. BAUERNFEIND, in their edition of *De Bello Judaico* (Vol I; München 1959, 414) give the following note (*BJ* 1, 279): "Es handelt sich um den Winter zu Beginn des Jahres 40 v.Chr. Die Unruhen in Italien beziehen sich wohl auf die Spannungen zwischen Antonius und Oktavian (41-40), die im Jahre 40 mit dem Fall Perugias wieder beigelegt wurden". See also Appendix 2.

[47] Josephus, *BJ* 1, 343 (συνήγετο δ'αὐτῷ τρίτον ἔτος ἐξ οὗ βασιλεὺς ἐν Ῥώμῃ ἀπεδέδεκτο), cf. *Ant.* 14, 465.

appears that he consciously figures from an appointment of Herod at the end of the winter of 40 a.n. This results in a dating — according to Josephus — of January or February of 40 a.n.

8. Conclusions

8.1. Herod's year of death

Herod died shortly before or shortly after 1 Nisan 4 a.n. It is not necessary to set his death *after* 1 Nisan, because the last year of his reign is considered to be the 1 Tishri 5 a.n. — 1 Tishri 4 a.n.

8.2. The years of the reigns of Herod's successors

The years of Herod's successors are counted in such a way that 1 Tishri 5 a.n. — 1 Tishri 4 a.n. is considered the first year.[48] This means that Philip's death can be more precisely determined in the year 33 p.n., namely, before 1 Tishri of that year. From this we may also conclude that Antipas did not reign longer than 43 years.[49]

8.3. Josephus' method of counting the years

The supposition that Josephus counts the years of kings over Israel from 1 Nisan in each year is untenable for the chronology of Herod and his successors. With them, Josephus figured at least from 1 Tishri. This justifies the question, therefore, whether he did not also elsewhere calculate in this way.

The "accession-year-method", applied by Filmer as coming from Josephus, is certainly not used in Josephus' information regarding the duration of the reigns of Herod and his followers.

8.4. The history concerning Antonius

Since Josephus places the appointment of Herod as king in the beginning of 40 a.n., it is good to reexamine the whole history of the Antonius period in the light of this information, in order to come to a certain conclusion regarding the (in)accuracy of Josephus' dating in this matter.[50]

---

[48] An exception, probably, should be made for *BJ* 2, 111, where Josephus does not cite 10, but 9, years of reigning for Archelaus : Did his source or he himself originally calculate from the appointment by Augustus, so that 1 Tishri 4 a.n. — 1 Tishri 3 a.n. counts as the first year? Or are the 9 years net years of reigning, not calculated according to calendar years?

[49] See also note 15.

[50] See Appendix 2.

APPENDIX 1

Dio Cassius and the dating of Herod's capturing of Jerusalem

According to Josephus, Herod captured Jerusalem in 37 a.n. with the help of the Roman general, Sosius (*Ant.* 14, 487). According to many, Dio Cassius dates this same event in 38 a.n. W. E. FILMER is even of the opinion that Dio states the year 36 a.n. Because Dio Cassius can be at least as well informed about the manoeuvres of the Roman troops in the East as Josephus about the memorial days of Herod, the discrepancy noted by many between Dio Cassius and Josephus on this point is not insignificant. Upon closer examination, the thought that Dio Cassius would not set the date of the capture of Jerusalem in 37 a.n. appears to be based on a misunderstanding.

Dio Cassius, in his *Historiae* 49, 22, 3-6, describes how Antonius delegates the supreme command over Syria and Cilicia to Sosius during the time in which he will be absent because of a journey to Italy, and how this Sosius restrains the until now unsubdued Aradii and also captures Jerusalem. Then follows the information (49, 23, 1): "This happened during the consulate of Claudius and Norbanus. During the next years, the Romans did nothing in Syria worth mentioning". From this information, we may infer that Jerusalem was captured in 38 a.n. (the consulate of Claudius and Norbanus), and not in the peaceful year 37 a.n.

The information of 49, 23, 1 regarding dating, however, refers back to a larger unit and not to the immediately preceding facts in the first place. In 49, 19 up to and including 49, 33, Dio Cassius deals with the subject "Antonius and the Barbarians (the Parthians)". In 49, 18, 6, concerning Italy he had already come to the death of Octavianus' opponent, Sextus, in 35 a.n. *That* story he will continue in 49, 34, 1. However, before he can do this, he first must continue the story about the situation in the East again. In 48, 39, 1 to 48, 41, 6 he already had told about Antonius' wars in the East in the period 39 a.n. — 38 a.n., but after that, without any great interruptions, he only had followed the events in Italy. When he, with this information, has come to 35 a.n. (Sextus' death), he first turns to Antonius again and must return, then, to the year 38 a.n. Therefore, 49, 19, 1 begins with the description of Ventidius' victory over Pacorus and Antonius' siege of Samosate. These much encompassing episodes in 38 a.n. are dealt with extensively (49, 19, 1 — 49, 22, 2). After that Dio tells how Antonius departs from the East temporarily and delegates the authority to Sosius. In this connection, he mentions at the same time what Sosius did as Antonius' representative. He subdued the Aradii and captured Jerusalem: two matters which had to be finished yet after the fall of Pacorus. That Dio Cassius tells in short what Sosius achieved in the entire period of Antonius' absence appears from the fact that he ends by mentioning that Antigonus was scourged and killed by *Antonius*. Antonius can only have done this *after* his return and as the last act in the matter of Jerusalem now completed by Sosius. Therefore, when mention is made in 49, 23, 1 of the year of Claudius' and Norbanus' consulate, this information refers to the entirety of Antonius' actions, described in 49, 19, 1 to 49, 22, 2: all this happened with respect to the barbarians in 38 a.n. However, in the following year, 37 a.n., the Romans did nothing worth mentioning: i.e. they did nothing of importance over against the *Parthians* with which these chapters deal. That Dio Cassius thinks about them appears also from the fact that he continues thereafter with a number of remarks about the situation in the kingdom of the Parthians (49, 23, 2ff.). Dio Cassius does not mean to say that Sosius did nothing of importance in 37 a.n. : he already had described his (few) deeds in the preceding section. Sosius' deeds are typically those of someone who settles current affairs, but who does not initiate anything new. Aradii and Jews, the last troublesome groups in a territory just recovered, are called to order, but in 37 a.n., the Parthians are not troubled by the Romans : Antonius is absent almost the whole year.

From Dio Cassius' manner of narrating it not only appears that the fall of Jerusalem does not *have* to be dated in 38 a.n., but also that it, in fact, *should* be dated in 37 a.n. after all. Antonius returns to the East only towards the end of 37 a.n. and he is the one who kills the conquered king of Jerusalem (Antigonus). This indicates that the fall of Jerusalem should be dated not immediately after his departure, but rather, shortly before his return.

In summary, we can conlude that Dio Cassius also dates the fall of Jerusalem in 37 a.n., or that, in any case, his description does not conflict with such a dating in any way. On the basis of Dio Cassius and Josephus together, we can say with certainty that Herod captured Jerusalem in 37 a.n.

APPENDIX 2

Josephus and the dating of Herod's appointment as king

Josephus dates Herod's appointment as king in the first half of the year 40 a.n. and, more precisely, in the beginning of that half year.

At the time of Herod's appointment, both Octavianus and Antonius were present in Rome. Josephus can make no mistake at this point, because it was exactly Antonius whom Herod sought and to whose mediation he owes his kingship.

Josephus, however, must have erred in *calculating* the exact *moment*. From a review of Herod's road to kingship in Jerusalem,[51] it appears that, after the battle of Philippi (November 42 a.n.), Antonius travelled via Ephesus, Tarshish, and Antioch to Egypt, where he spent the winter of 41/40 a.n. In the early beginning of 40 a.n. he sails to Greece via Tyre. From there he goes to Brundisium, where he takes actions against Octavianus. When this conflict is settled and the threat of a new civil war has disappeared. they march into Rome together in the autumn of 40 a.n. Antonius remains in this area until the spring of 39 a.n. Then he sails to Greece. Thus, it is clear that he was not in Rome in the winterperiod of 41/40 a.n., while he indeed *did* remain there in the winter of 40/39 a.n. Herod, therefore, was appointed king during *this winter*.

One can only guess at the cause of Josephus' error. It is clear, though, that Josephus *as a rule* proceeds from the year 37 a.n. when counting Herod's years, and that he calculated the year of his appointment in Rome for a certain occasion and made an error while doing so. Josephus also mentions how Cleopatra warns Herod, when he is about to sail out of Alexandria : not only the perils of the sea in winter, but also the tumults in Italy were to restrain him (*Ant.* 14, 376). Commentators, here, think about the conflicts between Octavianus and the consul Lucius Antonius (Antonius' brother), who died after the capturing of Perusia in January or February of 40 a.n. This concurs with Josephus' dating, but not with the historical situation. However,

---

[51] Published in the *Almanak 'Fides Quadrat Intellectum' 1976*. Kampen 1976, 137-148.

it would be possible that Cleopatra meant the confrontation between Octavianus and Antonius. The situation in Italy was extremely critical at the time of the confrontation near Brundisium. The report, that both parties had suddenly come to a reconciliation in the autumn of 40 a.n., reached Alexandria only later. When Herod, shortly after this reconciliation, with winter approaching, set sail from Alexandria, he still could have reckoned with a conflict-situation between Octavianus and Antonius, and an intensifying civil war in Italy. Later on, since peace was made, the tensions between Octavianus and Lucius appeared to be more serious in retrospect than the subsequent tensions between Octavianus and Antonius, but at that time, it was not so. If Cleopatra's warning is historical — and it is not likely that Josephus devised this for the sake of his dating — then the source of confusion may be found therein. Although *she* meant the conflicts which seemed to be resulting in a fatal civil war, *others* rather may have thought of the troubles in 41 a.n., especially since it was sufficiently known that Herod crossed the sea in the *winter* : Rhodes still owes part of its restoration to this (*Ant.* 14, 378). The troubles of 41 a.n. lasted into the winter of 41/40 a.n., but those of 40 a.n. were over in the beginning of the winter. In this way, one can come to think of the winter of 41/40 a.n., as long as one does not forget that Herod, at his departure from Alexandria, did not yet know that the tensions of 40 a.n. would be settled, or meanwhile had been settled, even though news of this had not yet reached Alexandria.

Because Josephus dates the invasion of the Parthians into Syria, under the leadership of Pacorus, after the autumn of 41 a.n. (*Ant.* 14, 330), and because he, moreover, mentions only *two* winter seasons between Herod's appointment as king and the capture of Jerusalem in 37 a.n., it must be stated that a certain discrepancy exists with Josephus between the course of the events as he describes it *and* the dating of Herod's appointment as king in the beginning of 40 a.n. His description of the course of events corresponds with other historians : his dating of Herod's appointment, however, deviates from it. These findings confirm the thought that this dating was erroneously calculated by him and was not taken from sources.

In summary, we can draw *two* conclusions. (1) When interpreting Josephus' data regarding datings, we must proceed from an appointment of Herod in the beginning of 40 a.n. (2) With the description of Herod's appointment as a historical event, we should maintain a dating in the beginning of 39 a.n.

THE STORM ON THE LAKE

Mk iv 35-41 and Mt viii 18-27 in the light of Form Criticism,
"Redaktionsgeschichte" and Structural Analysis

B. M. F. VAN IERSEL AND A. J. M. LINMANS

1. *Introduction*

The about-face which has been carried out in linguistics, from an almost exclusively historical to an almost totally synchronistic and structuralist study of language, has not only occurred in the study of the single grammatical sentence but equally so in the study of texts which consist of more than one grammatical sentence. Above all a number of French structuralists and German text linguists ("Generative Poetik") have occupied themselves with the Bible because on one hand the various texts which the Bible contains can make a contribution, too, to a universally valid text grammar, and on the other hand because through this method new light can be thrown upon the text concerned and hereby the interpretation of the text can be made more fertile.

Although it is not abnormal that such reversals contain an antithetical element which often leads to polemics, it can be stated that not the French structuralists, true, but the German text scholars who apply the structural method to the New Testament, and E. GÜTTGEMANNS above all, indeed assume a very polemic stance toward the historical study of the New Testament as that appears in the form-critical and "redaktionsgeschichtliche" method. For them the form-critical and "redaktionsgeschichtliche" method is not only finished, but is also in principle irreconcilable with the structural starting points, which they consider to be the only correct ones.

Therefore it seemed to the two authors of this contribution of no little importance to study a section of a text with a parallel according to the two methods and thence to draw provisional conclusions regarding the reconcilability of the two methods.[1] To this end the story of the storm on the lake in the versions of Mk and Mt was chosen.

---

[1] For a previous confrontation of "Redaktionsgeschichte" and structural analysis cf. J. DELORME, Luc 5:1-2: Analyse structurale et histoire de la rédaction, *NTS* 18 (1971), 331-350.

2. Form-criticism and "Redaktionsgeschichte" of Mk iv 35-41

2.1. Tradition and redaction in Mk iv 35-41

In the event that Mark used a tradition in his version of the story of the storm on the lake, it is clear that it at least showed structural similarities with the so-called miracle stories. It is also clear that at least *one* element is highly salient, namely the statement of Jesus in vs. 40. Likewise this is the only miracle story in which Jesus' disciples are saved from distress, a fact which has as yet gone unnoticed as far as we know.[2]

Although almost all authors are of the opinion that the beginning of the story contains editorial elements, the efforts to trace down the editorial elements have not been very successful. Something similar also holds true for vs. 40. Nevertheless it is not difficult to indicate, with the required degree of probability, a number of editorial elements.

The opinion of K. KERTELGE that vss. 35-36 are editorial only to a very slight degree[3] is difficult to sustain. The opening words καὶ λέγει αὐτοῖς are characteristic for Mark. The same holds true presumably for διέλθωμεν and for the combination of both.[4] Furthermore a certain

---

[2] Mt xvii 24-27 and Lc v 1-11 are, structurally considered, certainly not miracle stories.

[3] K. KERTELGE, *Die Wunder Jesu im Markusevangelium*, München 1970, 91.

[4] The combination of words καὶ λέγει αὐτοῖς with Jesus as its subject occurs all together in the frequency 5/22/0. Calculated according to the total number of words in the narrative text (5868/5909/7647) the expected frequency would be 8.2/8.2/10.16 and the deviation from this in Mt —3.2 (39%), in Mk +13.8 (168%), in Lc —10.6 (100%). If one takes only the cases in which the three immediately succeed each other (and thus function somewhat as a set formula), then the frequency is 5/16/0. The expected frequency is then 6.3/6.4/8.3 and the deviation in Mt is —1.3 (20%), in Mk +9.6 (150%), in Lc —8.3 (100%). (Worthy of notice is the fact that the combination occurs only once in two parallel sections of texts, namely Mt xxii 20 par. Mk xii 16).

The cohortative occurs in the following cases :

Mt			xxi 38; xxi 38; xxvi 46; xxvii 49.	
Mk	i 38; iv 35; ix 5;	xii 7;	xiv 42; xv 36.	
Lc ii 15; ii 15;	viii 22; ix 33; xv 23; xx 14.			

The frequency is 4/6/6. Calculated at the total extent of the direct discourse, which contains 12472/5353/11800 words (the cohortative does not occur outside of this), the expected frequency is 6.7/2.9/6.4 and the deviation from that in Mt is —2.7 (40%), in Mk +3.1 (106%), in Lc —0.4 (6%). Calculated at the total number of verbs in the direct discourse (2582/1174/2615) the deviation is almost identical. The expected frequency is then 6.5/2.9/6.6 and the deviation in Mt —2.5 (38%), in Mk +3.1 (106%), in Lc —0.6 (9%). The low numbers make it impossible, however, to express more than a conjecture here.

The combination of the introductory formula with the cohortative occurs exclusively in Mk i 38; iv 35 (diff. Lc viii 22); xiv 41-42 par.; Mt xxvi 45-46. The cohortative in these four cases is of a verb which expresses movement.

degree of tension exists within the two sentences because in vs. 35 Jesus takes the initiative for the crossing while in vs. 36 the disciples are the ones who take Jesus with them in the boat. Precisely the initiative of Jesus is one of the elements which make the story resemble that of Mk vi 45ff. and viii 13ff. This is also true in part for ὀψίας γενομένης (cf. vi 47). Finally, there is likewise a certain degree of incongruency between the beginning and the end of the story. Indeed the question in vs. 41 is less appropriate in the mouth of the disciples. In the only other miracle story which ends with such a question it forms a true "Chorschluss" uttered by those present (Mk i 27 par; Lk iv 36). Thus, there is sufficient reason to assume that vs. 35 comes entirely from Mark himself. In vs. 36 some text elements occur which establish the connection with iv 1, namely ἀφέντες τὸν ὄχλον, ὡς ἦν and the article before πλοίῳ. These, too, are probably due to redaction by Mark. The tradition would begin, then, with the words καὶ παραλαμβάνουσιν αὐτὸν ἐν πλοίῳ, καὶ ἄλλα πλοῖα ἦν μετ' αὐτοῦ. This implies that the original miracle story did not tell about Jesus' disciples but about anonymous passengers who crossed the lake together with Jesus, as G. SCHILLE has already proposed, albeit on other grounds.[5]

It is not difficult to recognize the hand of Mark also in vs. 40 if one follows the reading οὔπω ἔχετε πίστιν, which is qualified by *The Greek New Testament* (edited by K. ALAND a.o.) as "virtually certain". Indeed the word οὔπω taken alone already indicates the hand of Mark. It occurs in the frequency 2/5/1, while the two cases in Mt coincide with two in Mk (Mt xvi, 9 par. Mk viii, 17; Mt xxiv, 6 par. Mk xiii 7) and the only instance in Lk occurs in his Sondergut (Lk xxiii 53; further still in Mk iv 40; viii 21; xi 2). At the beginning of an interrogative sentence in the second person plural οὔπω occurs three times in Mk (iv 40; viii 17.21) and once in a parallel text in Mt (Mt xvi 9 par. Mk viii 17), always bearing a relation to the lack of comprehension in Jesus' disciples, a point so characteristic for Mark. The rest of vs. 40 shows no editorial traces. The position, however, is still strange. One can surmise that καὶ εἶπεν αὐτοῖς, Τί δειλοί ἐστε; stood originally between vs. 38 and vs. 39 and that Mark displaced this question and added on to it in order to bring it out in full relief, since right after Jesus' intervention οὔπω ἔχετε πίστιν; especially assumes a much sharper tone.

---

[5] G. SCHILLE, Die Seesturmerzählung Markus iv 35-41 als Beispiel neutestamentlicher Aktualisierung, *ZNW* 56 (1965), 31.

2.2. The pre-given miracle story

The original miracle story, then, sounded approximately as follows :

36a καὶ παραλαμβάνουσιν αὐτὸν ἐν πλοίῳ,
   b καὶ ἄλλα πλοῖα ἦν μετ᾽ αὐτοῦ.
37a καὶ γίνεται λαῖλαψ μεγάλη ἀνέμου,
   b καὶ τὰ κύματα ἐπέβαλλεν εἰς τὸ πλοῖον,
   c ὥστε ἤδη γεμίζεσθαι τὸ πλοῖον.
38a καὶ αὐτὸς ἦν ἐν τῇ πρύμνῃ
   b ἐπὶ τὸ προσκεφάλαιον καθεύδων·
   c καὶ ἐγείρουσιν αὐτὸν,
   d καὶ λέγουσιν αὐτῷ,
   e Διδάσκαλε, οὐ μέλει σοι ὅτι ἀπολλύμεθα;
40a καὶ εἶπεν αὐτοῖς,
   b Τί δειλοί ἐστε;
39a καὶ διεγερθεὶς ἐπετίμησεν τῷ ἀνέμῳ
   b καὶ εἶπεν τῇ θαλάσσῃ, Σιώπα, πεφίμωσο.
   c καὶ ἐκόπασεν ὁ ἄνεμος,
   d καὶ ἐγένετο γαλήνη μεγάλη.
41a καὶ ἐφοβήθησαν φόβον μέγαν,
   b καὶ ἔλεγον πρὸς ἀλλήλους,
   c Τίς ἄρα οὗτός ἐστιν
   d ὅτι καὶ ὁ ἄνεμος καὶ ἡ θάλασσα ὑπακούει αὐτῷ;

The structure of the miracle story is transparant and corresponds to a great extent to the standard structure. Vss. 36-38b describes the dire situation in which the passengers find themselves and thereby Jesus' sleep is contrasted with the raging of wind and waves. The reproach of vss. 38c-38e implies a request for help with the reproachful counter-question of Jesus in 40a-b. Vss. 39a-b gives Jesus' intervention and vs. 39c-d its effect, while vs. 41 can be considered as a so-called Chorschluss. Only the question of Jesus in vss. 40a-b still disrupts the structure of a miracle story. For the rest, the construction is very well-balanced.

It is striking that the miracle story does not tell of the saving of Jesus' disciples but of anonymous passengers. It is incorrect, then, to see it as an epiphany story or a natural miracle. It is less a matter of subduing the wind and waves and more a matter of saving people from an imminent shipwreck, caused by storm.

Furthermore it can be said that the story has a strong christological touch. Although the story attracts attention because of the complete anonymity — neither the miracle worker nor the other passengers are mentioned by name — it nevertheless does concern a name. The partial parallelism with Jonah I is hereby of essential importance. The fact that it was intended for this story to be read in the light of this O.T. story is evident not only in a number of noteworthy corresponding details but also in the correspondence of the total situation.[6] In both cases there is a connection between the imminent shipwreck and a prophet sleeping on board. The stilling of the storm, too, is related to the prophet, although in differing ways. In Jonah I the storm is stilled after the prophet is thrown overboard and in the miracle story by the fact that the prophet intervenes and subdues sea and wind with his powerful word. Jonah I, thus, concerns a disobedient prophet and the miracle story concerns an obedient prophet. The miracle story could be an elaboration on the words καὶ ἰδοὺ πλεῖον Ἰωνᾶ ὧδε, which we read in Mt xii 41 par. Lk xi 32, and which could function as the answer to the question in vs. 41.

The connection with the Jonah story also makes it improbable that the Sitz im Leben should be sought in a milieu other than a Judaic-Christian one. The choice between a Palestinian and a Hellenistic milieu is less easily determined. Although the story would fit in quite well in a θεῖος ἀνήρ — tradition, true indications of a hellenistic milieu are absent. One can indeed say that the paratactic sentences, the relatively numerous cases of the impersonal plural (vss. 36.38.41), the unrelated imperatives in vs. 39, the interrogative pronoun in vs. 40, and ὅτι and φοβέομαι φόβον μέγαν in vs. 41 indicate rather a milieu whose native tongue was not Greek but Aramaic. Thus the chance of a Palestinian tradition is greater than a non-Palestinian tradition.

2.3. *The editorial elements in Mk iv 35-41*

Although the editorial additions are few in number they nevertheless have a great effect. First of all by both the position as well as by the changes the result is achieved in the beginning that the story no longer concerns an anonymous group of travellers, but rather Jesus and the disciples. Subsequently the situation, too, is changed by Jesus

---

[6] Cf. X. LÉON-DUFOUR, *Études d'évangile*, Paris 1965, 175-177; otherwise K. KERTELGE, *o.c.*, 96; M. E. BOISMARD, *Synopse des quatre évangiles en français* II, Paris 1972, 196-197 is of the opinion that the similarities are the greatest in Mt. One should note, however, that φοβέομαι φόβον μέγαν in the LXX occurs exclusively in Jonah i 10 (cf. vs. 16) and I Macc x 8.

himself explicitly taking the initiative for the crossing. This creates the impression in the reader that Jesus himself provoked the situation which necessitates his intervention. Precisely in the accentuation of this initiative the story receives more the character of an epiphany, a demonstration of Jesus' power over wind and water, which should at least evoke the question in vs. 41.

The addition of vs. 40b does not seem unrelated to the additions in the beginning. Indeed the question as to οὔπω concerns in other cases, too, the disciples and there, too, involves their lack of understanding and trust in Jesus. The story, therefore, comes to stand on one line with Mk vi 45-52 and viii 13-21 and possibly via viii 18 with iv 10-13 and vii 17-18. The three stories which take place on the lake are closely inter-connected. This comes forward in terminological agreements[7] but especially in the theme which is central to Mk, that of the incomprehension and the lack of faith of Jesus' disciples.[8] Hereby the story of the storm becomes an important structural element in Mk. In i 16-viii 26 the incomprehension of the disciples comes to the forefront, as Th. J. WEEDEN[9] rightly observes. But this is nowhere so strongly accented as right where Jesus reveals to them the meaning of the parables (iv 10-13; vii 17-18), and where he manifests himself to them at sea (iv 35-41; vi 45-52; viii 13-21).

The story no longer functions as a miracle story. Indeed, it is not a miracle story, as HELD[10] proposes, which would have as an appendix a word of Jesus; but rather it is much more an introduction to the word of Jesus. That word attracts all the attention, just as in the other two

---

[7]

Mk iv 35-41	Mk vi 45-52	Mk viii 13-21
35 ὀψίας γενομένης	47 ὀψίας γενομένης	
35 διέλθωμεν εἰς τὸ πέραν	45 προάγειν εἰς τὸ πέραν	13 ἀπῆλθεν εἰς τὸ πέραν
36 ἀφέντες τὸν ὄχλον	45 ἀπολύει τὸν ὄχλον	13 ἀφεὶς αὐτοὺς
	45 ἐμβῆναι	13 ἐμβὰς
36 ἐν τῷ πλοίῳ	45 εἰς τὸ πλοῖον	14 ἐν τῷ πλοίῳ
37 λαῖλαψ μεγάλη ἀνέμου	48 ἄνεμος ἐναντίος	
39 ἐκόπασεν ὁ ἄνεμος	51 ἐκόπασεν ὁ ἄνεμος	
40 οὔπω ἔχετε πίστιν;	52 οὐ συνῆκαν	
		17 οὔπω ... συνίετε;
		21 οὔπω συνίετε;
	52 καρδία πεπωρωμένη	17 πεπωρωμένην ... καρδίαν

[8] Cf. especially Q. QUESNELL, The Mind of Mark, Interpretation and Method through the Exegesis of Mark vi 52, Rome 1969; K. G. REPLOH, Markus — Lehrer der Gemeinde, Stuttgart 1969, 75-86 and K. TAGAWA, Miracles et Évangile, Paris 1966, 174-185.

[9] Th. J. WEEDEN, Mark-Traditions in Conflict, Philadelphia 1971, 26-32.

[10] H. J. HELD, Matthäus als Interpret der Wundergeschichten, in : G. Bornkamm, et al., Überlieferung und Auslegung im Matthäusevangelium, Neukirchen 1961², 192.

passages, just by its unusual position in the sequence of the story. Inasmuch as one can speak of *Gattungen* of partial sequences at an editorial level, one could say that Mk iv 35-41 has a quasi-apophthegmatic structure.

Mk iv 35-41 has, too, a peculiarly powerful expressiveness. There are numerous indications that Mk was written with an eye to a situation of persecution.[11] The meaning of the passage in question in Mk comes fully to light only against this background. The exclamation of the disciples in vs. 38 Διδάσκαλε, οὐ μέλει σοι ὅτι ἀπολλύμεθα; receives its full meaning then, just as the awakening of Jesus from his sleep. This part of the story suggests associations with the way in which Israel calls upon Yahweh in times of oppression to rise up and bring salvation (Ps xliv 24-25; cf. vii 7; xxxv 23; lix 5-6; lxxviii 65-66). But the almost dispairing call to intervene because otherwise the community fears of succumbing is unmasked by vs. 40 as lack of faith.

As a consequence of this accent the attention is no longer directed to the specific christological tint. The accent lies much more on the attitude of the community to which Mark addresses himself and which he summons to faith and trust in Jesus, even when he does not make his presence felt[12] whereby the community has the feeling that it has been left in the lurch and approaches its ruination.

In the event that Mark indeed had a persecuted community in mind, there is an undeniable tension between what the disciples in the boat indeed do experience and what this community does not. Precisely because of that the intriguing question of vs. 41 can and should remain open. The answer can not be given before the resolution to bring Jesus to his fall has been carried out (iii 6; xi 18 both times with ἀπόλλυμι), and it has been made clear that Jesus' follower does not escape from a similar undoing and precisely therein gets the chance to save his life (viii 35 likewise with ἀπόλλυμι). Only when it is clear that the identity of the Son of Man entails first death and only then resurrection (viii 31-33; ix 31; x 33-34) and that this sequence is inescapable for Jesus' followers, too, (e.g. viii 34-38) can the question be answered, albeit not by words alone (viii 34). Hereby the tension continues to exist between the unprotected community and the disciples in the little boat which was saved by Jesus from going under.

---

[11] Cf. e.g. Th. J. WEEDEN, *o.c.*, 81-90.
[12] Cf. *o.c.*, 83ff.

3. *Mt viii 18-27 as an elaboration upon Mk iv 35-41 ("redaktions-geschichtlich")*

3.1. Comparison between Mt and Mk

Although we are of the opinion that the two-sources hypothesis should not be considered as dogma and should be tested continually anew, there is sufficient reason to assume that Mt viii 18-27 is dependent upon Mk iv 35-41. Due to the limited space there is no opportunity here to deal with this extensively. The main indication is indeed that vss. 26-27 presuppose that in the preceding verses mention has been made of the wind, which is not the case in Mt, but indeed in Mk (iv 37 cf. Lk viii 23). A "redaktionsgeschichtliche" reflection should start thus from a comparison with the version of Mk on one hand and on the other hand with the total conception of Mt. Again due to the limited space we can scarcely delve into this second aspect here.

Although the version of Mt is considerably longer than that of Mk and Lk nevertheless a number of elements in Mk are missing. We restrict ourselves to the main exclusions which are important for the meaning. Vss. 35-36 of Mk has been left out : the coming of evening, Jesus' word in the direct address, the dispersion of the crowd, the disciples' taking Jesus with them, and the mention of the presence of other boats. From Mk vs. 37 that the ship already is filling up with water. From Mk vs. 38 the place where Jesus sleeps and the circumstance that he sleeps on a cushion. From vs. 39 again the direct address as well as the quieting of the wind. From vs. 40 the second question of Jesus.

The following elements of Mk have been changed : From Mk vs. 35 is the proposal of Jesus to cross changed into an order (Mt vs. 18). From Mk vs. 36 the bringing along of Jesus in the boat has been changed into Jesus' embarking, followed by his disciples (Mt vs. 23). From vs. 37 the gale of wind (λαῖλαψ ἀνέμου) has become a quake (σεισμός). From vs. 38 the personal address διδάσκαλε has been changed into κύριε, while the reproach has become a prayer for salvation σῶσον. The lack of faith in vs. 40 has been changed in Mt vs. 26 into little faith. From vs. 41 the reaction of fear has been substituted by that of amazement.

The order of a number of parts in the sequence of the story has been changed. Thus the mention of the crowd in Mk vs. 36 has been brought further to the forefront (Mt vs. 18). The main transposition, however, is that of the words of Jesus, which in Mk are placed in vs. 40 after the storm and the sea have been subdued, and in Mt vs. 26, before the saving intervention has taken place.

In conclusion rather extensive additions can be indicated. Such is the case with the passage derived from Q, Mt viii 19-22 (cf. Lk ix 57-62), in which is told how Jesus talked with a scribe and "another man, one of the disciples", and in which a number of conditions are set which a disciple of Jesus must meet. This addition is connected with other revisions. First of all there is the note in vs. 23 that his disciples follow him when he embarks, which is not without relationship to the theme of vss. 19-22. Other changes, too, seem to have something to do with the circumstance that the whole text is consistently oriented toward people who followed Jesus. Thus in vs. 25 the change from a reproach into a prayer formula Κύριε, σῶσον, ἀπολλύμεθα, related to similar prayer formulas in Mt, such as Κύριε, σῶσόν με (xiv 30), Κύριε, ἐλέησον ἡμᾶς (xx 30.31) and Ἐλέησον ἡμᾶς, υἱὲ Δαυίδ (ix 27, cf. xx 30.31 which have at the end once more the address υἱὲ Δαυίδ). The disciples in the boat become well-nigh a Christian community. Also the address ὀλιγόπιστοι in vs. 26 can be related to this. Rightly therefore it is concluded that Matthew in this story wishes to confront the readers with the lot of the Christian community. Finally the addition of the logion in vs. 20 ὁ δὲ υἱὸς τοῦ ἀνθρώπου οὐκ ἔχει ποῦ τὴν κεφαλὴν κλίνῃ can be related, too, to the elimenation of the description in Mk vs. 38 ἐπὶ τὸ προσκεφάλαιον καθεύδων, which is not so compatible with this logion.

Within the added piece, vss. 19-21, too, the hand of Matthew is recognizable in a number of details. In vs. 19 one can point to προσελθὼν[13] and εἷς γραμματεὺς[14] and possibly the direct address διδάσκαλε.[15] In vs. 21 the absolute τῶν μαθητῶν,[16] while the direct address κύριε can be transmitted from the subsequent ix 61 in Lk. The reduction to two statements of Jesus enclosed within a frame — whether they be from Matthew or not — produces at any rate a striking effect. On one hand the two pieces 19-20 and 21-22 are much more clearly related to each other than in the three passages in Lk ix 57-62, and due indeed to the εἷς-ἕτερος construction in vs. 19 and

---

[13] Προσέρχομαι 52/5/10.

[14] Εἷς in the sense of τις with a noun occurs in Mt viii 19; ix 18; xviii 24; xxi 19; xxii 35; xxvi 69; Mk xii 42, i.e. in the frequency 6/1/0; εἷς with the genitive plural in the frequency 6/7/13 and with ἐκ + gen. plur. in the frequency 2/2/0.

[15] Cf. S. VAN TILBORG, The Jewish Leaders in Matthew, Leiden 1972, 130.

[16] The absolute οἱ μαθηταί occurs in the narrative text in the frequency 33/6/9.

vs. 21, and further by the fact that, unlike Lk viii 59, the words of the first speaker ἀκολουθήσω are pre-supposed together by the second speaker, who wants to do something else first, however (πρῶτον is not as strange, then, as T. W. MANSON[17] would make it seem). To a certain degree the two pieces have become mutual counterparts. The scribe who wants to follow Jesus wherever he goes comes up against a certain restriction (vs. 20) on Jesus' part. The disciple who wants to set restrictions himself (vs. 21) is told exactly this, that he must follow Jesus without any restrictions.

3.2.   The form of Mt viii 18-27

In regard to the form of Mt viii 18-27, which must be considered per se as a unit, we can limit ourselves to some observations, which, true, are in full agreement with what HELD[18] has said about the miracle stories, but which he himself, oddly enough, did not comment upon. First of all here, too, the dialogue is more important than the miracle performed, which is much more an illustration of what Jesus says in the dialogue. In this respect it is certainly of importance that Matthew drops the direct discourse of Mk iv 35 — the proposal to cross over — and of Mk iv 39 — the words of Jesus to wind and sea. Hereby all direct discourse becomes a dialogue between Jesus and his disciples (Mt viii 25-26a), just as that is the case in some miracle stories,[19] as HELD[20] had already observed. What he did not observe is that the story has two culminations, one in the double dialogue of vss. 19-22 and one in the dialogue of vss. 25-26. Possibly the double dialogue of vss. 19-22 also has something to do with ὀλιγό-πιστία, namely when the logion of vs. 20 about the difference between foxes and birds on one hand and the Son of Man on the other implies the suggestion that the γραμματεύς indeed considers that as a hindrance for actually following Jesus and inasmuch as the words of the other disciple explicitly refer to his own reservations. At any rate, there is reason to relate these dialogues with each other because the interlocutors confronting Jesus are placed in one series: εἷς γραμματεύς ... (vs. 19), ἕτερος τῶν μαθητῶν ... (vs. 21), οἱ μαθηταὶ αὐτοῦ ... (vs. 23). Comparable extensions with logia which either do not occur in Mk or Lk or which are transposed can be found in Mt viii 5-13 (Lk vii

---

[17] T. W. MANSON, The Sayings of Jesus, London 1949, 73.
[18] o.c., 200-234.
[19] Cf. HELD, o.c., 221-224, 229-234.
[20] o.c., 192.

1-10) and Mt xv 21-28 (Mk vii 24-30), while in both cases the words of Jesus are directed to the disciples (Mt viii 10; Lk vii 9: τῷ ἀκολουθοῦντι αὐτῷ ὄχλῳ; Mt xv 23-24, no parallel in Mk). Hereby the structure of the miracle story, especially in Mt viii 18-27, has been effaced even further, than BORNKAMM and HELD had discerned, although it is still recognizable.

These supplements sustain the opinion of BORNKAMM and HELD that what is primarily involved here is the community of Jesus' disciples and what is expected of it in the eschatological crisis.

3.3. The place within Mt

The position within the entire story of Mt deserves attention, too.[21] The story is first of all part of a trio of salvation stories of which Mt viii 18-27 is the first and the third of which also contains the theme of faith. This cycle of three stories (viii 18-ix 8) forms a larger cycle with three preceding stories of healing (viii 1-4.5-13.14-16) rounded off with a quotation from Scripture (viii 17), and with three succeeding ones (ix 18-34), which are separated from the middle cycle by the vocation of Matthew and a number of associated logia (ix 1-17). The total cycle is larded with dialogues which do not necessarily belong to the stories concerned (viii 10-12.19-22; ix 11-13.14-17.33-34), so that on this point, too, the two dialogues in vss. 19-22 do not fall out of line. The cycle is concluded with the summarizing ix 35, which is mainly a repetition of iv 23 and which makes the aforementioned cycle one entity with the sermon on the mount (v 1-vii 29). This part of Mt (iv 23-ix 35) gives a survey of what Jesus preached and did. It is preceded by the vocation of the first four disciples (iv 18-22) and is succeeded by the task given to the twelve to preach and act as Jesus (ix 36-x 8), which develops into a speech to the twelve, which is concluded by xi 1. One can say, then, that both the preaching of Jesus as well as his deeds are recounted within the cadre of the preparation of the twelve. It is thus not coincidental that the introduction to the Sermon on the Mount mentions that Jesus utters it in order to instruct his disciples (v 1b-2) and that the disciples in the "miracle stories" receive so much attention. The addition of viii 19-22 is a perfect example of this.

---

[21] Cf. F. NEIRYNCK, La rédaction matthéenne et la structure du premier évangile, in: De Jésus aux évangiles, Gembloux 1967, 41-73, W. G. THOMPSON, Reflections on the Composition of Mt 8:1-9:34, CBQ 33 (1971), 365-388.

For the rest, Matthew's theme of the weakness of faith is also an important element here which places the story on one line with the others. The word ὀλιγόπιστος is familiar to Matthew through Q (Mt vi 30 par. Lk xii 28) and concerns there a lack of trust in God who keeps his own alive (Mt vi 25.27) by providing them with food and clothing. It is introduced by Matthew in viii 26 and — oddly enough — also in xiv 31 and xvi 8, the two stories which are mutually connected in Mk and which are related to the story of the impending shipwreck by the theme of "not yet believing or understanding". Finally it can not be regarded as a coincidence either that the noun ὀλιγό-πιστία, which occurs only once, has a place within the story where it becomes clear that the μαθηταὶ are unable to heal a boy (xvii 14-21), and the disciples clearly fall short of that which according to iv 18-x 8 is their task and assignment. Therefore, the emphasis is consistently distinct from that of Mk. There is no longer any mention of a καρδία πεπωρωμένη (Mk vi 52; viii 17) in Mt. And even the οὔπω νοεῖτε of Jesus in Mt xvi 9 is quick relativated by the τότε συνῆκαν of the narrator in vs. 12.

4. Structural analysis of Mk iv 35-41

4.1. The text as an interweaving of codes

Structuralist linguistics, since F. DE SAUSSURE,[22] makes a sharp distinction between language ("la langue") on one hand, i.e. the code,[23] the system, the organization which makes the message possible and with which one has to confront every element of the message in order to grasp the meaning; and "la parole" on the other hand, i.e. the concrete application of the code in a message.[24] In the footsteps of structuralist linguistics, structural text analysis, which goes beyond the level of the single sentence and studies text structures of greater extent, has attempted to expose the codes which regulate the production of texts (and especially narrative texts) in order to come to a sort of universal text grammar or narrative grammar.[25] We are quite

---

[22] F. DE SAUSSURE, Cours de linguistique générale, Paris 1916.

[23] For the concept "code", which often has a looser meaning in structural text analysis than in linguistics, cf. G. MOUNIN, La notion de code en linguistique, in: Introduction à la sémiologie, Paris 1970, 77-86.

[24] CHOMSKY and his followers use instead of the terms "code" and "message" usually the terms "competence" and "performance".

[25] Well-known authors who have done research in this field are, among others, V. PROPP, Cl. LÉVI-STRAUSS (especially for the myths), R. BARTHES, A. GREIMAS, T. TODOROV. For the structural analysis of biblical texts cf. the review Linguistica Biblica, ed. E. GÜTTGEMANNS.

aware that great differences of opinion still exist regarding this structural text analysis and that many questions are as yet unanswered : to what extent e.g. may one regard this as a scientific method? In connection with this is the question whether one can formalize the codes? Which codes can one distinguish[26] and what are the criteria? May the structural analysis interpret the text, i.e. to read one particular meaning into the text, or does the text remain for it a structure with pluriform meanings? Etc. Nevertheless we are of the opinion that modern exegesis can hardly bypass it and should gain experience with structural text analysis by the practical application of the proposed analytical techniques. We discern in our structural analysis of Mk iv 35-41 six codes : the code of actions, the code of personages, the temporal organization, the spatial organization, the hermeneutic code[27] and the code of narration. Every code organizes a certain level of the text. One traces down this organization by investigating how the elements of the story are mutually correlated : e.g. the rising of the storm is clearly connected with the calming of the storm. By observing this one has reconstructed a small part of the code of actions. The structural text analysis considers each text as a kind of texture : every piece of text weaves elements of a number of various codes together (and can thereby serve as a starting point for the reconstruction of the codes).

The six codes aforementioned are all related to the articulation of the contents of the story. Besides this the codes which are connected with the "signifier character" of the text should merit attention (linguistic, rhetorical, stylistic codes), but to avoid overburdening the argument we will practically pass over these in silence.

4.2. *Code of actions*

The mutual organization of actions in Mk iv 35-41 is undoubtedly one of the most important structural facts of this story. The other codes (leaving the hermeneutic codes aside for the moment) have only

---

[26] Traditionally the most attention has been paid to the code of actions (going back to the analysis of popular Russian fairy tales by V. PROPP in 1928, who constructed a repertoire of 31 narrative actions or "functions"; later authors, especially GREIMAS and GÜTTGEMANNS, have tried to order these elementary narrative actions logically in binary pairs); besides this also the code of the personages has attracted much attention, especially through the "actantial analysis" of GREIMAS, who thought that the figures in the story could be classified in a schema of six "actants". The organization of time and space, too, is often studied.

[27] The word has here, as will appear later, another meaning than it usually has in exegesis.

a subservient role. When one traces down the mutual correlations on
the level of the actions one can observe that the story is constructed
from the following elementary action sequences:

PASSAGE : 1. Embarking (iv 1), 2. Departure (iv 35-36), 3. Arrival (v 1),
    4. Disembarking (v 2).

ENCOUNTER : 1. The multitude flocks toward Jesus (iv 1), 2. Dismissing
    the multitude (iv 36).

STORM : 1. The rising of the storm (iv 37), 2. The calming of the
    storm (iv 39).

SLEEP : 1. Sleeping (iv 38), 2. Being awakened (iv 38).[28]

The narrative sequences PASSAGE and STORM each contain an element
which is realized by a new narrative sequence : COMMAND. The departure
i.e. (iv 35-36) occurs upon a COMMAND : 1. Command of Jesus to cross
over (iv 35), 2. The disciples' obedience (iv 36). Also, the quieting
of the storm evinces this structure : 1. Command to the storm to be
still (iv 39), 2. The storm's obedience (iv 39).

The elementary narrative sequences are all very simple in structure.
Apart from the first one, they all consist of two mutually correlated
elements. The sequence PASSAGE, too, which consists of four elements,
can be considered as being constructed of two separate pairs (1+4 and
2+3). The simplicity of these sequences indicates that the sequence
of action as a whole, too, should have a very transparent structure.
The following schema shows how the various sequences of action are
brought together into a whole :

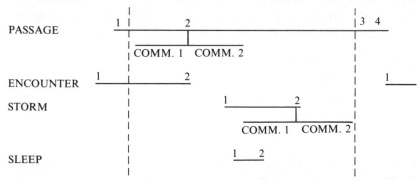

Only that which lies between the two horizontal dotted lines belongs
to Mk iv 35-41; the elements occurring outside them are connected

---

[28] One could add yet an action sequence here, namely CONFLICT : 1. reproach of
the disciples (iv 38), 2. counter-reproach of Jesus (iv 40).

by correlation with Mk iv 35-41.[29] Mk iv 40-41 are not yet represented in this schema but later on more will be said about these verses.

The PASSAGE and the STORM are two very important narrative sequences. One can represent their mutual relationship by considering PASSAGE as the axis of desire (Jesus desires to attain to the other side of the lake), and the STORM as the axis of trial because the storm is an obstacle to the realization of the desire and must be eliminated by struggle. Jesus wins this struggle because the storm obeys his command. As such the story deviates here from the sequence, that would have been probable according to the normal logic of the narrative : 1. Command to the storm to be still, 2. The *dis*obedience of the storm. This "normal" sequence would have meant that Jesus was the loser. Hence the very central meaning of the narrative sequence COMMAND : 1. Command to the storm to be still (iv 39), 2. The storm's obedience (iv 39).

It is also precisely on behalf of this sequence, that the story of the storm on the lake should be ranked among the miracle stories. It is characteristic for the code of the miracle story that the central sequence of action has a sequence which disrupts the "normal" code of actions, which is the sediment of a sort of collective empirical experience. In the miracle story the current grammar of the story is trespassed against. This is not to say, for the rest, that this breaking of certain rules of the normal code of actions in the Gospels occurs arbitrarily. On the contrary, it is itself bound to very clear rules. One of them is e.g. that when Jesus performs such an action it always occurs because certain people are in mortal danger or are affected in important human faculties.[30]

Among the miracle stories the story of the storm on the lake occupies a special place. In the form-critical part of this article it has already been observed that this is the only miracle story[31] in which Jesus' disciples are saved from peril. Furthermore it is one of

---

[29] Form-criticism, which has the hypothesis that the story of the storm on the lake originally existed independently, eliminates these elements in iv 35-41 from the original story, because they have correlates outside the text. Structural analysis, which proceeds from the whole of the Mk text, can not perform such eliminations.

[30] Mk xi 12-14.20-21 is an exception; one can pose the question whether it is a real miracle story or not. The rule explains, too, why Jesus refuses to perform demonstration miracles (Mk viii 11-12 par. Mt xvi 1-4). The miracle stories in the Gospels obey therefore an entirely different code than that of fantastical literature and science fiction, where disrupting certain laws of our world has more of a play function.

[31] Perhaps Mk vi 45-52, too, should be named here.

the few[32] miracle stories in which the miracle did not occur in someone who is ill or possessed by a demon, but rather in inanimate
natural objects (Jesus speaks to sea and wind; a paradox, since speaking
is a form of communication par excellence among living beings).

Not only are the narrative sequences constructed from mutually
correlated elements. Correlations occur, too, between the narrative
sequences, namely the sequences STORM and SLEEP. The rising of the
storm and the sleep of Jesus form an opposition of movement and rest.
The awakening of Jesus and the stilling of the storm, too, show this
opposition, although less clearly.[33]

There should be no doubt that the story of the storm on the lake
owes a great deal to the manner in which the Old Testament describes
God's actions in its own special code with a logic and with possibilities
which deviate from the logic and the possibilities of human actions.
It was a part of this "divine" code that Yahweh had unlimited power
over natural forces. There, too, the natural forces were represented,
especially in the poetic books, as being addressable and as listening
to the voice of Yahweh (cf. Job xxxviii 11). In Mk iv 35-41 the code
of divine actions of Yahweh becomes the code of the actions of
Jesus.

Until now the vss. 40 and 41 have been left outside the discussion.
Regarding vs. 41 a few things will be said in the discussion of the
hermeneutic code. In respect to the highly important vs. 40 a few
comments follow here. Jesus' reproach of the disciples Τί δειλοί ἐστε;
οὔπω ἔχετε πίστιν; introduces an entirely new element into the miracle
story. One can consider the cowardice of the non-faithful as a unity
of action within the code of actions,[34] but one must immediately
remark thereby that this unity of action differs greatly in a number
of respects from those mentioned until now:

---

[32] Cf. the stories of the multiplication of the bread (Mk vi 30-44; viii 1-10), the
walking on the water and the stilling of the storm (Mk vi 45-51) and the withering
of the fig. tree (Mk xi 12-14.20-21). It is noteworthy that these miracles, in contrast to the
healing miracles and the exorcisms, always have in Mk only the disciples as witnesses
and are related to their (dis)belief.

[33] Perhaps it is not entirely coincidence that, at least in Dutch, the verbs which
are used in combination with "wind" and "storm" are often dead metaphors which
are related to sleep: "to lie down", "to rise up".

[34] If one counts even still the action sequence CONFLICT, as was proposed in
footnote 28, one can consider this sequence as the sequence through which the theme
of faith enters the storm story. Via the CONFLICT the miracle story is made into a
conflict-story with the disbelief of the disciples as its subject.

1. Through the addition of οὔπω the non-believing is situated within a sequence of action FAITH in which the remaining elements must be sought outside of Mk iv 35-41. The difference with the aforementioned sequences is that this sequence FAITH does not consist of a very limited number of clearly localizable elements but that the parts are spread here and there over the entire Gospel (cf. the clearest cases vi 52; vii 18; viii 17-21).

2. Believing or not believing is more an inner quality which expresses itself in or is peculiar to certain other, more exterior actions such as the aforementioned.

3. In connection with the preceding, the attesting of faith or the lack of faith is always the result of an interpretation. This is precisely what is happening in vs. 40. Jesus interprets in a direct discourse the preceding conduct of the disciples as cowardly and unbelieving.

With the addition of vs. 40 the entire story becomes noticeably more complicated. Apart from this verse it was a fairly simple miracle story in which Jesus restrains the storm. Now, besides the description of a number of actual events (the storm and its being restrained), a judgment enters the picture in the words of Jesus about what went wrong. The whole story tells, in other words, not only the actual course of events but also tells an evaluation of them as to how things should have gone. One can also say that the story includes two trials : the trial with which Jesus is confronted (the storm) is won by him; the trial with which the disciples are confronted (to conduct themselves in the storm as men of faith) is lost by them. In conclusion it can be observed that the SLEEP sequence plays a very important role in combining these two lines in the story. Although it played a clearly secundary role within the actual miracle story beside the sequences PASSAGE and STORM (contrast with the STORM sequence), it now appears that it offers the points of contact for Jesus' judgment in vs. 40. The awakening of Jesus by the disciples (and naturally above all the words with which this occurs) indicates their lack of faith and Jesus' sleep functions thereby as an example of confiding faith.[35]

---

[35] We have made no attempt here to reduce the actions in the story to the repertoire of 32 narrative actions (also called motifemes), like that constructed and applied by GÜTTGEMANNS in imitation of PROPP and GREIMAS in regard to the Gospel stories. These are much more abstract than the actions discerned by us. The STORM-sequence e.g. would, according to this schema, be made into the abstract sequence Lack — Lack Liquidated.

4.3. Hermeneutic code

R. Barthes[36] has called attention to the fact that in stories it often occurs that questions, mysteries, puzzles are posed which are solved later in the story, often after all sorts of intermediate stages in which the question is posed anew or whereby the question receives a partial, a false or a misleading answer. Barthes has bundled all these phenomena under the name hermeneutic code.

In Mk this code plays a highly important role because the question : who is Jesus? runs like a thread throughout the Gospel. Mk iv 41, where the disciples ask among themselves Τίς ἄρα οὗτος ἐστιν ὅτι καὶ ὁ ἄνεμος καὶ ἡ θάλασσα ὑπακούει αὐτῷ; is a very important moment in the hermeneutic structure of Mk and is therefore together with οὔπω ἔχετε πίστιν; of vs. 40 the part of Mk iv 35-41 which most clearly ties this story with the whole of the Gospel. In order to determine clearly the place of Mk iv 41 more should be said about the larger hermeneutic structure of Mk. In order to understand the mutual relationship of the texts mentioned and the progression they show, one must ask oneself at every turn various things : is an answer or a question involved? If it is an answer, is it true or false? Who is the speaker? Who is spoken to? What was the possible inducement? What is the possible reaction of Jesus?

The question as to who Jesus actually is, is in Mk i 1 answered at once for the reader through the words of the narrator Ἰησοῦ Χριστοῦ υἱοῦ θεοῦ. That which is established for the reader from the very beginning is not at once so for the persons in the story. Jesus gets to hear at his baptism who he is; a voice from heaven says to him (and to no one else) : Σὺ εἶ ὁ υἱός μου ὁ ἀγαπητός. The evil spirits, too, appear to know who Jesus is (i 24 ὁ ἄγιος τοῦ θεοῦ; i 34; iii 11 ὁ υἱὸς τοῦ θεοῦ; v 7 υἱὲ τοῦ θεοῦ τοῦ ὑψίστου), but Jesus enjoins them to silence. Nor does he inform either the people nor his disciples who he is. Nevertheless the people and the disciples, due to his manner of acting, begin to ask questions about him. At the very beginning of his public appearance (i 21-28) the people are surprised at the novelty of his instruction and at his first exorcism and pose, then, the question among themselves : vs. 27 Τί ἐστιν τοῦτο; διδαχὴ καινὴ κατ᾿ ἐξουσίαν · καὶ τοῖς πνεύμασι τοῖς ἀκαθάρτοις ἐπιτάσσει, καὶ ὑπακούουσιν αὐτῷ. The question here is as yet impersonal (τί). The

---

[36] R. Barthes, *S/Z*, Paris 1970.

same sort of amazement of the people at the novelty of Jesus' manner of action appears in ii 12 Οὕτως οὐδέποτε εἴδομεν. Later in the Gospel (vi 14f; viii 28) it will appear that the people have tried in different ways (all mistaken) to determine his identity: he could be John the Baptist resurrected, Elias or one of the prophets. Relatives are of the opinion that he is not in his right mind (iii 21); scribes think that Beelzebul dwells in him (iii 22-30); his mother and brothers think unrightly to be able to claim him on the grounds of blood-relationship (iii 31-35); the people from his native city Nazareth pose the question Πόθεν τούτῳ ταῦτα, καὶ τίς ἡ σοφία ἡ δοθεῖσα τούτῳ ἵνα καὶ δυνάμεις διὰ τῶν χειρῶν αὐτοῦ γίνωνται; (vi 2) but they appear to be unable to give the right answer because they see Jesus merely against the background of his profession and his family relationship (vi 3). What is the case with the disciples? Here Mk iv 41 comes in sight. This is the place where Jesus' disciples pose the question among themselves for the first time explicitly as to who Jesus is; they do not as yet attempt an answer. Mk iv 41 brings to mind the formulation in i 27 where the people ask for the first time, Τί ἐστιν τοῦτο;[37] Instead of the impersonal question of the people induced by Jesus' instruction and his exorcism, the question of the disciples now arises directed to the person of Jesus and induced by the restraining of the storm (Τίς ἄρα οὗτός ἐστιν ...). The question will become even more urgent at the occasion of the multiplication of the loaves and through the walking of Jesus upon the water, but the lack of understanding continues (vi 5 v; viii 14-21). Only in viii 29 does Peter, when questioned by Jesus, give the answer Σὺ εἶ ὁ Χριστός. This is then confirmed for three of Jesus' disciples by a voice from heaven Οὗτος ἐστιν ὁ υἱός μου ὁ ἀγαπητός (ix 7; cf. i 11). Knowing the identity of Jesus does not mean, however, that all the misunderstandings have been eliminated. The part of the Gospel after Peter's confession shows that the disciples can not understand that the Son of God will have to suffer and die (viii 31-33 and many other places). Because these implications must first become clear, Jesus enjoins the disciples to silence (viii 30; ix 9). In the story of the passion Jesus will make his identity known explicitly to outsiders for the first time, at the occasion of the question of the high priest Σὺ εἶ ὁ Χριστὸς ὁ υἱὸς τοῦ εὐλογητοῦ; by answering affirmatively Ἐγώ εἰμι (xiv 61 f). After that, in answer to the question

---

[37] Cf. the use of ὑπακούω in i 27 and iv 41; ἐθαμβήθησαν in i 27 and ἐφοβήθησαν φόβον μέγαν in iv 41; φιμώθητι in i 25 and πεφίμωσο in iv 39 (the only two times that this verb occurs in Mk).

of Pilate Σὺ εἶ ὁ βασιλεὺς τῶν Ἰουδαίων, he gives the equivocal response Σὺ λέγεις (xv 2). This leads to the salutation of the Roman soldiers (xv 18), the inscription on the cross (xv 26) and the mockery by the high priests and scribes (xv 32). Paradoxically it will finally be not one of Jesus' disciples who makes the confession under the cross, that Jesus is the Son of God, but a Roman centurion: Ἀληθῶς οὗτος ὁ ἄνθρωπος υἱὸς θεοῦ ἦν (xv 39).

The hermeneutic code in Mk aims at giving an answer to the question who Jesus is by giving him a name and by determining his family relations. To do this an appeal must be made to other codes than those of the usual names (Jesus) and the natural family ties (son of Mary). Mk could do this by appealing to the codes which were developed in the O.T. and in the succeeding period to indicate the Messiah : a new complex of names and a new kind of family relations. Just as the "normal" code of actions is broken by Jesus, so also the question who Jesus is shows that the "normal" answers are insufficient.

4.4. *The remaining codes*

The code of actions and the hermeneutic code were undoubtedly the most important codes of the story about the storm on the lake. Regarding the remaining codes we can be less extensive.

Code of the personages. The personages and their mutual relations possess a structure which can be studied separately.[38] Characteristic of our story (as for practically all Gospel stories by the way) is that the personages receive no individual psychological description but rather are characterized by what they do.

Two groups are confronted with Jesus : the disciples and the ὄχλος. The last group appears only marginally in the storm story (vs. 36). Thereby the story becomes a story of Jesus and his disciples, beginning with a departure from the ὄχλος and followed by a new encounter with a possessed man (v 2). The function of the other ships in vs. 36 is not made clear and one gets the strong impression that one is dealing here with a structural remnant.

The relationship between Jesus and the disciples is asymmetric. This is indicated by Jesus' initiative for the departure (vs. 35), παραλαμβάνουσιν αὐτὸν (vs. 36; i.e. Jesus does not have to do any work), the addressing of Jesus as διδάσκαλε (vs. 38, for the first time

---

[38] We make no attempt here to rank the personnages of the storm story according to the actants-scheme of Greimas.

in Mk) and the entire subsequent course of the story. Jesus as an individual is confronted with the collectivity of the disciples as someone who possesses power.

Temporal organization. The only indication of time in the story is in vs. 35 ἐν ἐκείνῃ τῇ ἡμέρᾳ ὀψίας γενομένης. The indication that it was late is correlated with the action-sequence SLEEP and motivates Jesus' sleep. The same indication of time shows furthermore that the crossing took place in the dark and thereby it accentuates the perilous character of the crossing.

Spatial organization. The spatial structure of the story is determined by the sea of Galilee with its two shores; on one side Galilee and on the other side the land of the Gerasenes. This structure represents on a spatial level what the sequence PASSAGE represents on the level of the action.

Another important spatial structure is connected with the sequence STORM : water and boat are contrasted with each other in the sense that the boat serves to separate the seafarers from the water; a storm can lead to the boat's losing this function by the water's exceeding its limits and making the boat sink (vs. 37).

Code of the narration. This code involves the elements in the story which point to the narrator and/or the reader and not to the structure of the events, the story as such.[39] Mk iv 35-41 shows a very objective manner of narration, just as the rest of the synoptic Gospels; there are scarcely any direct indications of the narrator and the reader to be observed.[40] The entire story is placed in the third person and tells itself, as it were. The referential function dominates and other functions are scarcely present.[41] One may not put this objective method of narration on the same line with neutrality of the narrator, of course, in respect to his subject. The effacing of the narrator and listener

---

[39] For the distinction between narration and history, or discourse and history, cf. E. BENVENISTE, Les relations de temps dans le verbe français, in : *Problèmes de linquistique générale*, Paris 1966.

[40] For an inventarization of the various types of narration and the place of the objective manner of narration therein, cf. e.g. L. DOLEŽEL, The Typology of the Narrator : Point of View in Fiction, in : *To Honor Roman Jakobson I*, The Hague, Paris 1967, 541-552.

[41] For the concept "function" and the six functions of language which one can discern (referential, emotive, conative, poetic, phatic and metalingual), cf. R. JAKOBSON, Linguistics and Poetics, in : Th. A. SEBEOK (ed.), *Style in Language*, Cambridge, Mass. 1960.

from the story seems here on the contrary subservient to the absolute authority and universal validity of the story.

4.5. *Context and situation*

Has this unravelling of a number of codes in the story of the storm on the lake grasped all the meaning which is enclosed in this text? We think not. Two amplifications seem necessary to us. The text functions namely within a textual context (the whole of Mk) and within an extra-textual situation[42] (the actual situation of the reader with all his cultural and personal presuppositions) and both elements help to enrich the meaning of the story. Just a few remarks here about the context of the story of the storm on the lake. What we mean is not so much that separate elements of the story enter into correlation with other elements of Mk. outside of it (we already saw this on various levels of the story, namely the code of actions and the hermeneutic code), but that the story as a whole enters into correlation with other parts of Mk. The story about the storm on the lake actually enters into correlation with all the stories in Mk where there is reference to threat and peril and about salvation therefrom. The story especially functions as a symbolic presage of *the* description of mortal danger and salvation therefrom: the suffering and the death of Jesus Christ. There are a number of indications which sustain this assumption. We can indicate here the elements in Mk iv 35-41 which in one way or another return in the story of the passion : dying and restraining death (in the resurrection) show a structural similarity with the PASSAGE and the restraining of the storm; both times Jesus is the subject; ὀψίας γενομένης returns litterally in xiv 17 (at the Last Supper) and has a certain parallel with the important role of the night and darkness in the passion story; the weakness of the disciples occurs very clearly, too, in the story of the passion (Judas, Gethsemane, betrayal of Peter); the ἐφοβήθησαν φόβον μέγαν as the reaction of the disciples to the restraining of the storm (iv 41) has a parallel in the fear of the women after being confronted with the message of the resurrection (xvi 8).

If this is correct and if one relates to this the suffering of Jesus in Mk as a presage of the persecution of his disciples, then one will be justified in connecting the story of the storm on the lake with this

---

[42] We mean by this not the Sitz im Leben of form-criticism; this is only one of the extra-textual situations. The situation, too, of the reader in 1975 is such an extra-textual situation.

persecution, without considering this as the only interpretation of the story.

5. Structural analysis of Mt viii 18-27

5.1. Mt viii 18.23-27

One could defend the opinion that a structural analysis of the story of the storm in the version of Mt. should be restricted to Mt viii 18-27 and that one should not look sidelong toward the Mk-version. Nevertheless we think that also another method of operation is possible, namely to analyze the text of Mt structurally and *simultaneously* investigate which transformation the Mt version applies to the Mk version. This method of approach nears in many respects quite closely that of "Redaktionsgeschichte". One difference, however, is that the structural analysis will continually have to indicate how the various levels of the Mt text are structured, from which codes the text is constructed, what belongs to the surface and what to the deep structure, and likewise at which level and within which code the transformations occurred in comparison with the Mk text. In "Redaktionsgeschichte" these matters will all often play a role but less explicitly and less systematically than in a structural analysis.

One important part of the transformations which Matthew applies to Mk lie close to the surface level of the text; they are expressed in the choice of words, the set combinations of words, the sentence structure, certain figures of style, the rhythm, the use of direct and indirect discourse, etc. They are directly connected, in other words, with the linguistic and stylistic or rhetorical codes, which have been neglected by us until now and which concern more the signifying aspect than the signified aspect of the text.[43] He who compares the texts of Mk and Mt with each other will notice that here a shift occurs from a more concrete, more visual description to a less concrete, more stereotype, less vivid description, but it would be beyond our scope to elaborate further on this here.[44]

Also what regards the codes which were mentioned, there are a

---

[43] Cf. R. BARTHES, Style and its Image, in : S. CHATMAN (ed.), *Literary Style : A Symposium*, London, N.Y., 1971, i 3-10.

[44] Cf. only the elimination in Mt. of the direct discourse Mk iv 35 and iv 39, the much lower frequency of the praesens historicum in Mt (Mk v, Mt i), the dropping of all sorts of concrete details in Mt. (the stern, the cushion, the words with which Jesus stills the storm, the other boats), the more stereotyped use of language in Mt (ἀκολουθέω, the apocalyptic turn σεισμὸς μέγας, cf. Apoc. *passim*).

number of clear transformations. Within the *code of actions* Matthew
has intervened especially in the sequence of FAITH by substituting lack
of faith with ὀλιγόπιστία. Hereby important differences arise : 1. While
Mk has a contrast of faith vs. lack of faith without an intermediate
term, Mt. clearly does leave room for gradations; 2. With the disappearance of οὔπω (Mk iv 40) no clear connection is present anymore
in Mt. with other texts of the Gospel.

The weakening of the reproach of Jesus by the introduction of this
ὀλιγόπιστοι has as a correlate the transformation of the sharply
reproachful question of the disciples Διδάσκαλε, οὐ μέλει σοι ὅτι
ἀπολλύμεθα; (Mk iv 38) into the much milder words in Mt. Κύριε,
σῶσον, ἀπολλύμεθα, which are more of an anxious prayer than a
reproach. One could summarize this transformation as follows : in both
Mk as well as Mt there is a reference to an action-sequence CONFLICT,[45]
but in Mk this consists of 1. reproach of the disciples, 2. counter-
reproach of lack of faith; in Mt of 1. anxious prayer of the disciples,
2. reproach of little faith.

Other transformations of Matthew are that he changes the order
of action in two places. In the sequence PASSAGE with him the command
to cross over precedes embarkation, a change which is connected with
the fact that the context of Mk (Mk iv 1 f!) has been changed by him.
Another change is that he no longer, as in Mk, separates the two
terms of the sequence CONFLICT from each other by the restraining
of the storm, but lets them succeed each other immediately. Thereby
the story receives a very regular construction, with a dialogue between
Jesus and his disciples in the middle, preceded by the description of
the rising of the storm, and succeeded by the description of the
restraining of the storm.

The weakening of the conflict between Jesus and the disciples in
Mt also has important consequences for the *hermeneutic code* and the
code of personages. After the confession of the disciples which is
implied in the use of the word κύριος, it is difficult for Matthew to have
the disciples pose the question as to Jesus' identity in the same way as
in Mk iv 41; furthermore the prayer for a saving intervention is difficult
to reconcile with amazement at the salvation. Matthew resolves the
problem by placing the question, then, in the mouths of οἱ ἄνθρωποι.
Thereby he then weakens τίς to ποταπός. Hereby Mt viii 27 receives
an entirely different function in the hermeneutic structure of Mt than

---

[45] Cf. footnote 28.

Mk iv 41 had in Mk. We will not delve further into this here. With οἱ ἄνθρωποι a third group enters the picture in Mt, besides Jesus and the disciples. This changes considerably the network of mutual relationships within the story. The relation between Jesus and the disciples is still asymmetrical as in Mk but while in Mk Jesus was contrasted with unbelieving disciples, in Mt Jesus is contrasted on one hand with disciples who in principle are faithful but weak and, on the other hand, amazed outsiders.

5.2. *Mt viii 19-22*

The small piece of narrative which Matthew adds via viii 19-22 to the version of Mk contains four statements in the direct discourse : two from Jesus himself (the answers) and two from others. Whereas in the actual storm story the story of the events by the narrator was just as important as the dialogues between Jesus and the disciples in the vss. 25 and 26; in viii 19-22 that which falls outside the direct discourse is merely a subordinate frame which is limited to the naming of the speakers. This implies that viii 19-22 introduces a new element into the actual miracle story viii 18.23-27 : the latter is predominantly narrative (third person indicative, narrative tense), the first (true, in a narrative frame) exclusively "discursive" (with a much more varied complex of personal categories, modes and verbal tenses).[46] In the actual miracle story the referential function dominates, in viii 19-22 the conative and poetic function becomes very pronounced.[47] Mt viii 19-22 is not composed according to the codes of narrative, but according to the code of the dialogue and, as far as the statements of Jesus go (vss. 20 and 22), also according to the code of the saying.

The contrast between vss. 19-22 and vss. 18.23-27, however, must not be exaggerated. That was already proven by the fact that vss. 19-22 contains introductory formulas of narrative character, which tie these

---

[46] Cf. for the distinction narrative-discursive H. WEINRICH, *Tempus : Besprochene und erzählte Welt*, Stuttgart ²1971.

[47] The conative function comes forward in the imperative of Mt viii 22. The poetic function appears above all in viii 20 where via all sorts of lexical and syntactical parallelisms a very ordered whole emerges. The three lines of the logion show a unity in that they all refer to living beings and their resting place. Besides this there are important contrasts, in the first place, between line 1 + 2 and line 3 (connected by δέ) and in the second place, subordinated to the first opposition, between 1 and 2. The first opposition consists herein that animals are contrasted with a human being, classes (αἱ ἀλώπεκες, τὰ πετεινὰ) contrasted with an individual (ὁ υἱὸς τοῦ ἀνθρώπου) and having a resting place is contrasted with not having one. The second opposition contrasts animals that mainly live in the air with animals that live on land.

verses in with the rest of the storm story and by the fact that in vss. 25, 26, and 27 discursive direct discourse is also found. However, one should go even further and state that a clear thematic connection exists between the verses added by Matthew and the miracle story. Much has already been discussed in the "redaktionsgeschichtliche" treatment of the Mt text. The following could be added to it. The two direct addresses in vs. 21 and vs. 25 rhyme with each other (Κύριε followed by an imperative). The fact that Jesus has nothing to lay his head upon has a counterpart on one hand with the lack of Mk iv 38 ἐπὶ τὸ προσκεφάλαιον, and corresponds on the other hand to the unsafe stay on the ship which thereby comes into contrast with the holes of the foxes and the nest of the birds, which at any rate offer a certain shelter from the elements. The storm narrative in Mt functions thereby as a translation into narrative form of a common saying, whereby the indefiniteness of time and place which is peculiar to a saying is transformed in the story into a concrete here-and-now; reversely the logion of vs. 20 is a generalization of the storm narrative which thereby is uncoupled from its direct reference and implies all situations of jeopardy to which following Jesus can lead.

Less clear is whether vss. 21-22, too, have a direct relation with what is said in vss. 23-27. One can assume that in both cases death enters into sight, in vss. 21-22 as a circumstance which includes responsibilities which must yield way, in vs. 25 as the death which threatens the passengers on the ship (ἀπολλύμεθα).

5.3. The broader context of Mt

Also the broader context of Mt enriches the meaning of the storm story. For instance, we would like to point out one thematic correlation. At a very important place in Mt, namely at the end of the Sermon on the Mount (Mt vii 24-27), Jesus compares everyone who listens to his words and who does them with a sensible man who builds his house on a rock, so that it can withstand rain, torrents and wind (οἱ ἄνεμοι cf. Mt viii 26f). He who does not listen to his words and does not do them builds his house on sand, so that it is destroyed by the elements. What is involved here is a figurative story (ὁμοιωθήσεται) pronounced by Jesus while Mt viii 23-27 is a literal story about Jesus. Nevertheless there are similarities. Both times reference is made to a threat and to danger on the part of nature. Both times, too, there is an opposition between dangerous nature and a human construction which should offer protection against it (one time a house, another time a ship).

But the similarity extends even further. In the storm story Jesus is the one who offers salvation from the storm and in the Sermon on the Mount it is said that if the house has a firm foundation, i.e. if one follows the words of Jesus, he is shielded against catastrophes. Through this correlation with the end of the Sermon on the Mount the meaning of the storm story is enriched; it extends beyond its direct, literal reference and indicates, too, the role of Jesus as teacher, so important to Matthew, and the security which this gives.

6. *Conclusions*

Finally we will try to draw some conclusions regarding the question whether the two methods are mutually exclusive in principle or in fact.

The first conclusion is that both the historical (form-critical and "redaktionsgeschichtliche") as well as the structural research methods are based on observation of the empirical text data. In the observation in both cases, furthermore, comparison plays an important role. But there are important differences too. We will try to discover the similarities and differences in regard to three main points: the presuppositions, the text material to be compared, and the structuring principle. These three points of difference are clearly inter-connected.

In regard to the *presuppositions* it seems incorrect to us to purport that the form-critical and "redaktionsgeschichtliche" method are built upon a series of presuppositions and that the structural analysis is not. Both prescind from presuppositions. Those of the form-critical and "redaktionsgeschichtliche" method involve the manner in which the text came into existence; those of structural analysis involve the opinion that systems underlie texts in general and comparable kinds of texts therein.

However much it might be desirable to distinguish Formkritik and Gattungskritik from Form(en)geschichte, as W. RICHTER[48] does, these distinctions are in actual practice generally not applied. The form-critical method is distinct from structural research inasmuch as form-criticism does not restrict itself to the determination of structure in a given section of text. Rather it attempts to bring this structure into a temporal relationship with pre-given text structures, indicable in Hellenistic or Rabbinic literature and furthermore in a direct relationship to an extra-textual situation, certain circumstances (preaching, discussion) from or within a local and cultural milieu which more-or-less

---

[48] W. RICHTER, *Exegese als Literaturwissenschaft*, Göttingen 1971.

determine a Christian community (Hellenistic or Palestinian). Hereby
it is clear that exactly the latter case, determining the Sitz im Leben
in general had to and still must be hypothetical. Structural analysis
restricts itself to the inner structure of a given text and renounces
attempts to determine the situation. Form-criticism is based on the
presupposition that various Christian communities exist which are
mutually discernible and that these have formed the concrete text data
in correspondence with the cultural milieu of which they are a part.
Furthermore form-criticism presupposes that the sections of text involved existed independently in the same state as in which they now
form a part of the whole or in a state which can be reconstructed from it.
That which connects both methods is the attention which is paid in
principle to the structure of the sections of texts, whereby form-
criticism suffices with a simple schema of similarities and occasionally
with naming the "Gattungen", which concerns more the — assumed —
contents than the structure (e.g. miracle stories). In contrast structural
analysis has at its disposal much more nuanced possibilities for
analyzing the texture of texts. The presupposition of form-criticism
is that the structural characteristics of a text have something to do
with the situation around its origin and the history of its development. It aims thus at reconstructing this process. Structural analysis
sees these structures against the background of the presupposition
that a relatively small number of set rules exist which determine the
surface structures of all texts. What is involved is discerning this
entire complex of rules. It should be clear that in both cases the
most attention is not paid to the message of the concrete text, but
that in both cases the conclusions which they draw are important for
discerning it.

"Redaktionsgeschichte" can be considered as a continuation of the
form-critical inquiry. It renewed interest in aspects to which form-
critical research gave too little relief: that which the final author
intended to communicate to his readers with his work. Here, too,
attention was and is directed to the genetic aspect to a large extent.
That leads to differences with the approach of the structuralists. The
interest for the genetic aspect leads to the comparison of a book with
its (presupposed) source, e.g. Mt with Mk, which is supposed to have
been used by the author of Mt. The point is that "Redaktionsgeschichte" attaches the most value to what the author revised in his
source. Generally that which the author added or changed is considered
more important than what he adopts. One can ask oneself what the

reason for this is. One will receive nowhere an explicit answer, but one can surmise that this sort of active operations on a given text are assumed to require more attention from the author than the more passive acceptance. Therefore "Redaktionsgeschichte" is of the opinion that these elements are more important for what the author actually intends to say with his text. Structural analysis does not make this distinction. For it all the text data have the same value, to begin with. When it attaches more value later on to one fact above another this is only because it finds in the text itself structurizing elements which motivate the application of a hierarchical ordering. In any event, it seems to us that on this point the structural approach is an important correction of insufficiently thought-out presuppositions. We would prefer not to keep this criticism abstract but would like to indicate an example in the article in question where this tendency of "Redaktionsgeschichte" raises its head. In 2.3 it was said that the storm narrative in Mk no longer functions as a miracle story but as a quasi-apophthegma. The motivation for this conclusion was the observation that vs. 40b was an editorial addition. The line of reasoning is, then, implicitly the following. The editorial addition places in the mouth of Jesus a statement about the disbelief of the disciples. Because this addition is editorial it determines in fact the meaning of the entire story and thus the story no longer functions as a miracle story, as it did in the pre-given tradition. The question is whether in the light of the criticism given above one should not also refer to a miracle story in the case of Mk (how does one explain otherwise vs. 41, which is highly important for Mark?), although it must be admitted that the miracle story has got an additional point by the addition of vs. 40b.

On a second point, too, i.e. *the text material used as a comparison*, important differences come to light. The form-critical and "redaktions-geschichtliche" method limit their research in principle to the text material which can supply information about the historical genesis of the Gospels. Form-criticism directs its attention thereby above all to the material which shows a structural similarity with the section of text being studied; "Redaktionsgeschichte" considers the pre-given text which is the direct source for a certain Gospel. The principle starting point of both "Redaktionsgeschichte" as well as form-criticism has two consequences. In the first place : the form-critical and "redaktions-geschichtliche" method always look back in time. Text material from the time after the genesis of the text being studied is not important except when conclusions can be drawn from that text material for the period before or during the origin of the text being studied. This is often the case with later Rabbinic text material. In the second place the importance of the text material being used as a comparison becomes greater to the extent that this text material was more directly involved in the origin of the text being studied. In "Redaktionsgeschichte" this requirement is very strict : only those texts are important which were known and digested by the author of the text being studied. Form-criticism on the contrary usually involves more texts in its research : all texts from a certain cultural milieu which belong to a certain sort of text can be of importance to it. There is yet an other important characteristic of the form-critical and "redaktionsgeschichtliche" method : they work not only with the actually present text material but they also, via hypothetical reconstructions, make up texts and let them function as well in their research. The research method inspired by structuralism usually does not show much interest in a genetic inquiry. This has important consequences for the text material to be investigated. Especially when one sets as ones aim (as many structuralist do) to construct a kind of narrative grammar, then in principle no limit is set to the text material which can be used as a comparison. The aim of the study is to establish a limited number of rules whence *all* stories can be derived. In actual practice the researcher naturally does have to limit himself to a restricted body of texts. Because he is not interested in the horizontal-genetic ties, but rather in the vertical relation of texts with the same system of rules he will direct his attention to texts with the same basic underlying system. This can be very generally the narrative system, but on a smaller scale the system of a fairy tale, the miracle story, etc. It will be clear that here not only differences but also similarities lie between the structural analysis and form-criticism. Form-criticism, too, tries to bring together texts which show a similar structure. The differences remain nevertheless very great : 1. in form-criticism the "structural analysis" is subordinate to the study of the history of development of separate texts, 2, in form-criticism the "structural analysis" will always remain more implicit while structuralist analysis will aim at as much explicitness and completeness as possible in its description of the rules of text production.

A third difference between the two study methods occurs in the *structuring principle*. This difference is closely connected with what has already been said. One can say that the form-critical and "redaktionsgeschichtliche" method in fact use two structuring principles. On one side diachronism is important: one makes distinctions within a Gospel between the redaction and the tradition preceding it, and the latter is then carried back to a certain Sitz im Leben (actually more of a sociological category than a strict diachronical one). However, this is not the only structuring principle of form-criticism and "Redaktionsgeschichte". Form-criticism compares as well texts with each other which are very similar and arrives thereby at constructing kinds of texts (Gattungen), such as miracle stories, debates, etc., whereby structural considerations play an important role. "Redaktionsgeschichte", too, structures the redactional material of the Gospel being studied, especially on thematic grounds. Form-criticism and Redaktionsgeschichte contain thus on one hand a historical, diachronical aspect and on the other hand a structural, synchronical aspect. The structuralistic method on the contrary has had until now almost no thought for the historical aspect of texts; the structural aspect, however, is analyzed much more systematically because one discriminates all sorts of text levels and tries to expose the codes which are active on all these levels.

If the preceding is correct, then there is in principle no opposition between the two methods of approach. We have found nothing in the presuppositions of form-criticism and "Redaktionsgeschichte" which is essentialy in conflict with the structuralist approach. No less have we found anything in the presuppositions of structural analysis which might be in opposition with the form-critical and "redaktionsgeschichtliche" method. Both have their own area of inquiry and complement each other.

It is a different question as to what extent the two methods of approach can make use of each other. If we see things correctly an important distinction occurs here between the two approaches. Form-criticism and "Redaktionsgeschichte" appear in principle to be open to the use of structural analytical techniques; in fact they have always applied them implicitly. Without having to give up their own historical inquiry form-criticism and "Redaktionsgeschichte" can thus find advantage in incorporating structuralist methods of reflection. Reversely the case is not such that the structuralist method of reflection might stand open to the way the problems are posed in form-criticism and "Redaktionsgeschichte". Since it is not interested in the history of development of separate texts it will never be able to integrate form-criticism and "Redaktionsgeschichte" in its own method of research.

Is one then justified in concluding from the greater integrative capacity of form-criticism and "Redaktionsgeschichte" that this method makes the purely structuralist approach superfluous? Thus one could suffice with a form-critical and "redaktionsgeschichtliche" approach which incorporates the structuralist one. This consequence seems incorrect to us. Structural analysis will always remain merely an aid within form-criticism and "Redaktionsgeschichte" and will remain subordinated to the historical inquiry. This implies that there will always be room for an independent structural analysis, apart from every historical inquiry.

In conclusion it can still be remarked that the structuralist method has a clearer relevance to the average reader of the Gospels than the form-critical and "redaktionsgeschichtliche" method. The reason for this is that the former is more clearly connected to the process of reading than the latter. The latter works with entities which do not belong to the text concerned itself, e.g. a hypothetical tradition which Mark digested, or Mark's text which was an auxiliary source for Matthew, and distinguishing within the text various layers which must be considered as the sediment of a kind of history of development. This history of development does indeed lead to the text which the reader has before him but this text was intended to be read as one homogenous whole. Even though the text may resemble a mosaic somewhat, it is nevertheless in conflict with its nature to pay attention to the origin of the parts (like the stones in a mosaic) instead of considering the totality of the text as the actual data (the mosaic). Reading is a process in time whereby the reader gradually absorbs the whole of the text. Thereby the text itself offers him in many ways the structurizing elements. But these can never be borrowed from another text with which the reader should compare it. That is in conflict with the nature of the text as such.

CRÉÉ À L'IMAGE DE DIEU

La question du divorce dans Marc x[1]

B. HEMELSOET

Deux manières de lire

Le texte de Marc x 1-12, peut être lu de deux manières. Il peut être reçu comme information sur l'enseignement de Jésus en matière de divorce. Le texte donne ainsi réponse à la question; "qu'a enseigné Jésus pendant sa vie terrestre au sujet du divorce, qu'a-t-il répondu aux questions s'y rapportant". Ou pour s'exprimer plus prudemment : quelle est la réponse de la tradition des premiers décennies après Jésus Christ, à la question du divorce?

Dans ce premier cas, le texte est lu comme un document historique, l'autorité reconnue à Jésus garantit les réponses données. De plus, celles-ci, peuvent faire prévoir la manière d'enseigner de Jésus et des premières communautés.

Il est certes permis de lire le texte autrement, et de se demander, non pas ce que Jésus et les premières communautés ont enseigné à propos du divorce, mais bien : "que nous enseigne cette question à propos de Jésus". Cette lecture est possible si le texte est considéré comme organisé en soi-même. Au lecteur de déchiffrer lui-même cette organisation. Le texte de l'évangile veut présenter Jésus dans un contexte donné, qui est celui de l'évangile. Les differentes périscopes

---

[1] A part des commentaires v. E. BAMMEL, Markus x 11 und das jüdische Eherecht, *ZNW* 61 (1970), 95-101. — K. BERGER, Hartherzigkeit und Gottes Gesetz, die Vorgeschichte des antijüdischen Vorwurfs in Mark x 5, *ZNW* 61 (1970), 1-47. — T. A. BURKILL, Two into One : the Notion of Carnal Union in Mark x 8, 1 Cor vi 16, Eph v 31, *ZNW* 62 (1971), 115-120. — H. G. COINER, Those Divorce and Remarriage Passages (Matt v 32, xix 9, 1 Cor vii) with brief Reference to the Mark and Luke Passages, *CTM* 39 (1968), 367-384. — T. P. CONSIDINE, Two in one Flesh. The meaning in Sacred Scripture, *ACR* 39 (1962), 111-123. — D. DAUBE, Concessions to Sinfulness in Jewish Law, *JJS* 10 (1959), 1-13. — G. DELLING, Das Logion Mark x 11 und seine Abwandlungen im Neuen Testament, *NT* 1 (1956), 263-274. — F. J. LEENHARDT, Les Femmes aussi ... à propos du billet de répudiation, *RThPh* 19 (1969), 31-40. — F. NEIRYNCK, Het evangelisch echtscheidingsverlof, *CBG* 4 (1958), 25-46. — H. J. RICHARDS, Christ on Divorce, *Scrip* 11 (1959), 22-32. — B. SCHALLER, Commits adultery with her, not against her, *ET* 83 (1972), 107-108.

sont ordonnées et juxtaposées de telle façon que le lecteur puisse en recueillir une image cohérente de Jésus. Ainsi, dans cette cohérence présupposée, l'évangile se présente comme un programme de lecture.

La réalisation de ce programme n'en est pas pour autant accomplie. C'est au lecteur de réaliser le programme. Les différentes études sur la structure et la théologie de l'évangile selon Saint Marc, où l'on trouve des indications pour le lecteur, en sont une preuve convaincante.[2]

La question du divorce, comme question concernant Jésus, en implique beaucoup d'autres. Elle occupe en fait une place bien définie dans l'évangile. Dans le mouvement que fait Jésus dans l'évangile de Marc, de Galilée vers Jérusalem, elle prend même une place décisive. Le départ hors de Galilée, qui inaugure l'orientation vers Jérusalem en est marqué. Cette tendance vers Jérusalem définit par conséquent la question du divorce. De plus, qu'est ce qui conduit l'évangéliste à poser cette question à cette place, sous forme de tentation?

Comparaison synoptique

L'évangile de Marc compte parmi les évangiles synoptiques. C'est pourquoi il peut être lu en concordance avec Matthieu et Luc, et leur être comparé. Dans une comparaison des trois évangiles synoptiques, telle que la présentent habituellement les synopses, on remarque que la péricope en question se trouve bien dans Matthieu (xix 1-12) mais non dans l'évangile de Luc. La synopse de Aland présente en regard de Matthieu xix 1[3] et Marc x 1, la phrase éloquente de Luc ix 51. Suivant cette présentation, les trois évangélistes décrivent chacun à sa manière, l'orientation décisive vers la Judée, vers Jérusalem. Des trois évangélistes Luc se montre le plus décisif et le plus explicite. Étant si explicite, il n'éprouve pas la nécessité à cet endroit (Luc ix 51) de poser la question du divorce. Par contre dans l'évangile de Marc et Matthieu la dite question est liée à l'orientation de Jésus vers Jérusalem.

Ainsi est donnée la première impulsion vers une méditation de Marc x. Jésus part définitivement de Galilée vers Jérusalem. L'orientation de Jésus de Nazareth quittant la Galilée pour Jérusalem est soulignée et interprétée par la question des Phariséens à propos du

---

[2] M. SABBE (ed) *L'Evangile selon Marc, Tradition et Rédaction* (BEThL), Gembloux 1974. — E. SCHWEIZER, Neuere Markusforschung in USA, *EvTh* 33 (1973), 533-537.

[3] K. ALAND, *Synopsis Quattuor Evangeliorum*, Stuttgart 1964, 255 (n° 174: Iter ingreditur, Aufbruch aus Galiläa, Decision to Go to Jerusalem!).

divorce. Luc décrit en parallèle le refus des habitants d'un village de Samarie et la mission des soixante douze disciples.

Le Royaume de Dieu est proche

Dans le discours sur l'envoi en mission (Luc x) on entend pour la première fois dans le troisième évangile, la phrase : "Le royaume de Dieu est proche" (Luc x 11). L'évangile de Luc en a déjà parlé plusieurs fois, mais c'est dans ce discours que le Royaume de Dieu se trouve pour la première fois employé avec l'expression "est proche". C'est le contenu de la prédication des soixante-douze. Une conclusion s'impose : il est donc possible que Luc souligne la correspondance entre l'approche du royaume et la montée de Jésus vers Jérusalem, lorsque Il tend son visage vers la ville (Luc ix 51).

Bien que différente cette concordance se retrouve dans l'évangile de Marc. Lui aussi met en rélation Jérusalem et l'approche du royaume. Le verbe ἐγγιζειν (s'approcher) n'apparaît que trois fois dans le deuxième évangile ; dans Marc i 15 pour dire que le royaume de Dieu s'est approché, dans xi 1 pour noter "et lorsqu'ils s'approchaient de Jérusalem", et enfin dans xiv 42 où il est écrit : "celui qui me livrera s'est approché". On est tenté de lire ces trois versets dans une perspective commune : le Royaume de Dieu s'est approché parce qu'ils se sont approchés de Jérusalem, et parce que là s'est approché celui qui le livrera. Autrement dit : ils s'approchent de Jérusalem parce que le Royaume de Dieu s'est approché et parce que s'est approché celui qui le doit le livrer. Ou encore : celui qui doit le livrer s'est approché, parce que le royaume de Dieu s'est approché, c'est pourquoi ils s'approchent de Jérusalem.

Dans Marc x on ne trouve rien d'expressément mentionné concernant l'approche du royaume, ni rien d'explicite sur la proximité de Jérusalem. Mais la voie vers Jérusalem est engagé, et son accomplissement est déjà écrit dans Marc x 32, à la fin des péricopes qui commencent au chapitre x.

L'ordre des péricopes

La façon dont les différents évangélistes ont ordonné leur matière est plus qu'un pieux caprice. L'ordonnance elle-même est un enseignement (sur Jésus). Les différents récits tracent d'eux-mêmes le chemin que Jésus suit de Galilée à Jérusalem, et ils éclairent l'un après l'autre la figure de Jésus. Ainsi dans Marc x.

La question posée par les Phariséens est placée ici pour mettre en lumière le chemin que Jésus emprunte vers Jérusalem, pour souligner l'attraction de cette ville, et pour rendre tangible l'alliance de Jésus et de Jérusalem. Cette péricope fait apparaître la raison pour laquelle Jésus n'a pas voulu divorcer avec Jérusalem.

Marc x

Au début de ce chapitre, verset 1, Marc écrit qu'Il, — le nom de Jésus n'est pas encore mentionné — enseignait une fois de plus selon son habitude, aux foules rassemblées. Une fois de plus également, comme d'habitude, le contenu de sa prédication n'est pas précisé. Cependant, pour le lecteur de Marc viii 31, cet enseignement est clair : Jésus se fait connaître lui-même à travers son enseignement ; il faut que le Fils de l'homme souffre beaucoup. Si l'on considère l'ordonnance des péricopes dans l'évangile de Marc, il faut tenir compte de ce qui précède Marc x 1, à savoir Marc ix 48-50 : "... où leur ver ne meurt pas et où le feu ne s'eteint pas. Car chacun sera salé au feu. C'est une bonne chose que le sel...". Marc cite ici le dernier verset du prophète Isaie. Le feu que brûle dans le verset 48 s'étend jusqu'au verset 49 et se prolonge dans le verset 50 : feu et sel (Is. lxvi 24). Le premier verset de l'évangile de Marc reprend le début du livre des consolations d'Isaïe. Si Jésus, au ch. x de Marc peut prendre son départ pour Jérusalem c'est que le livre des consolations du prophète Isaïe est accompli ; des lors il est clair que celui qui a assimilé le livre des consolations peut être emmené avec Jésus vers Jérusalem. Car bien qu'il sache qu'à Jérusalem le Fils de l'Homme doit souffrir, il sait aussi qu'à Jérusalem doit être donnée la consolation de Isaïe (lii 7) : Ton Dieu est Roi, et là est l'évangile : le royaume de Dieu est proche (Marc i 15).

Dans cette lumière nous voyons Jésus se lever, de nouveau, et comme à son habitude, enseigner aux foules, et cette prédication ayant Jérusalem pour horizon, est interrompue par la question des Phariséens. Ils lui démandent : Est-il permis à un homme de répudier sa femme ? L'évangéliste commente cette question en l'interprétant : c'était pour le tenter. Ce dernier commentaire doit éveiller l'attention du lecteur. Il ne s'agit pas, en l'occurrence, de savoir à quelle école Jésus appartient celle de Hillel ou celle de Sjammai. Cette seule question ne contiendrait pas la tentation dont parle Marc. Qu'est ce qui pousse l'évangéliste à présenter la question des Phariséens comme une tentation ? La réponse de Jésus semble bien claire (Marc x 10-11). Le divorce n'est pas permis. Mais il n'est pas permis parce que d'autres choses sont en jeu, bien plus transcendantes, que la seule union d'un homme et d'une femme.

C'est pourquoi la question du divorce est présentée comme une tentation.

La tentation

La tentation de Jésus est mentionnée quelque fois dans l'évangile de Marc. Au chapitre i 13 Jésus est tenté par Satan; au chapitre viii 11 les Phariséens demandent un signe du ciel. Ici aussi l'évangéliste indique qu'il s'agit d'une tentation. C'est d'ailleurs pourquoi Jésus refuse le signe qu'ils attendent. Par contre, Jésus rencontre leur question dans x 3 comme dans xii 15: apportez-moi une pièce d'argent. De même demande-t-il au chapitre x 3: qu'est-ce que Moïse vous a préscrit? Ici comme là, il renvoie la question à ceux qui veulent le tenter.

La réponse à la question

Elle se donne en deux temps. Tout d'abord, Jésus leur demande ce que Moïse a ordonné; ensuite, il poursuit sur la réponse reçue des Phariséens. L'étonnant est de trouver par deux fois, le nom de Moïse avant que celui de Jésus soit mentionné. Au verset 3, il est écrit: *Il* répondit et leur dit, alors qu'au verset 5 on peut lire: mais *Jésus* leur dit. Faut-il n'y voir que l'effet du hasard? La conclusion du verset 9: Ce que Dieu a mis sous le même joug, l'homme ne le séparera pas, ne semble pas encore répondre à la question des Phariséens, alors qu'un simple recours au précepte de Moïse apporterait le réponse "oui" ou "non", plus ou moins nuancée, que les Phariséens attendent.

Au surplus, au verset 9, le mot ἀνήρ (mari) employé par les Phariséens devient ἄνθρωπος (homme). Si l'on considère le verset 9 comme une réponse concluante, il faut cependant prendre garde au remplacement de "mari" par "homme". Les Phariséens semblent envisager les relations de l'homme et de la femme dans le mariage. C'est pourquoi ils demandent s'il est permis au *mari* de répudier sa femme. La réponse du verset 9 parle de l'*homme*. L'explication de ce changement doit se trouver dans les versets 4 à 8. D'autant plus que, au verset 9, le mot habituel "répudier" ἀπολῦσαι est remplacé par se séparer χωρίζειν, lequel mot signifie davantage que le mot "divorcer" au sens technique du terme.

Ce verset 9 va révéler au lecteur la réponse qu'il espère; il montrera clairement pourquoi Jésus ne peut se contenter d'un oui ou d'un non. Comme s'il ne s'agissait que de mari et de femme, de oui et de non...

Le précepte de Moïse

Jésus commence par demander le précepte de Moïse : "Qu'est-ce que Moïse vous a préscrit?" Ils disent : "Moïse a permis d'écrire un certificat de répudiation et de renvoyer sa femme". Jésus n'accuse pas Moïse, mais souligne la dureté du cœur, l'endurcissement de l'esprit qui n'est plus capable d'entendre ce que fut proclamé au commencement. Car la dureté de cœur s'oppose à l'intelligence des mots de la Génèse. Mais le bon entendeur comprend à demi-mot.

Au commencement, dans la Génèse, il est écrit : "Dieu *les* fit mâle et femelle". Le verset n'est ici qu'à moitié repris. L'évangéliste n'écrit pas : "et Dieu créa l'homme à son image à l'image de Dieu il *le* créa". De tout ce texte, il ne retient que "mâle et femelle il *les* créa". Il n'envisage que le redoublement, le pluriel, qu'il rattache au verset de la Génèse ch. ii, en guise de conclusion : "c'est pourquoi l'homme quittera son père et sa mère, et les deux ne feront qu'une seule chair". Ainsi, ils ne seront plus deux, mais une seule chair. N.B. Ici l'évangéliste ne mentionne pas que l'homme s'attachera à sa femme. De la première citation de Gen. i il élimine tout ce qui peut rappeler le singulier (à son image il *le* créa). De la seconde, il néglige tout de qui a trait à l'attirance de l'épouse pour l'époux. L'accent est posé sur l'aspect double de l'être-homme, créé à l'image de Dieu, mâle et femelle... Il *les* créa. Ceci doit être souligné, étant donné que Matthieu, quant à lui, est apparemment plus "facile" et cite le verset Gen. ii 24 intégralement parce qu'il s'agit toujours de divorce. Il ressort de la comparaison de Marc et de Matthieu que Marc dépasse de loin la simple question du divorce.[4] Marc ramène l'interrogation des Phariséens à l'origine de l'homme, à la création de l'homme à l'image de Dieu, c'est-à-dire mâle et femelle, au pluriel. Il s'est servi de la distinction entre mari et homme.

D'où le lecteur conclura que l'homme de verset 7 n'est pas seulement le mari, mais mâle-femelle, mari-femme. Ainsi homme et femme sont en jeu quand il est écrit : c'est pourquoi l'homme quitera son père et sa mère. Et Marc peut intentionellement négliger l'autre membre de phrase : et il s'attachera à sa femme.

Marc signifie par là que le fait de quitter ses père et mère est dans ce contexte, le sort de chaque homme, mâle-femelle et ce fait

---

[4] Pour cette raison nous avons donné la préference au texte de Marc qui se trouve dans le synopse de K. ALAND.

débouche sur : "et les deux ne feront qu'une seule chair". Dans cette double unité est accomplie ce que Dieu a réalisé dès le commencement, ce qu'Il a donné comme programme à l'homme : "Il *les* créa, mâle et femelle", et ce qui est écrit : "A l'image de Dieu il les créa". La remarque de Matthieu : "si telle est la condition de l'homme envers sa femme, il n'y a pas intérêt à se marier", est superflue dans l'optique de Marc. S'attacher à une épouse, à sa femme, est transcendé et peut-être approfondi, interiorisé.

Le plus important n'est pas de savoir si ce que Dieu a conjugué est une institution indissoluble, — et Dieu sait si elle est représentée comme telle ici, — mais bien d'accomplir la tâche, le programme donné dans la double unité qui est l'image même de Dieu. L'homme ne pourra se soustraire à ce programme, de même que cette tâche ne pourra le détruire ou le partager, ni dans le mariage, ni en dehors. Dans le mariage car mâle et femelle sont les témoins de l'homme créé à l'image de Dieu, hors du mariage parce que l'homme créé à l'image de Dieu, ne peut pas davantage se soustraire à ce programme. Ce texte contient bien plus que ce qui peut servir à édifier l'assistance dans une cérémonie de mariage ! En conclusion, Marc ajoute : Ainsi ils ne seront plus deux, mais une seule chair. Dans cette double unité, un témoignage sur terre. "Que l'homme ne sépare donc pas ce que Dieu a uni". Les choses étant telles, la discussion s'éteint, les Phariséens disparaissent de la scène, et la tentation est surmontée. Si l'homme se convertit à cette parole initiale, son cœur guérira de l'endurcissement, et ce que Moïse a permis à cause de la dureté de son cœur deviendra superflu.

Le certificat de répudiation

On ne rencontre que deux fois dans l'écriture ce certificat dont Marc fait mention, et qui se réfère à Deut. xxiv 1. Les prophètes en parlent (Is. l 1 et Jér. iii 3).

Pour Jérémie, c'est limpide ; le certificat de répudiation est cité pour proclamer que la répudiation (de Jérusalem !) n'est pas définitive, et que le jugement n'est pas sans appel : toutes les tribus se rassembleront à Jérusalem, au nom du Seigneur. Dans Is. 1 la plainte du Seigneur est éloquente : Où donc est la lettre de répudiation par laquelle j'ai renvoyé votre mère ? Le Seigneur n'a pas répudié son peuple. C'est lui-même qui s'est éloigné.

Isaïe et Jérémie se servent de cette formule pour exprimer la possibilité de conversion, d'orientation et de retour vers Jérusalem.

La tentation surmontée

Dans le réponse de Jésus, la tentation est surmontée. Les accents se sont déplacées, les Phariséens ont disparu. L'image de Dieu d'après laquelle l'homme fut créé, est plantée au centre. Cette réponse est donnée à la main de Moïse au moment où Jésus se dirige vers Jérusalem et où sa relation avec Jerusalem va apparaître au grand jour. Cette relation de Jésus à Jérusalem, cette double unité, décide de la relation mâle-femelle. Tout est mesuré d'après la venue de Jésus à Jérusalem, d'après la bienveillance de Dieu quand il déclare à Sion : Votre Dieu est Roi. De même pour le divorce, de même pour la relation homme et femme.

La tentation des Phariséens doit être lue avec en filigrane cette interprétation de l'image de Dieu. Ils tentent Jésus, ils le provoquent à répudier son épouse Jérusalem.[5] Mais l'homme doit quitter son père et sa mère en faveur de cette double unité. Jésus ne veut pas se soustraire à cette obligation. La réponse de Jésus ne laisse pas seulement entendre qu'une lettre de répudiation à Jérusalem est inpensable, mais aussi qu'en ne la donnant pas, Jésus réalise un programme bien supérieur à la simple relation mari et femme suggéré par les Phariséens. Jésus se réclame de la Genèse. Il va plus avant dans la voie de Jérusalem. Son Nom doit être lié à cette ville. Cette alliance garantit l'unité de l'homme, l'unité du programme "être créé mâle-femelle".

La question des disciples dans la maison

À la maison les disciples posent la question "ordinaire". "Ils interrogent Jésus sur ce sujet". Ils ne le tentent pas. Ils cherchent la protection de la maison. Quelle maison? Celle où les élèves posent toujours leurs questions; celle où l'explication leur est consentie, où le sens profond des mots est dévoilé. La maison séparé extérieur et intérieur. L'on sait que, à l'intérieur, la question des Phariséens ne peut être posée. Elle a été clairement résolue dans la réponse de Jésus en

---

[5] Cf. R. H. LIGHTFOOT, *The Gospel Message of St. Mark*, Oxford 1962 (1958), 114n. The thought of Israel as the bride of Yhwh is familiar in the Old Testament, e.g. Isa l 1; lxii 4 and the Lord in Mark ii 19 has spoken of Himself as a bridegroom. But by x 1-12 the reader has already learned, and not only in the two predictions of the passion, that He will be rejected; and on the interpretation suggested the Lord finds Himself faced with the neccesity of deciding whether at all costs to Himself He will maintain the Union and remain faithful to His people, however they may treat Him. In this light the words : "What God hath joined together, let not man put asunder" x 9 acquire very great significance.

référence à la Génèse. Mais cette réponse plane si haut au-dessus des réalités quotidiennes qu'elle surprend. Cependant, les disciples veulent savoir, — et qui ne le voudrait, — ce qu'il en est de cette réalité de tous les jours. Est-ce permis ou non? L'explication de Gén. i les laisse perplexes, et nous de même; c'est pourquoi ils interrogent Jésus sur ce sujet. Mais alors ils se trouvent devant la même difficulté : le sujet, est-ce le divorce ou l'homme?

Leur question vise l'homme à la lumière de l'interprétation donnée d'une image de Dieu, à la lumière de Jésus en marche vers Jérusalem. C'est alors que Jésus prononce les mots "homme et femme", et cela semble écrit pour tous ceux qui attendent de lui une réponse explicite. "Si quelqu'un répudie sa femme et en épouse une autre, il est adultère à l'égard de la première. Et si la femme répudie son mari et en épouse un autre, elle est adultère. Cette conclusion ne répond pas à la question de savoir si le divorce est permis ou non, car les disciples n'ont pas posé leur question de la sorte. Ils l'ont interrogé "sur ce sujet". La réponse de Jésus se fonde sur l'intelligence acquise de ce que signifie "être créé à l'image de Dieu". C'est à cause de cette image que Jésus ne veut pas se séparer de Jérusalem afin que s'accomplisse la parole donnée à Sion dans l'évangile du Royaume : Votre Dieu est Roi.

THE SENSE OF ΣΥΛΛΟΓΙΖΕΣΘΑΙ AT LUKE XX 5

G. MUSSIES

Diogenes of Sinope, it is said, used to reason (συνελογίζετο: D.L. VI 37) as follows : "All things belong to the gods; the wise are friends of the gods, and friends hold things in common as you know,[1] so all things belong to the wise". The conclusion he draws here might as well have been "so all things belong to me", because unlike previous philosophers Diogenes was in no doubt whatsoever about the fact that he himself was a wise man. As he is elsewhere not very serious about religious matters — he used, for instance, a wooden statuette of Heracles as fire wood to cook his meal on — it may well be, that the above two statements about the gods are not to be taken too seriously either. And although he probably may have meant the words that make up the inference, the syllogistic form of the whole was certainly intended as a parody, too, and belongs as such under the same heading as his ridiculing criticism of philosophical and scientific problems in general, such as the alleged non-existence of motion, all kinds of astronomical questions, the lectures of Plato and the definition he gave of man (D.L. VI 24, 39-40). The closest parallel to his mockery of syllogisms, however, is his own refutation of the well known sophism of the horns as preserved in the "Life of Chrysippus" (D.L. VII 187) : "If you have not lost something you are still in possession of it; you have not lost horns, so you have horns". Our Cynic's typical answer to someone who believed he had proved by this syllogism that he had horns (πρὸς τὸν συλλογισάμενον ὅτι κέρατα ἔχει), was to touch the man's forehead and to say "I don't see them", in his favourite way supporting his words by an action of some kind.

While doing work on the theme of "Diogenes Traditions and the New Testament" as a future contribution to the Corpus Hellenisticum Series, I hardly expected to find in the New Testament anything remotely corresponding with such anecdotes on Greek philosophers

---

[1] A common saying : Euripides *Orestes* 735, Plato *Phaedrus* 297C, Corpus Paroemiographorum Graecorum I 106, 266; II 76, 481; Dio Chr. III 110, XXXVII 7. Terentius *Adelphoe* 5, 3, 18 vetus verbum hoc quidem est : communia esse amicorum inter se omnia.

as we find them in the biographical sketches made by Diogenes Laertius. But as there is a parallel in this case, one would expect the N.T. passage that contains such a technical word as συλλογίζεσθαι to have already been commented upon so intensively that there is nothing left to be said. This, however, is not the case: H. A. W. MEYER, PLUMMER, ZAHN, KLOSTERMANN, to mention only these, make very brief remarks *ad locum*, mainly of the content that the verb is a N.T. hapax; only LAGRANGE is a little more informative: "συλλογίζομαι (*au lieu de* διαλογίζομαι) *insiste davantage sur la conséquence logique pesée d'avance*";[2] if we turn away from the commentaries to the N.T. lexicons we learn that the latter are no exception to this general brevity since none of them devotes any special attention to the word. But before we ourselves start to say anything about it it is in place to give some statistics. Συλλογίζεσθαι, as far as known, was introduced by Herodotus (at II 148 only) but does not seem to have been very frequent in the Classical period: the other two famous historians, Thucydides and Xenophon, do not have it at all, neither does any of the great tragedians, or Aristophanes; of the rhetoricians only Isocrates and Demosthenes have some rare instances (2× and 4×). Those who had more reason to apply it were the philosophers, because they gave an extra, technical sense to the verb: in Plato's writings the word is found already fourteen times, while Aristotle uses it at least 48 times according to BONITZ.

In the Hellenistic period the verb seems to have been favourite with Polybius (13×) and Philodemus (7× and *passim* in his writings on rhetoric). By comparison, many other authors whose preserved works cannot precisely be called small, use it only sporadically, such as Philo of Alexandria (4×), Plutarch (*Moralia*: 4×, *Lives*: 2× according to WYTTENBACH's lexicon, but *Pomp*. LX 2 should be added), Josephus (2×), and Lucian (2× according to REITZ' index).

Within this general picture it may cause some surprise that the verb does occur at all in the not so extensive New Testament, and also that it has not been considered important enough to be the subject of a separate article in KITTEL's *Theologisches Wörterbuch zum Neuen Testament* or in the *Begriffslexikon* of COENEN *c.s.*, the more so since Luke deviates here from the parallel versions of the story: the other Synoptists have διελογίζοντο, a usual word to refer to discussions or considerations, for which Luke has substituted a comparatively rare

---

[2] M. J. LAGRANGE, *Evangile selon Saint Luc*, Paris 1921, 506.

and technical word. Since several translators render Luke xx 5, we believe, in a somewhat flat and colourless way, which, it seems, is backed by *"überlegen, bedenken"* given in BAUER's lexicon *s.v.*, a periphrasis wholly absent from LIDDELL-SCOTT's dictionary *s.v.*, the *raison d'être* of the following "one word article" may be obvious.

If we survey first what shades of meaning have been registered by the different general dictionaries and by the indexes to the works of one author, we perceive that on the whole lexicographers are unanimous about a coherent complex of meaning which we should like to present as follows :

1) *to add*, originally numbers only : 1a) *to count, reckon*; later also arguments : 1b) *to reason*; or circumstances : 1c) *to summarize, recapitulate*; or entries : 1d) *to book*; figuratively : *to reckon among*;

2) *to compute*, with numbers : 2a) *to calculate*; with arguments : 2b) *to conclude*; with circumstances : 2c) *to take into account*; 2d) in philosophy sense 2b has been narrowed down to be the technical term for those special forms of reasoning which to-day are still called *"syllogistic"*.

Senses 1a, b, c and 2a, b, c were generally used, whereas both 1d and 2d tended to be restricted to more technical use of language, the latter as has been said, belonging to the vocabulary of logic, the former to that of administration and book keeping, mostly preserved in papyri from Egypt, *e.g.* Stud. Pal. I 69, 371; of the figurative sense of 1d we know of only one example as yet : Numbers xxiii 9 in the Septuagint version : *"Lo, a people dwelling alone, and not reckoning itself among the nations"* (R.S.V.). Of course, the above grouping of the different senses is only one out of several possibilities. We have endeavoured to place together those senses which in our opinion are most contiguous, but we are quite aware that others would prefer a different order. On the whole these senses still link up with the semantic sum total of the constituent parts : συν– in the sense of "together" and –λογίζομαι in the sense of "to count, reckon". The meanings of the rare re-compounds ἀντι–, ἐπι–, κατα– and προ–συλλογίζομαι combine a modal or temporal notion and sense 2b "to conclude" or sense 2d "to syllogize", for instance ἐπισυλλογίζομαι "to conclude in addition".

As λογίζομαι is a deponent verb, the compound συλλογίζομαι and its re-compounds are deponents as well; the voice value is mostly

active, sometimes passive,[3] rarely middle (*e.g.* Numbers xxiii 9). By
the side of this deponent there occurs, be it extremely seldom, an
active verb συλλογίζω which cannot be considered to belong to the
same paradigm as our συλλογίζομαι, because it has quite a different
meaning: "to collect", being a derivative from συλλογή "collection".
The only instances that we know of are found in the writings of
Dionysius of Halicarnassus, for example in *De Imitatione* fr. VI where
he relates how the famous Zeuxis painted a Helen in the nude for the
inhabitants of Croton. First he made separate copies only of the ideal
limbs and members which he perceived with the girls who had been
sent to him from Croton to serve as models; thereupon he combined
all these copies into one single painting of a woman of outstanding
beauty: κἀκ πολλῶν μερῶν συλλογίσαντι (*sc.* αὐτῷ) συνέθηκεν ἡ
τέχνη τέλειον καλὸν εἶδος.[4]

a) In addition to the above sketched, "generally accepted" meaning
of συλλογίζομαι some dictionaries list senses that are not mentioned
by others and are sometimes backed by a very restricted number of
instances from literature. One of the latter kind is "to plan" at
Polybius XIV 4, 4, which is mentioned by LIDDELL-SCOTT "*he had
planned to*" and by E. A. SOPHOCLES "*it was his plan to*",[5] both
probably going back to SCHWEIGHÄUSER's lexicon which has "*constitu-
tum ei erat*" (he had determined, decided to).[6] The passage adduced
deals with an episode of the Second Punic War, when in 203 B.C.
Scipio Africanus wanted to destroy both the winter camps of his
enemies. In order to achieve this end he divided his army: one part
under the command of Laelius was to attack the camp of the Numi-
dians, the other part was conducted by Scipio himself against the
Carthaginian camp under Hasdrubal. Now comes the event referred
to in our passage: ἦν δ᾽ αὐτῷ (*sc.* Scipio) συλλελογισμένον μὴ
πρότερον ἐγχειρεῖν ἕως ἂν οἱ περὶ τὸν Λαίλιον πρῶτοι τὸ πῦρ
ἐμβάλωσι τοῖς πολεμίοις "it had been ... to/by him not to attack
before Laelius and his men had set fire to the enemy camp". The
context of the verb shows us a situation in which the right moment
to make an attack is carefully weighed and made dependent on the

---

[3] H. BONITZ, *Index Aristotelicus*, Darmstadt 1960, 711b.

[4] But USENER-RADERMACHER make here the conjecture: συλλογῆς ἔν τι.

[5] H. G. LIDDELL-R. SCOTT, *A Greek-English Lexicon*, Oxford 1968, 1673a, *s.v.*
(II.3). E. A. SOPHOCLES, *Greek Lexicon of the Roman and Byzantine Periods*, New York,
repr. (1887), II *s.v.*

[6] J. SCHWEIGHÄUSER, *Lexicon Polybianum*, Leipsic 1795 (vol. VIII, 2 of his Polybius
edition).

visible success of another, parallel attack. This story is brought out
in more relief if we stick to one of the most current senses of
συλλογίζομαι and translate here "it had been calculated by him" or,
more fluently, "he had calculated not to"; this would be more precise
than "to plan, determine, decide" or PATON's translation "*he had made
up his mind*".[7] Of course one could argue that "to calculate" in this
case comes under the heading of planning, but there is no reason here
why we should supplant a specific term by a more general one which
includes the former, let alone to insert the latter in a lexicon as an
extra sense without the support of further passages.

b) In his Plato lexicon AST included "*reputo*" in the first heading
of his description of the total meaning of συλλογίζομαι: "*colligo h.e.
computo, rationem subduco, etiam reputo*".[8] Except for the last word,
this part of his description is covered by the semantic survey given
above. Since AST makes use of that language we have to make some
remarks here about the meaning "*reputo*" has in Latin. Now if one
makes a semantic comparison between "*computo*" and "*reputo*" it
turns out that the two run parallel for the greater part, except that the
latter can also convey the senses "to think over, ponder, meditate,
reflect upon", and that these were the reason why "*reputo*" was
added at all.

Under this first heading then have been enumerated eight passages
from Plato and if one checks these in a translation of his works, for
instance in the one that is part of the BUDÉ edition[9] and which was done
by several scholars, it turns out that in none of them συλλογίζομαι
has been rendered by a verb comparable to "*reputo*", "to think over",
or the like, but as follows: *rendre raison* (Tim. 87C), *calculer* (Leg.
670C), *découvrir* (Pol. 531D), *observer que* (Politic. 280A), *bien
considérer* (Charm. 160E), *tirer la conclusion* (Pol. 618D), *ordonner
d'avance* (Leg. 799A), *trier* (Leg. 957B). Some of these may be a little
free: *rendre raison* might have been: "en faire le compte",[10] *observer
que* equally well: "conclure", and *ordonner d'avance*, as it is about
Egyptian festivals: "calculer", but at any rate a simple "en penser"
was nowhere chosen to render συλλογίζομαι. The Plato lexicon by

---

[7] W. R. Paton, *Polybius, The Histories*, (Loeb Classical Library), London-Cambridge
(Mass.) 1960, *vol.* IV, 441.

[8] F. Ast, *Lexicon Platonicum sive Vocum Platonicarum Index*, Darmstadt 1956
(= repr. 1835-1838), *vol. III*, 295.

[9] *Platon. Œuvres Complètes* (ed. Association Guillaume Budé), Paris 1956-1968.

[10] So the version by L. Robin-J. Moreau (Monaco 1964, vol. II, 517).

DES PLACES which forms the closing volumes of the BUDÉ edition mentions only the following senses : "*calculer, tenir compte de, récapituler, conclure*".

If we take another "one author lexicon" in hand of still older date, SCHWEIGHÄUSER's Polybius lexicon, we see that he also had a heading "*reputare, secum cogitare*"; the five passages listed there appear to have been rendered in the LOEB edition by : "*calculating*" (I 44, 1), "*take into consideration*" (I 63, 8), "*reflecting*" (III 61, 2), "*reckoned on*" (*i.e.* calculated) (III 81, 12) and again "*reflecting*' (IV 71, 1).[11] We shall only discuss the two instances of the colourless "*reflecting*", since the other passages are evidently capable of being rendered without making use of such an equivalent of "reputare" and appear to be in line with the meaning as given in the introduction.

III 61, 2 : Hannibal who has just descended the Alps, is surprised to learn that his adversary Publius Scipio has already crossed the Po "reflecting (ἐνθυμούμενος) that he had left him near the crossing of the Rhone only a few days previously, and that (καὶ συλλογιζό-μενος) the coasting voyage from Marseilles to Etruria was long and difficult". PATON has rendered the two bracketed verbs by one, but we think there can be no objection against translating the latter separately : "and calculating that the voyage from Marseilles to Etruria would be (εἴη) long and difficult".

IV 71, 1 : Ταῦτ᾽ οὖν πάντα συνορῶν καὶ συλλογιζόμενος ὁ Φίλιππος etc. "*Philip* (*sc.* the Vth of Macedonia) *observing and reflecting on all this*" ... was in two minds about attacking the town. Ταῦτ᾽ refers to the strong strategical position of the town of Psophis in Arcadia. Polybius uses almost the whole preceding chapter to give a detailed picture of the topography of Psophis with a subdivision according to the four sides of the town. The two participles, therefore, can quite well be rendered by "viewing together and recapitulating all these points", which is more specific than "*observing and reflecting*".

Reputo as a special sense of συλλογίζομαι is also mentioned by the *Thesaurus Linguae Graecae*, but as follows : "*Accipitur etiam pro* ἀναλογίζομαι, *Mecum reputo, Perpendo*".[12] This is illustrated by : Plato *Leg.* 670C ("*Reputant, Intelligunt*"), *Tim.* 87C, *Rep.* 531D, Polybius I 44, 1, Plutarchus *Pomp.* 60, 2 ("*de Caesare Rubiconem transituro*"), Polybius III 98, 3 ("*Consilium cepit*"), I 26, 10; I 32, 2; pass. XIV 4, 4.

---

[11] W. R. PATON, *Polybius, The Histories* (see n. 7), *vol.* I, 123, 173; *vol.* II, 145, 201, 469.

[12] *Vol.* VII, Paris 1848-'54, 1037 A-B.

Apart from the Polybius passages (see above sub b and sub c below) the only addition here is Plutarch *Life of Pompey* LX 2 αὐτὸς ἄρα πρὸς ἑαυτὸν συλλογιζόμενος τὸ μέγεθος τοῦ τολμήματος "*reasoning with himself, of course, upon the magnitude of his adventure*".[13] In the Caesar biography of Plutarch this same event is related without συλλογίζομαι : XXXII 4. λογισμὸς αὐτὸν εἰσῄει μᾶλλον ἐγγίζοντα τῷ δεινῷ (*i.e.* the crossing of the Rubicon) καὶ περιφερόμενον τῷ μεγέθει τῶν τολμωμένων: "*he ... began to reflect, now that the drew nearer to the fearful step and was agitated by the magnitude of his ventures...*"[14] If we should have to choose from among the three senses constituting the separate heading in the *Thesaurus* (see above) it would undoubtedly be the intensive "*perpendo*" (to weigh carefully) and not so much the rather flat "*mecum reputo*" or ἀναλογίζομαι which is semantically hardly different from συλλογίζομαι itself.

The dictionary of PASSOW, too, has a heading, "*bei sich überlegen, bedenken, reputare*", quoting ten passages to illustrate this sense,[15] but only one of these is not already found in the lexicons discussed thusfar. This is Demosthenes *Or.* XIX 47 ἐπειδὰν δὲ τοὺς καιροὺς συλλογίσηταί τις ἐφ' ὧν ἐγράφη "*but if you will take into account the occasion on which it (sc. the decree) was proposed*".[16] According to LIDDELL-SCOTT the verb means here "to recapitulate", but because the context is hardly informative it does not allow us to discard the rather vague "bedenken" on the one hand, or to make a definite choice between "to take into account" and "to recapitulate". We think it a typical instance of those passages that have to be interpreted in the light of clearer ones, and for that matter it can hardly be used as evidence.

As a final alleged instance of "reputare" we should like to discuss Plutarch *Life of Sertorius* XVII 4 because of the translation "*reflecting*" given by PERRIN in the LOEB edition.[17] The story is about how this opponent of Sulla outmaneuvered the Characitanians, a barbarian tribe in Central Spain who were hiding themselves in unconquerable

---

[13] B. PERRIN, *Plutarch's Lives* (Loeb Classical Library), London-Cambridge (Mass.) 1961, *vol.* V, 273.

[14] *O.c.*, 1958, *vol.* VII, 523.

[15] F. PASSOW, *Handwörterbuch der Griechischen Sprache*, Leipsic 1857, 1615.

[16] C. A. VINCE and J. H. VINCE, *Demosthenes* (Loeb Classical Library), London-Cambridge (Mass.) 1971, *vol.* II, 277.

[17] B. PERRIN, *Plutarch's Lives* (Loeb Classical Library), London-Cambridge (Mass.) 1959, *vol.* VIII, 45.

caves in a mountain slope facing North. Sertorius perceived that there was often blowing a rather strong north wind in this area and also that the soil opposite these caves was so loose that every foot step made it fly up: ταῦτα δὴ συλλογιζόμενος ... καὶ ἀκούων παρὰ τῶν ἐγχωρίων, he had his soldiers make a mound of this loose soil just in front of the caves until nightfall stopped them. This mound was mistaken for some kind of siege-works and caused much hilarity. At sunset, however, the north wind began to blow very gently and the Roman infantry and cavalry were ordered to walk over the mound and pulverize it. When the wind gradually increased it blew enormous clouds of dust into the faces of the Characitanians, so that they were choked and had to surrender after three days without having been able to offer any armed resistance at all. The crucial phrase containing our verb is rendered by PERRIN as follows: "*reflecting on these things and getting information about them from the natives of the country*". In our opinion ἀκούων refers here to what Sertorius could not know from his own observation, that is, when and for how long this wind would blow. The version "*reflecting*", we think, gives less than Polybius means to convey, which is rather that Sertorius had a brain wave and combined three things for a special purpose: the loose soil, the northern cave entrances and the northern wind. The notion of "adding" up is here clearly present and can be maintained in English if we use the idiom "putting two and two together".

By way of summary we might remark that translators are far from unanimous about those passages that figure in the dictionaries mentioned under a heading (which comprises) "reputare" or the like. The few that we found actually rendered by "to reflect upon" *etc.* are all capable of being assigned a more specific and emphatic sense, not too remote from "to count" or "to reckon". The ones whose sense cannot easily be judged on the ground of their own context are, of course, no proof to the contrary. The deceptive point about such a general notion as "to reflect" is that it *comprises* in a way more specific ones like "to reason" or "to recapitulate", and for that reason can be substituted in almost any context for these finer distinctions without doing any apparent harm. As to its insertion in dictionaries it seems better, as long as such a faded, general sense cannot be verified, to consider the use of the verb in a context where no actual adding or counting is done, as a metaphor, which retains the general idea of mental activity, and the accuracy or intensiveness inherent in counting; as a consequence "to reflect" or "to consider" should not figure in descriptions of the meaning of συλλογίζεσθαι without "carefully" or "thoroughly" being added. If possible, translations must pass on such a metaphor and make use of "to count" or "to reckon"; if not, one should take care to render by a factual equivalent of equal force and colour.

c) SCHWEIGHÄUSER also has a heading "*excogitare, capere consilium*" *s.v.* συλλογίζομαι; against the former no objection can be raised, but "*capere consilium*" diverges from what other dictionaries have, although it comes close to sense 2b) "to conclude". If we check these passages once more in the LOEB edition we find the following versions : "*taking into consideration*" (I 26, 10), "*he at once reached the conclusion*" (I 32, 2), "*he reasoned with himself*" (III 98, 3). Since the last mentioned place has been taken over by the *Thesaurus Linguae Graecae* with the special remark "*Consilium cepit*",[18] it may be worth a closer look. Polybius tells us there how the Iberian Abilyx persuaded the Carthaginian commander of Saguntum at the approach of the Roman army to send home the Iberian hostages whom Hannibal had taken from the Spanish towns that he did not trust. Three quarters of the whole chapter (*ch.* 98) are needed to display the sly piece of reasoning done by Abilyx to achieve his end, allegedly to help this Carthaginian, but in reality in favour of himself. Polybius summarizes all this by making an introductory remark in which the verb συλλογίζεσθαι is combined with a cognate object, the only example that became known to us : συνελογίσατο παρ' ἑαυτῷ περὶ τῆς τῶν ὁμήρων προδοσίας συλλογισμὸν Ἰβηρικὸν καὶ βαρβαρικόν. PATON translates this by "*he reasoned with himself in a manner thoroughly Spanish and barbarian on the question of betraying the hostages*",[19] which better suits the whole situation than "*Consilium cepit*"/"he took the decision".

d) Finally, the verb can be used "*De meditando et philosophando*" as the *Thesaurus* says, quoting only Dio Chrysostom XXXV 22 as an example,[20] a passage which deals with the people of the Indians to whom indeed one might safely ascribe the invention of meditating. Having given a vivid picture of their beautiful, paradisian country which is intersected by many rivers, and of their happy life and the old age they attain, Dio goes on to say that in spite of all this there are still men called Βραχμᾶνες, οἵ, χαίρειν ἐάσαντες τούς τε ποταμοὺς ἐκείνους καὶ τοὺς παρ' αὐτοῖς ἐρριμμένους ἐκτραπέντες, ἰδίᾳ τι ξυλλο-

---

18 *Vol.* VII, Paris 1848-'54, 1037 A-B.

19 W. R. PATON, *Polybius, The Histories* (see n. 7), *vol.* II, 241.

20 *Vol.* VII, Paris 1848-'54, 1037, A-B.

γίζονται καὶ φροντίζουσι, πόνους τε θαυμαστοὺς ἀναλαβόμενοι τοῖς σώμασιν οὐδενὸς ἀναγκάζοντος καὶ καρτερήσεις δεινὰς ὑπομένοντες. In Passow's dictionary (1857) this passage is considered as an instance of the sense "*sich versammeln*", but this is not well possible in combination with τι and not in line, moreover, with the period of hermit's life or *vanaprastha* which every Brahman had to go through. The verb φροντίζειν does not have here any connotation of worry or anxiety but is more or less a synonym of συλλογίζεσθαι : "Although these people are in such good health and so many blessings are present, there are men called Brahmans who say farewell to those rivers and the people scattered along them, withdraw from life, and meditate and speculate in seclusion on a theme (? τι), while physically they undertake amazing labours though nothing compels them to do so, and endure fearful hardships".

The only further instance of συλλογίζεσθαι "to meditate" that we know of is in Perrin's translation of the *Life of Brutus* XXXVI 1-3 where Plutarch relates how his hero, who usually slept little, was particularly bothered by the future in the time immediately preceding the battle of Philippi : τεταμένος τῇ φροντίδι πρὸς τὸ μέλλον. The only sleep he permitted himself now was a short doze after supper : the further evening and night were devoted to urgent matters, and after these had been dealt with he used to read (ἀνεγίνωσκε βιβλίον) up to the third night watch when the officers came again to report to him. So before crossing over to Europe from Abydus he was sitting, as usually, in his tent at a very late hour, συλλογιζόμενός τι καὶ σκοπῶν πρὸς ἑαυτόν (XXXVI 3), "*meditating and reflecting*" in Per-rin's translation,[21] when suddenly there came to him an apparition, which proved to be his own evil genius who announced that the two of them would meet again at Philippi, an episode well known from Shakespeare's *Julius Caesar*. Plutarch's *Life of Caesar* contains the story as well (LXIX 5-7), but more briefly, so that the phrase important to us has no exact counterpart : ἀνεπαύετο, ὥσπερ εἰώθει, κατὰ σκηνήν, οὐ καθεύδων ἀλλὰ φροντίζων περὶ τοῦ μέλλοντος; next comes the remark that Brutus never slept much, which is immediately followed by the appearance of the ghost. Although φροντίζων περὶ τοῦ μέλλοντος matches *Life of Brutus* XXXVI 2 τεταμένος τῇ φρον-τίδι πρὸς τὸ μέλλον, which was not restricted to one night, it func-tions in the *Life of Caesar* LXIX 5 to depict Brutus' mood in the

---

[21] B. Perrin, *Plutarch's Lives* (see n. 17), *vol.* VI, 207.

night of the apparition and is therefore, in that respect, on a par with *Life of Brutus* XXXVI 3 συλλογιζόμενός τι *etc.* The latter phrase, therefore, is certainly to be interpreted in the light of the whole picture of Brutus' tension, and for that reason the pronoun τι, which like πρὸς ἑαυτόν, may be syntactically connected with both participles at the time, has not so much the sense of "somewhat", which would weaken συλλογιζόμενός to a mere musing without the notion of worry, but rather means "something" or "a matter". In view of the context this matter can hardly have been a subject Brutus had just been reading about, but more likely some military or political problem. For these reasons we prefer to *"meditating and reflecting"* a translation like "recapitulating and considering some matter with himself".

e) *Summary.* With the exception of d) "to meditate" the disputed senses cannot be shown to result with necessity from the respective contexts. For that reason we consider their incidental insertion in dictionaries at least as superfluous and as giving an unreal extension to the meaning of this word.

f) If we now bend our eye upon the Hellenistic-Jewish literature we perceive that our verb is much less frequent there than elsewhere. In the different Greek versions of the Old Testament it occurs only in the Septuagint, at Leviticus xxv 27, 50, 52, where it renders the pi'el of חשב and has the senses "to reckon" (*vss.* 27 and 50) and "to make a reckoning with" (*vs.* 52); it further occurs at Numbers xxiii 9 rendering the hithpa'el of חשב: καὶ ἐν ἔθνεσιν οὐ συλλογισθήσεται *"and not reckoning itself among the nations"* (R.S.V.), and finally, more important for comparison with the New Testament, at Isaiah XLIII 18 in chiastic parallelism: μὴ μνημονεύετε τὰ πρῶτα, καὶ τὰ ἀρχαῖα μὴ συλλογί-ζεσθε. The last two words are evidently the equivalent of the Masoretic אַל־תִּתְבֹּנָנוּ, for which Symmachus has: μὴ ἐννοεῖσθε. The Revised Standard Version renders the Hebrew by *"nor consider the things of old"*, the New English Bible has: *"and* (cease) *to brood over past history"*. It is only in this passage in the Septuagint that the hithpa'el of בין, which occurs 22 times in the Masorah, is matched by the verb συλλογίζεσθαι, elsewhere it is mostly represented by: (κατα-)νοέω, νουθετέω, συνίημι.

The Hebrew lexicon of Brown-Driver-Briggs circumscribes the meaning of this hithpa'el (or rather hithpo'lel) as *"shew oneself attentive, consider diligently, get understanding, understand, shew oneself to have understanding"*. From among these senses it is clearly *"consider diligent-ly"* which is the best equivalent of συλλογίζεσθαι, and therefore we would prefer, both for the Masorah and the Septuagint passage, a version as given in the New English Bible.

In the Old Testament Apocrypha and related literature συλλογί-ζεσθαι does not occur[22] but it is present, be it at four places only, in Philo's works.[23] In *De Iosepho* XXIV 113 the words τοῦ συλλογισθέν-τος, which are hardly clarified by the immediate context, seem to refer to the inventorized quantity of grain stored away by Joseph for the seven years of famine, a sense comparable to 1d) "to book". Greater difficulties are provided by the three occurrences in his cryptic *Legum Allegoriae*.

At II 99 an allegorical interpretation is given of the blessing of Dan as found in the Septuagint version of Genesis XLIX 17 : καὶ γενηθήτω Δὰν ὄφις ἐφ᾽ ὁδοῦ ἐγκαθήμενος ἐπὶ τρίβου, δάκνων πτέρναν ἵππου καὶ πεσεῖται ὁ ἱππεὺς εἰς τὰ ὀπίσω. The "horse" figuring in this blessing equals, according to Philo, the "passions of man" and the "horseman" his "mind" : Τὰ πάθη δὲ ἵππῳ ἀπεικάσθη (or rather : ἀπεικασθῇ, *cf.* the parallel νοητέον below)· τετρασκελὲς γὰρ ... (the Stoa distinguished four passions). Ὁ δὲ σωφροσύνης λόγος δάκνειν καὶ τιτρώσκειν φιλεῖ καὶ ἀναιρεῖν τὸ πάθος. Ἱππέα νοητέον ⟨τὸν⟩ ἐπιβεβηκότα τοῖς πάθεσι νοῦν, ὃς ἀποπίπτει τῶν παθῶν ὅταν αὐτὰ συλλογισθῇ καὶ πτερνισθῇ.

MONDÉSERT translates this : "*On doit comprendre le cavalier comme l'intelligence montée sur les passions : elle tombe des passions lorsque celles-ci ont été remises à la raison et qu'on les a fait trébucher*"; in a note he gives the following comment on this version : "*Ce mot de συλλογισθῇ est assez difficile à traduire : il semble que Philon songe à une intervention de la raison (λόγος) plutôt qu'à une reddition de comptes*"[24]. COLSON and WHITAKER have here "*... when they are brought to a reckoning and overthrown*",[25] COHN *etc.* on the other hand : "*... wenn sie vernünftig beurteilt und niedergerungen werden*".[26] If MONDÉSERT's remark is correct it seems reasonable to suppose that πτερνισθῇ as a metaphor corresponds with δάκνειν, τιτρώσκειν, ἀναιρεῖν, and that συλλογισθῇ refers then in a *non*-metaphorical way

[22] According to C. A. WAHL-J. B. BAUER, *Clavis Librorum Veteris Testamenti Apocryphorum Philologica*, Graz 1972.

[23] According to G. MAYER, *Index Philoneus*, Berlin-New York 1974.

[24] R. ARNALDEZ - J. POUILLOUX - Cl. MONDÉSERT, *Les œuvres de Philon d'Alexandrie*, Paris 1962, *vol.* II, 159 and 158 *n.* 2.

[25] F. H. COLSON - G. H. WHITAKER, *Philo* (Loeb Classical Library), London-Cambridge (Mass.) 1956, *vol.* I, 326-327.

[26] L. COHN, *etc.*, *Philo von Alexandria*, Berlin 1962, 2nd *ed.*, *vol.* III, 83.

to the action of the σωφροσύνης λόγος, the controling and moderating ratio. In that case we should have to do here with a diverging sense of συλλογίζεσθαι, based on λόγος "thinking" instead of λόγος "reckoning". Of course this is not impossible, especially not where it concerns Philo, but yet we believe that this passage can be interpreted in a more usual sense.

In order to prove this we shall have to deal first with *Legum Allegoriae* III 37 where another, still more far fetched allegory is given, on Exodus ii 12, the story of how Moses killed the Egyptian supervisor and hid him in the sand. According to what Philo writes in the next section (*par.* 38) the "Egyptian" stands for τὸ ἀνθρώπειον καὶ ἐπίκηρον πάθος "the human, mortal passion" (of loving bodily pleasure), whereas "the sand" is supposed to symbolize ὁ σπορὰς νοῦς "the incoherent mind" (*par.* 37). Now Philo says that the wicked man descends into his own incoherent mind when he tries to escape from God (τὸν Ὄντα, *cf.* Rev. I 4), which is shown by Moses, who smote the Egyptian and hid him in the sand: ὁ πατάξας τὸν Αἰγύπτιον καὶ κρύψας ἐν τῇ ἄμμῳ. This quotation is explained as follows: ὅπερ ἦν· συλλογισάμενος τὸν προστατεῖν λέγοντα ⟨τὰ⟩ τοῦ σώματος *"c'est-à-dire qu'il a supputé la valeur de celui qui dit que les choses du corps ont la priorité"*;[27] *"this means that he took full account of the man who ..."*.[28] From *par.* 38 where our verb recurs, one gets the impression that it explains or even equals κρύψας only: πατάξας καὶ συλλογισάμενος τὸν φιλήδονον *"il a frappé et réglé son compte à l'ami du plaisir"*,[29] *"after smiting and thoroughly reckoning up the lover of pleasure"*;[30] in this latter case both translations introduce unnecessary variation in rendering our verb: it is abundantly clear that it refers here to exactly the same thing as in the preceding paragraph 37.

Although the context of III 37-38 is no more revealing than at II 99, the three passages have at least in common that they are about the πάθη, either about ἡδονή alone, or about all four, and also that the νοῦς plays some part in them. However, at II 99 the νοῦς is meant *in bonam partem*, whereas it is said to be in a bad state, σπορὰς, incoherent, at III 37-38. Nevertheless we think it possible to assume that in the three of them the verb has one and the same

[27] ARNALDEZ-POUILLOUX-MONDÉSERT, *o.c.*, 191.
[28] COLSON-WHITAKER, *o.c.*, 326-327.
[29] ARNALDEZ-POUILLOUX-MONDÉSERT, *o.c.*, 191.
[30] COLSON-WHITAKER, *o.c.*, 327.

sense, namely "to evaluate", in accordance with the version "*supputer la valeur*" given by MONDÉSERT for III 37. At II 99 where the νοῦς itself is positive, its judgment of the passions can only be negative, disapproving: "when the νοῦς takes them (the πάθη) for what they are worth". At III 38, however, where the νοῦς is wrong being in favour of pleasure, one of the passions, the verb συλλογισάμενος as a consequence has a more positive tone, for instance "having valued (the life of) the lover of pleasure". This sense of "determining the value of", which is not in the general semantic description above, can be seen as a variant in between the senses 1c, 2a and 2c.

Passing on to that other Hellenistic Jew, Flavius Josephus, we see that he uses the verb συλλογίζεσθαι still more sparingly than Philo did, namely twice in the *Bellum Judaicum*, but the two places are much easier to interpret: I 560 συνελογίζετο δὲ τὸ ἑαυτοῦ μῖσος καὶ τὸν τῶν ὀρφανῶν ἔλεος ἐκ τοῦ ἔθνους "*Er* (*i.e.* Antipater) *stellte aber auch den Hass des Volkes gegen seine Person und dessen Mitleid mit den Waisen in Rechnung, ...*"

IV 125 καὶ μεγάλα τῆς ἑαυτῶν ἁλώσεως συνελογίζοντο τὰ τεκμήρια (das Volk) "*das folgern musste, diese Vorgänge seien deutliche Vorzeichen für ihre eigene Gefangennahme*".[31]

g) The first Christian known to have used συλλογίζεσθαι after Luke is Justin Martyr, who certainly was acquainted with the Platonic uses of the verb. He asks his Jewish opponent Tryphon the question: ... οὐδὲ νῦν, ἀκούων ὅτι Ἰησοῦς ἐστιν ὁ Χριστὸς ἡμῶν, συλλογίζῃ οὐκ ἀργῶς οὐδ᾽ ὡς ἔτυχεν ἐκείνῳ τεθεῖσθαι τοὔνομα; The translation in the Anti-Nicene Library runs: "*... you consider not that the name was bestowed on Him not purposely nor by chance*"[31a]; but we would prefer something like: "even now, when you learn that Jesus is our Messiah, don't you draw the conclusion that it was intentionally and not by chance that this name was bestowed on Him?" The later Churchfathers, such as John Chrysostom, Epiphanius, Theodoretus, use the verb more frequently; in their writings there occur also instances of a new semantic development: συλλογίζεσθαι has adopted the further sense of: "to outreason, to overcome in argument" (with συν- as in συντρίβειν?). LAMPE's lexicon mentions as the earliest instance Acta Petri et Pauli LXVII where these two apostles say to the emperor Nero: Ἀγαθὲ βασιλεῦ, οὗτοι οἱ ἄνθρωποι συνελογίσαντο τὴν εὐμένειάν σου "Good King, these men have outreasoned

---

[31] As translated by O. Michel - O. Bauernfeind, Munich 1962-1969 (2nd ed.), *vol.* I, 149; *vol.* II, 1, 21.

[31a] *ch.* CXIII, Edinburgh 1867, *vol.* II, 240.

Your Grace".[32] But this new sense should not concern us to much, it is time to return to the New Testament.

h) Against the Classical and Hellenistic background συλλογίζεσθαι at Luke xx 5 does not seem to offer anything difficult or divergent. The chapter contains the wellknown dispute in the Temple between highpriests, scribes and elders on the one hand, and Jesus on the other, the issue being the authority of the latter : vs. 2 εἰπὸν ἡμῖν ἐν ποίᾳ ἐξουσίᾳ ταῦτα ποιεῖς ἢ τίς ἐστιν ὁ δούς σοι τὴν ἐξουσίαν ταύτην. It is now Jesus' tactics to make his answer hang on their reply to his own counterquestion : vs. 4 τὸ βάπτισμα Ἰωάννου ἐξ οὐρανοῦ ἦν ἢ ἐξ ἀνθρώπων; To the subsequent activity of his adversaries the other Gospelwriters do not refer by συλλογίζεσθαι; Mark (xi 31) has : καὶ διελογίζοντο πρὸς ἑαυτοὺς λέγοντες (ελογιζοντο: א al ΑΓΦ 700 pm; at illi cogitabant secum dicentes: Vulg.), and Matthew (xxi) 25) with a trifling variant : οἱ δὲ διελογίζοντο πρὸς ἑαυτοὺς λέγοντες (παρ εαυτοις: א CDΘ א pm: at illi cogitabant inter se dicentes : Vulg.). According to LIDDELL-SCOTT the verb used by Mark-Matthew can have, just like συλλογίζεσθαι, the senses "to calculate" and "to consider", but also "to debate, argue, discuss"; BAUER says that the sense "erwägen" prevails in the New Testament, especially when the verb is combined with prepositional phrases like πρὸς ἑαυτούς, ἐν ταῖς καρδίαις, etc.;[33] the Vulgate's "cogitabant" "to consider thoroughly, ponder, weigh, reflect upon" is a somewhat one-sided choice in that it only brings out the mental activity and no longer the verbal as well. In the Vulgate, moreover, where on the one hand Matthew and Luke's "at illi" (for οἱ δὲ) has also been used at Mark xi 31 where no pronoun is present in the Greek, and on the other hand Matthew and Mark's "cogitabant" (for διελογίζοντο) also serves to render συνελογίσαντο at Luke xx 5 without taking account of the semantic difference between the Greek verbs, the story has clearly fallen a victim to some tendency towards harmonization.

Let us now look more closely at this διαλογισμός of Jesus' opponents and pay special attention to its structure. In Mark xi 31-33 it runs :
ἐὰν εἴπωμεν· "ἐξ οὐρανοῦ" ἐρεῖ· "διὰ τί οὖν οὐκ ἐπιστεύσατε αὐτῷ;" ἀλλὰ εἴπωμεν· "ἐξ ἀνθρώπων";
(ἐφοβοῦντο τὸν ὄχλον· ἅπαντες γὰρ εἶχον τὸν Ἰωάννην ὄντως ὅτι προφήτης ἦν.)

---

[32] i.e. Martyrium Petri et Pauli 67, dated to c. A.D. 190.
[33] W. BAUER, Wörterbuch zum Neuen Testament, Berlin 1971[5],

The alternative ἐξ ἀνθρώπων to which they adhered in reality is
not mentioned in a parallel hypothetical phrase, but in a rhetorical
question which contains a dubitative subjunctive. Moreover, the scribes
themselves do not say what consequences might result from the answer,
but the impossibility of giving this answer is implied by the rhetorical
character of the question and by Mark's own comment that they were
afraid of these consequences: ἐφοβοῦντο *etc*. Formally there is here
no complete scheme of reasoning with parallel constituents : the second
part is incomplete and as we saw, its possible contents have been
phrased otherwise.

In Matthew xxi 25-26 the former part of the διαλογισμός is identical
with Mark xi 31b, except for the unimportant addition of ἡμῖν after
ἐρεῖ. The whole has become a little more balanced by the fact that
the alternative answer to Jesus' question is now also introduced by
ἐὰν εἴπωμεν, but here again, what this second answer would entail is
not specified : the scribes merely say that in that case they would
be afraid. That this is done in direct speech is a further step towards a
parallelism between the two parts of the discussion : ἐὰν εἴπωμεν·
"ἐξ ἀνθρώπων" φοβούμεθα τὸν ὄχλον· πάντες γὰρ ὡς προφήτην
ἔχουσιν τὸν Ἰωάννην. The variant reading ειχον makes indirect speech
again of the latter phrase, but it is only attested by λ, lat, sy. In
this structure the future indicative ἐρεῖ is paralleled by the present
indicative φοβούμεθα, which for this reason and also because the
consequences as such are here again omitted, is somewhat difficult
to translate; "we (shall) have to fear"? What one expects is a phrase
headed by μὴ and including a futural subjunctive, such as *μὴ
ἀποκτείνωσιν ἡμᾶς : "If we say 'From man' we are afraid they are
going to kill us".

In Luke's version finally, the scribes' conversation has taken the
shape of a harmonious, evenly balanced scheme, since in the latter
half the consequences feared are mentioned as such and in direct
speech. Both parts now run completely parallel in that they contain :
a) ἐὰν εἴπωμεν; b) either of the answers possible headed by ἐξ;
c) the consequence of this answer in the future indicative :

a) ἐὰν εἴπωμεν. b) "ἐξ οὐρανοῦ" c) ἐρεῖ · "διὰ τί οὐκ ἐπιστεύσατε
αὐτῷ;"

a) ἐὰν εἴπωμεν· b) "ἐξ ἀνθρώπων" c) ὁ λαὸς ἅπας καταλιθάσει
ἡμᾶς.

It is not surprising, therefore, that in contradistinction to Mark and
Matthew he has chosen a different verb in order to bring out, no

doubt, that what we have here is a piece of logical reasoning and not so much discussion only : xx 5 οἱ δὲ συνελογίσαντο πρὸς ἑαυτοὺς λέγοντες ὅτι (συνελογιζοντο: א..CDWΘ al; διελογισαντο: λ al; *at illi cogitabant intra se dicentes quia*: Vulg.). For all this we prefer versions like "*this set them arguing ...*" (N.E.B.) or "*now they reasoned...*" (MOFFATT) to "*and they discussed it...*" (R.S.V.), and WEIZSÄCKER'S "*sie aber berechneten...*" to LUTHER'S "*sie aber bedachten's ...*" Martin Luther may have been influenced by the Vulgate's uniform "*cogitabant*", which in that case he took in its most neutral sense; from his translation it probably found its way to BAUER'S lexicon which *s.v.* mentions two senses only : "*(bei sich) überlegen, bedenken*". In addition to the remark that the word occurs since Herodotus, and in Plato, Demosthenes, Polybius, the Septuagint, inscriptions and papyri, the following instances are given : Isaiah XLIII 18, Philo *Leg. all.* II 99, Josephus *Bellum* I 560, IV 125 and finally Plutarch *Pomp.* LX 3 (*i.e.* 2).

Now we hope to have demonstrated in the preceding lines that such senses as given by BAUER are much too weak in general and certainly unfit to circumscribe the sense of the verb in all the passages adduced, including Luke xx 5. With regard to two of them, Philo and Josephus *Bellum* I 560, they are even out of place as our discussion above may have shown. As a matter of fact we think that none of the places adduced offers a close parallel to the passage to be clarified, Luke xx 5. The different senses of συλλογίζεσθαι given by BAUER by way of semantic description represent only a restricted choice from the total meaning; the lemma, therefore, gives the wrong impression that the word had no further senses. The senses not present in the New Testament need not be dealt with extensively in a New Testament lexicon, but some sketchy survey such as given by THAYER is to be preferred to their wholly being unmentioned. THAYER'S lexicon has *s.v.* :

"a) to bring together accounts, reckon up, compute, (Hdt. et sqq.)
   b) to reckon with one's self, to reason, (Plat., Dem., Polyb., al) : Lk XX.5."[34]

The parallels which WETTSTEIN quotes to elucidate our passage are Plutarch *Pompey* LX 2 which we have seen, and Demosthenes XVIII 172:[35] ἀλλ᾽ ὡς ἔοικεν, ἐκεῖνος ὁ καιρὸς καὶ ἡ ἡμέρα 'κείνη οὐ μόνον εὔνουν καὶ πλούσιον ἄνδρ᾽ ἐκάλει, ἀλλὰ καὶ παρηκολουθηκότα τοῖς πράγμασιν ἐξ ἀρχῆς καὶ συλλελογισμένον ὀρθῶς τίνος

---

[34] J.H. THAYER, *A Greek-English Lexicon of the New Testament*, Edinburgh 1908⁴.
[35] J. J. WETSTENIUS, Η ΚΑΙΝΗ ΔΙΑΘΗΚΗ, *Novum Testamentum Graecum (etc.)*, Graz 1962 (repr. Amsterdam 1752), *vol.* I, *ad locum.*

ἕνεκα ταῦτ' ἔπραττεν ὁ Φίλιππος καὶ τί βουλόμενος "... *had rightly fathomed the purposes and desires of Philip"* [36] or, more literally "had drawn the right conclusions about ..." Again we hold the opinion that neither these two passages are very close to Luke xx 5. A better illustration would be offered by an instance of the verb συλλογίζεσθαι which is followed by an explicit example of reasoning, and from among all that we have come across the best instance thusfar seems to be the Diogenes anecdote which opened this article, although the types of reasoning are essentially different:

Συνελογίζετο δὲ καὶ οὕτως·
 Τῶν θεῶν ἐστι πάντα· φίλοι δὲ οἱ σοφοὶ τοῖς θεοῖς.
 "Κοινὰ" δὲ "τὰ τῶν φίλων"· πάντ' ἄρα ἐστὶ τῶν σοφῶν.

---

[36] C. A. VINCE and J. H. VINCE, *Demosthenes* (see n. 16), *vol.* II, 135.

TWO CREATIVE ENCOUNTERS IN THE WORK OF LUKE

Luke xxiv 13-35 and Acts viii 26-40

C. H. LINDIJER

Working at my commentary on the Acts of the Apostles and busy with the story of Philip and the eunuch I observed that there are points of contact between this story and that of the Men of Emmaus.[1] I was glad with this discovery and resolved to work out this matter some time. Afterwards I perceived that others before me had already seen the resemblance between the two pericopes.[2] In this article I want to raise this subject once again and enter into three questions:

1. What motifs have the two stories in common?
2. How did Luke come by the series of common motifs?
3. What is the theological importance of these common motifs?

1. The points of agreement in the two stories

Both stories deal with people being on the way: the two followers of Jesus and the Ethiopian eunuch. Minor points of resemblance are: the use of "and see" (καὶ ἰδού, Luke xxiv 13; Acts viii 27); the fact that both are coming from Jerusalem (Luke xxiv 13 and 33; Acts viii 26 and 27) and are going to a place where they belong (Acts viii 28; cf. Luke xxiv 29); the use of the words "road" (ὁδός, Luke xxiv 32 and 35; Acts viii 26, 36 and 39) and "go" (πορεύομαι, Luke xxiv 13 and 28 — twice —; cf. vs. 15 συμπορεύομαι; Acts viii 26, 27, 36 and 39). — Generally, the resemblance of the two stories is not due to the use of identical words.

The men of Emmaus are talking together. The Ethiopian has nobody to talk with, he is reading the prophet Isaiah, and in a way he has a talk with him. The subjects are related: the crucifixion of Jesus, the suffering servant.

---

[1] C. H. LINDIJER, Handelingen van de Apostelen I, Nijkerk 1975, 225.

[2] I found this question touched upon with the following authors (the great number of Roman Catholic authors is noteworthy): J. DUPONT, Les pèlerins d'Emmaüs (Luc. xxiv 13-35), Miscellanea biblica B. Ubach, Montserrat 1953, 361 ff. J. DUPONT, Le repas d'Emmaüs, LV(B) 31 (1957), 90 ff. J. A. GRASSI, Emmaus revisited (Luke 24, 13-35 and Acts 8, 36-40), CBQ 26 (1964), 463 ff. J. KREMER, Die Osterbotschaft der vier Evangelien, Stuttgart ³1969, 68 ff. X. LÉON-DUFOUR, Réssurrection de Jésus et message pascal, Paris 1971, 213 ff. J. WANKE, "... wie sie ihn beim Brotbrechen erkannten", Zur Auslegung der Emmauserzählung Lk 24, 13-35, BZ 18 (1974), 192.

Another traveller, a stranger, joins these travellers : Jesus comes up and walks with the men of Emmaus and a follower of his, Philip, a man "full of the Spirit and of wisdom" (Acts vi 3) comes to the Ethiopian at the initiative of an angel of the Lord and led by the Spirit. In both stories a conversation arises and in both cases it is opened by a question of the stranger. There is some agreement between that which the travellers bring out : the men of Emmaus are disappointed about what has happened to Jesus and the Ethiopian is incapable of understanding the prophesy. Another parallel is that in both stories the readers know who the stranger is : the risen Jesus, the follower and preacher Philip, and that the travellers do not know this. In Luke xxiv this is expressed: they do not recognize Jesus (ἐπιγινώσκω, vs 16), the time of recognition comes later (ἐπιγινώσκω, vs 31, cf. vs 35, γινώσκω). Parallel to this we may say that in a certain sense the eunuch has Jesus with him, in the text from Isaiah, but that he does not understand at first (γινώσκω, vs 30, a play upon words with ἀναγινώσκω, vs 30, also used in vss 28, 30 — second time — and 32).

In both stories the conversation about the Old Testament, the Scripture(s), γραφή, γραφαί (Luke xxiv 27 and 32; Acts viii 32 and 35) — cf. also "prophet", "prophets" (Luke xxiv 25 and 27; Acts viii 28, 30 and 34) — is an important element. The travellers to Emmaus are "fools, and slow of heart to believe all that the prophets said"; the Ethiopian does not understand what he reads with the prophet Isaiah. In both stories the stranger now interferes. Jesus explains the things concerning himself in all the Scriptures; He does so "beginning with Moses and with all the prophets" (Luke xxiv 27); He "opens the Scriptures" (vs 32). Philip begins with "this scripture", viz. the verses quoted from the prophet Isaiah, and preaches the good news of Jesus (viii 35, εὐαγγελίζομαι τὸν Ἰησοῦν). — In both stories Luke writes "beginning with" (ἀρξάμενος ἀπό), and uses the word περι (Luke xxiv 27; Acts viii 34). — In both cases Luke gives a somewhat more concrete form to the interpretation with regard to Jesus. The prophets had said that it was God's will and intention ("it was needful") that the Messiah suffered and (in this way) entered upon his glory (Luke xxiv 25 and 26). And in the text from Isaiah quoted in the Acts the Christian interpretation will have heard the message about Jesus' sufferings and resurrection, his exaltation and spiritual offspring. According to both stories the principal point in the Scripture is Jesus' cross, his resurrection and exaltation. Luke relates in both stories that the travellers understand this interpretation : the hearts of the men of

Emmaus (at first "slow to believe all that the prophets said") now begin "to burn within them" when Jesus opens the Scriptures to them; the Ethiopian wants to be baptized after the interpretation of the Scripture; obviously he gives credit to it.

Both in the Gospel-story and in Acts the interpretation is followed by what with a general term I would call a Sacred Act. This is clear without comment in Acts viii. The stranger baptizes the traveller. There is "no hindrance" to admit this non-Jew, this eunuch into the congregation. The baptism is described more or less in detail (the words "to go down" and "to come up", "to baptize" — twice —, "water" — four times —; Philip and the eunuch mentioned in vs. 38). With respect to Luke xxiv there is no unanimity, but in our opinion Luke has thought here of a Sacred Act too, viz. the Lord's Supper. The stranger serves it to the travellers. — The way of describing the facts speaks for finding the Lord's Supper here : the use of the words κλάσις (vs. 35; Acts ii 42) and κλάω (vs. 30; Acts ii 46; xx 7 and 11; Mark xiv 22 and par.; I Cor x 16 and xi 24); to take the bread (Mark xiv 22 and par.; I Cor xi 23), to give it (Mark xiv 22 and par.) and to bless it (Mark xiv 24; Matth xxvi 26). The fact that Jesus suddenly acts the host here[3] also points into the direction of the Eucharist. The recognition of the risen Jesus (mentioned twice, vss 31 and 35) is also well in harmony with the Lord's Supper : there Jesus is "seen", there the risen One is met.

An invitation precedes the meal : abide with us (vs 29). Acts also have an invitation : the Ethiopian asks Philip to get in and to sit with him (viii 31). This invitation, however, stands at an earlier moment, before the interpretation. The Ethiopian touches upon baptism (vs 36); this may also be considered a kind of invitation.

In both stories Luke, after the Sacred Act, abruptly puts an end to the meeting as a result of a miraculous disappearance of the stranger. Jesus became invisible to the travellers to Emmaus (Luk xxiv 31). The Spirit of the Lord caught Philip away (ἁρπάζω, to take by force) and the eunuch saw no more of him (Acts viii 39). — The Spirit led him to the carriage, now the Spirit takes him away. — In the Gospel story the sudden disappearance is more obvious than in the more "ordinary" story in Acts. The fact that Acts viii describes in such a way the end of Philip's presence, does accentuate that what had

---

[3] As a rule the host performed the opening ceremonial of the meal (benediction and breaking of the bread). He could also delegate this to a guest, however. Cf. H. L. STRACK - P. BILLERBECK, *Kommentar zum Neuen Testament aus Talmud und Midrasch* IV, München [4]1965, 621 and 623).

happened was most uncommon and significant. It is stated where Philip finds himself afterwards, in Asdod (viii 40). In a way we can compare this to the fact that Jesus, who had vanished from sight, is back in Jerusalem after some time (Luke xxiv 36).

At the end of both stories the travellers start on their way again. For the men of Emmaus it means a turn : they go back to Jerusalem at the same hour (Luke xxiv 33). The eunuch travels on to his country : for him a turn is indicated in "rejoicing" (Acts viii 39). The stranger continues his work : Jesus makes his appearance in Jerusalem (Luke xxiv 36) — and has appeared to Simon (vs 34) —; Philip brings the good news from Asdod to Caesarea (Acts viii 40), as he did to the Ethiopian. The work is going on. — That the work of preaching is going on also holds good for the travellers to Emmaus (Luke xxiv 35); preaching by the Ethiopian in his country may be presumed, but the story does not mention it.

It is also possible to find a resemblance in the two stories as regards the way in which various moments have been grouped. It is our belief that we can show the following structure in the two pericopes. For this purpose both stories have been noted down in form of a kind of horseshoe and corresponding elements are placed next to each other. The interpretation of the Scripture and the Sacred Act stand at a central spot.[4]

Luke xxiv

Women report to the eleven and others upon resurrection (9 and 10)	Cleopas and his fellow-traveller relate what has happened to them to the eleven and others (35)
they are not believed (11)	the eleven and others testify to their faith (33 and 34)
Cleopas and fellow-traveller go from Jerusalem to Emmaus (13)	they go from Emmaus to Jerusalem (33)
they talk together (14)	they talk together (32)
Jesus approaches and walks with them (15)	Jesus disappears (31)
their eyes are held from recognizing Him (16)	their eyes are opened and they recognize Him (31)
Jesus explains the Scriptures (27) — Before this He asks, pretending to be ignorant : what things? (19) —	Jesus serves supper (30) — Before this He pretends to continue his walk (28) —

THEY APPROACH EMMAUS (28)

---

[4] I was put on the right track by what Léon-Dufour writes about the structure of the story of the men of Emmaus (*o.c.*, 212 f.), and I also deviate from him. With the structure of this story also occupy themselves F. SCHNIDER and W. STENGER, *Beobachtungen zur Struktur der Emmausperikope* (Lk 24, 13-35), *BZ* 16 (1972), 94 ff.

Acts viii

Philip goes to the road Jerusalem-Gaza (26 and 27)

Ethiopian returns from Jerusalem to Ethiopia (27 and 28)

the Spirit leads Philip to the Ethiopian and he hears the latter read (29 and 30)

while they are in the carriage together (31) Philip explains the Scripture (35) after preceding question of the Ethiopian (34)

Philip goes as far as Caesarea (40)

Ethiopian continues his way rejoicing (39)

the Spirit of the Lord catches Philip away and the Ethiopian sees no more of him (39)

while they are in the water together Philip baptizes the Ethiopian (38) after preceding question of the Ethiopian (36)

THEY COME TO THE WATER (36)

2. The origin of the series of motifs

We presume that the series of motifs, to be found in the two pericopes, is a conception of Luke. We do not have the impression that he borrows it from others. Possibly individual motifs may be found elsewhere, but the combination seems new to us. H. GUNKEL wrote in view of the story of the men of Emmaus : "Christus erscheint hier unbekannt, als Wanderer — so wie es die Gottheit von alters liebte, in schlichter menschlicher Gestalt, etwa als Wanderer verkleidet, unter den Menschen zu wandeln — und offenbart sein geheimnisvolles göttliches Wesen an einzelnen Zügen; aber sobald er erkannt wird, ist er verschwunden. Dieser Aufriss der Geschichte ist ganz analog den ältesten Erzählungen vom Erscheinen der Gottheit; die Geschichte könnte ihrem Stil nach in der Genesis stehen!".[5] GUNKEL refers to places in his commentary on Genesis,[6] where he writes about "God's conversation with Hagar" (Gen xvi 7ff.) and the visit to Abraham (Gen xviii 1ff.). But these examples are not so striking yet. We find even more relation in the story of Jacob at Bethel (Gen xxviii). Related features are : the traveller is in a problematic situation; there is an unexpected meeting with the world of God; at first the traveller does not know what peculiar things are happening; there is a Sacred Act (with the stone). There is a special relation between the two stories in the version of D, who reads instead of Emmaus Οὐλαμμαους, which in a certain version of the Septuagint stands for Luz. L. VAN HARTINGS-VELD, who wrote about this, says : "On both stories goes : Surely the

---

[5] *Zum religionsgeschichtlichen Verständnis des Neuen Testaments*, Göttingen 1903, 71.
[6] *Genesis, übersetzt und erklärt*, Göttingen ²1902, 165, 170 and 174ff.

Lord is in this place, and I knew it not".[7] Yet we cannot say that the
story of Jacob has stood model for the story of the men of Emmaus or
for both stories dealt with by us. Parallels from other religions may
also be adduced,[8] but here too we are under the impression that it is a
matter of details, not of the whole series of motifs.

It seems to us that another pericope written by Luke is related to
our stories : the description of the conversion of Paul. Saul travels
from Jerusalem to Damascus. The risen Jesus suddenly meets him,
appears to him on the road (Acts ix 17 and 27 — cf. Luke xxiv)
and the follower sent by the Lord comes to him (cf. Acts viii). There
is question of Saul recovering his sight (cf. Luke xxiv), be it in a different
sense. It results in his being baptized. Yet here too the element of
interpreting the Scriptures is wanting. The affinity between our stories
and that of Saul's conversion certainly fortifies the impression that
the series of motifs was important to Luke.

We may ask ourselves how Luke came to creating these series of
motifs. We can guess that there was some influence of what regularly
took place in the congregations of Luke and his readers. Again and
again the congregation met the risen Lord in the Scriptures (the
Old Testament), in the interpretation of the Scriptures (which the
preachers gave and in them the Lord himself) and in de Lord's Supper
and baptism. — Cf. WANKE : "Die Unterweisung auf dem Weg (Lk
24, 17ff) spiegelt wohl die missionarische (antebaptismale?) Verkündi-
gung der Kirche jener Zeit wider, der Taufe (vgl. Apg 8, 26ff) und
Eucharistie folgen".[9]

We could go even further and see in both stories a reflection of the
liturgy of the congregational meetings in Luke's time, with Scripture +
interpretation and the Lord's Supper and baptism for central moments.
Compare the article by R. ORLETT, who points out the agreement
between the experience of the men of Emmaus and that of the early
Christian at his liturgical meeting.[10] Liturgical influence on an important
part of the series of motifs seems possible. But we know too little of
the liturgy of the early congregations to get further than suppositions.

---

[7] Codex D en Emmaus, *NedThT* 7 (1952-1953), 363 ff.

[8] Cf. H. GUNKEL, *Genesis, übersetzt und erklärt*, Göttingen [4]1917, 193 f.; R. BULT-
MANN, *Die Geschichte der synoptischen Tradition*, Göttingen [7]1967, 310; A. EHRHARDT,
The disciples of Emmaus, NTS 10 (1963-1964), 194 ff.

[9] *a.c.*, 191.

[10] An influence of the early liturgy upon the Emmaus account, *CBQ* 21 (1959),
212 ff.

We mention yet the conclusions GRASSI draws from the agreement between the two stories. He points to the travelling apostle in the early church, the stranger who meets new people in new places. Those who receive him with hospitality and listen with faith to his word in the explanation of the Scriptures come to know Christ himself, especially in the Eucharist. Christ shows his power both in the word and in the breaking of the bread. What Luke teaches is based on an experience that he and many others had in the early church — that of Christ manifesting himself as a mysterious stranger, a travelling apostle. If GRASSI's supposition is right, we have a key to the origin of Luke's series of motifs. Again we cannot say much but : it could be possible, but we do not know much about it. Was the presence of Christ strongly felt in the travelling apostle? And was he really felt to be a *mysterious* stranger?

3. *The kerugma*

We will now examine the theological significance of the series of common motifs in the two stories. What is the kerugma which Luke wants to bring in these common motifs, which he obviously thinks of importance? First a quotation of J. Kremer : "The way of the disciples respectively the eunuch to the belief in the Risen One via explanation of the Scripture and communion respectively baptism is an example for the readers".[11]

The stories are concerned with a man, who is on his way with his problems (being in flight, disappointed, he does not understand). It is the man who has not yet come to belief, who has not yet found somebody who shows him the way and who not yet "goes on rejoicing". Such a man may be a Jew or an gentile.

Something can happen to such people. There is a meeting, a dialogue begins, questions are put and answered to, problems are expressed. The meeting is not accidental. It is Jesus of Nazareth, raised from the dead by God, the fellow-traveller sent by his angel or Spirit, who accompanies these people on their way. In the human conversation with a more than human dimension conclusive things will happen. Inter-human meetings on the way can be extremely creative.

The Scripture has an important place in what happens to the travellers. Obviously things are not possible without the Scripture (the Old Testament!). Sometimes Luke is critical of the Jews, but

---

[11] *o.c.* 70.

for him it is a fact : it is to be found in the Old Testament; all
people who are on their way, Jews as well as gentiles, must go via
these Scriptures. We must read the Scriptures in such a way that they
become transparent and Jesus becomes visible. What Jesus was, did
and said was the deepest mystery of this Scripture. In order to make
people discover this it is necessary for the Scriptures to be interpreted
(διερμηνεύω), they must be opened and the mind must be opened
to understanding them (Luke xxiv 32 and 45). It is a human being
who interprets the Scripture and it is also the Lord himself who does
it.

The suffering, failing Messiah, the silent, humble servant, the small-
ness of the revelation of God in the world, is a problem to people.
But via Scripture and interpretation they can discover that God's way
to "glory" goes via the cross.

The Sacred Act takes an important place in what happens to people
on the way. It is an event : which makes something visible; which has
in it a personal decision (the invitation : "abide with us"; the request
to be baptized) and the character of receiving (the stranger baptizes,
the stranger passes the bread); which establishes a relation with the
Messiah (baptizing connects with Him; at the Eucharist they recognize
Him) and his congregation.

In the fact that the meetings take place unexpectedly and are abruptly
broken off again, we can hear first of all that man does not command
this creative happening himself : it comes on his way without being
expected and suddenly it is over. It also implicates that there is no
permanent presence, the relation is broken off again, the word and
the Sacred Act are present for a moment only. Cf. H. OOSTERHUIS :
"Then you. I hear your voice. I see — sometimes, for a moment
only".[12]

The road of people goes on after the creative meeting, but things
have changed by it. The direction is different, there is no longer a
flight (men of Emmaus), the state of mind is different (the Ethiopian
is full of joy now).

The stories also say that what happened on the way, will happen
elsewhere in course of time (Jesus appears in Jerusalem, Philip preaches
in the towns). "Die Sache Jesu geht weiter" (cf. W. MARXSEN).[13]
The men of Emmaus tell in Jerusalem later on what happened; from

---

[12] *Zien — soms even, fragmenten over God* (to see — sometimes, for a moment,
fragments about God), Bilthoven [2]1972, 8.

[13] W. MARXSEN, *Die Auferstehung Jesu als historisches und als theologisches Problem,*

the eunuch something like it could be supposed. It is somewhat like a chain-reaction; through those who had the meeting the cause of Jesus goes on too. — In Acts ix, a story with related features, this element is strongly present : Saul, who has the meeting on his way, becomes the "chosen instrument" to bear Jesus' name before gentiles, kings and sons of Israel (cf. vs 15). — From the agreement between the two stories we can also hear : what Jesus did then, now does his follower (Philip) in a similar way,[14] through the followers his "cause" goes on.

It is these things we hear Luke preach in the series of motifs of these two stories.

---

in MARXSEN, WILCKENS, DELLING and GEIER, *Die Bedeutung der Auferstehungsbotschaft für den Glauben an Jesus Christus*, Gütersloh ⁶1968, 29.

[14] Cf. J. WANKE : "Was in der Äthiopiergeschichte exemplarisch als missionarisches Bemühen der Kirche herausgestellt wird, hat nach Auskunft des Evangelisten seine Grundlegung im Tun (Lk 24, 25ff) ... des Auferstandenen" (*a.c.* 192).

JOHN XVIII 28 AND THE DATE OF THE CRUCIFIXION

H. MULDER

After having examined attempts to harmonize the synoptic gospels with John and attempts to harmonize John with the synoptics, as well as solutions concerning the slaughtering of the lambs on two different days and the eating of the Passover on different days, A. J. B. HIGGINS summed up the results regarding the harmonization of John with the synoptics in this way: "John xiii 1 and 29 are of little use in this connection; John xviii 28 contradicts the synoptics; the evidence in John xix[1] is best taken as in agreement with them. The attempts to entirely harmonize John with the synoptics must be judged a failure, while we have seen the impossibility of harmonizing the synoptics with the Johannine chronology of the Passion".[2]

It is evident: John xviii 28 is the main stumbling-block in determining the date of the crucifixion. For all other texts it is possible to give a satisfactory explanation, but in the case of the Passover, which the Jews — according to John, in contrast with the synoptics (cf. Mk. xiv 12-16; par.) — had still to await for, one encounters almost unsolvable problems up till now.[3]

In my opinion it is therefore sensible to take a closer look at John xviii 28. There are no problems concerning textual criticism.[4]

---

[1] Cf. Jn. xix 14, 31, 42.

[2] A. J. B. HIGGINS, The origins of the Eucharist, *NTS* I (1955), 208.

[3] An almost complete survey of all publications until 1950: H. LESSIG, *Die Abendmahlsprobleme im Lichte der neutestamentlichen Forschung seit 1900*, Bonn 1953; N. GELDENHUYS, *Commentary on the Gospel of Luke*, London-Edinburgh, 1951 ([5]1960), 649-670: Excursus: "The day and date of the crucifixion", with rich bibliographical material; H. MULDER, De datum van de kruisiging, I, *GThT* 51 (1951), 176-189, a review of the different solutions, their "pro's and con's", until 1950. Since 1957 the discussion was ruled by the solution presented in the book of: A. JAUBERT, La Date de la Cène, Calendrier Biblique et Liturgie Chrétienne (ÉtB), Paris 1957. Miss JAUBERT concluded that Jesus had stuck to the calender of Qumran. The description of the synoptics was based on this calendar. John on the other hand followed the indications of the calendar of Jerusalem. Against this solution: J. JEREMIAS, *Die Abendmahlsworte Jesu*, Gottingen [3]1960, 18-19; J. BLINZLER, *Der Prozess Jesu*, Regensburg [3]1960, 82-84; *idem, ZNW* 49 (1959), 238-251; P. BENOIT, *Exegese und Theologie*, Düsseldorf 1965, 259; E. LOHSE, *Die Geschichte des Leidens und Sterbens Jesu Christi*, Gütersloh [2]1967, 48-50; W. TRILLING, *Fragen zur Geschichtlichkeit Jesu*, Düsseldorf [3]1969, 125-131; E. LOHSE, *Umwelt des Neuen Testaments* (GNT I), Göttingen 1971, 80.

[4] B. M. METZGER, *A Textual Commentary on the Greek New Testament*, London-New York 1971, 252.

Ἄγουσιν οὖν τὸν Ἰησοῦν ἀπὸ τοῦ Καϊάφα εἰς τὸ πραιτώριον·
ἦν δὲ πρωΐ· καὶ αὐτοὶ οὐκ εἰσῆλθον εἰς τὸ πραιτώριον, ἵνα μὴ
μιανθῶσιν ἀλλὰ φάγωσιν τὸ πάσχα.

Who are those, who brought Jesus from Caiaphas to the house
where Pilate stayed in Jerusalem? We have to think here of two groups
of men, who played an important part in the arrest of Jesus. In the
first place the detachment of soldiers with the servants of the Jews,
who arrested Jesus in Gethsemane and in the second place the members
of the Sanhedrin, who pronounced the death-sentence in an official
session, and who did all they could in order to obtain the ratification
of this sentence from Pilate as soon as possible (Jn. xviii 12, 13, 24).
Nobody else took part in this procession to the praetorium, where
the governor had his residence, because it was early in the morning,
at the dawning of the day (Mt. xxvii 1), in the fourth nightwatch.
Pilate could expect the leaders of the people very early, for he had
placed at disposal a detachment of soldiers of the garrison, in view
of the arrest (Jn. xviii 3, 12).

In approaching the praetorium, the procession split up: the soldiers
went into the inner court with their prisoner, presumably being glad
that the nightly action was over, that they had not been involved in
severe skirmishes, and that they were able to return to their barracks.
The members of the Sanhedrin stayed outside, in order not to become
defiled. They still had to eat their Passover, they did not enter. The
prescriptions of the law were known to them and they did not want
to deviate from those over against the procurator. Just like the
members of the Sanhedrin, the men of the temple-guard too will have
stayed outside. They are mentioned once again in the sequel of this
lawsuit, then they are outside of the praetorium, with the chief priests
(Jn. xix 6). John does not mention any other people in his record on
this point. Since it was early in the morning, only gradually more
Jews will have gathered before the praetorium. The arrest had been
prepared and performed in full silence, and without the presence of
any stranger at the nightly trials before Annas and Caiaphas. So
nothing of an arrest of the rabbi of Nazareth had become known
among the population of Jerusalem. The only time the feasters in
the town noticed something of what had happened last night, was
when they saw Jesus in the power of the procurator and when the
members of the court pronounced the death sentence.

So we read in Jn. xviii 28 that the members of the Sanhedrin and the
servants of the Jews, the temple-guard that stood under the power

of the Sanhedrin, still had to eat the Passover. This verse does not say anything else. One can even go further on this point and say, that John does report more or less explicitly that the members of the court and their satellites stayed out of the praetorium on purpose, for they (still) had to eat the Passover. If John would have made here a correction of the reports of the synoptics, he certainly would have done it in another way.[5]

There is no contradiction here with the data of the synoptics, but rather a useful expansion. According to the synoptics, the Passover has been eaten in accordance with the law, in the evening preceding the day that the members of the High Court gathered before the praetorium, early in the morning (Mt. xxvi 17-29; Mk. xiv 12-25; Lk. xxii 7-23). As an extra detail however, the fourth evangelist can report that the members of the Sanhedrin and the servants who were at their disposal, did not sit at the table for the Passover supper. They postponed the celebration. Why?

In order to be able to answer this question, we have to represent the situation, just as it was before the arrest of Jesus. The synoptics show us that there have been planned attempts in two respects for clearing away Jesus Christ, and how the ideas, that had been formed on this point, have fused on a certain moment.

There is a plot in the palace of Caiaphas, the high-priest. The members of the court did agree there, that one had to dispose of the rabbi of Nazareth as soon as possible. However, they had to face many difficulties. Because of the feast to come, Jerusalem was completely packed. From all parts of the country the feasters came up. There was an enormous rush in the town and in the court of the temple, where Jesus did usually walk around with his disciples (Lk. xxi 37).

It was not possible to let Jesus be arrested in these circumstances. The crowd was easily inflammable and rapidly moved. The entry into Jerusalem had proven that again (Mt. xxi 1-9; Mk. xi 1-10; Lk. xix 28-38; Jn. xii 12-16). So the danger of a revolt was certainly not imaginary and the latter had to be prevented first of all. So only one possibility was left: in secret, unexpectedly, Jesus had to be arrested. But how?

Now Judas, one of the twelve disciples, came to the rescue. When the members of the court agreed that Jesus should be brought to death, the sooner the better, and when the deliberations reached a deadlock

---

[5] C. BOUMA, *Het evangelie naar Johannes II* (KVHS), Kampen 1950, 19.

about the question how to lay hands on Jesus without causing a sensation, a solution comes from a side from which they certainly never expected it. Satan went into Judas Iscariot's mind, and he went away and discussed with the chief-priests how he would deliver Jesus to them (Lk. xxii 3, 4). Undoubtedly Judas knew that he would find a willing ear with the members of the Sanhedrin, for these leaders of the people had issued the command that "if someone knew where He was, he would denounce it, so that they could catch him" (Jn. xi 57). However, since one could not arrest Jesus in full daylight, in view of the rebellion feared, it was an extraordinary occasion that one of the nearest followers of the Nazarene got in touch with them. This man was acquainted with Jesus' coming and going and thus could develop a plan for laying hands on Him in secret. So it does not surprise us that the chief-priests are very glad about this course of events and that they would gladly count out thirty pieces of silver as betrayer-payment, if the plan would show to be successful (Mt. xxvi 15; Mk. xiv 11; Lk. xxii 5). However, the plan of action was not yet all set at the time of the deliberation between Judas and the chief-priests. It remains an open question whether Judas would await for further indications from the leaders of the people, or would first make sure of sufficient aid before he offered an elaborated plan for the arrest. In any case, the members of the court and the false disciple have found each other and the latter will look for an opportunity — the synoptics say — to deliver Jesus without the people knowing — Luke adds (Lk. xxii 6).

As for this opportunity : it is true that the members of the Sanhedrin initially concluded that the arrest should not take place during the feast, but this limitation can be put aside if Judas sees a chance to carry out his evil plan "without the people knowing". The objection was not that the feastdays should not be desecrated by the arrest, but that a rebellion might arise! If there was none or little chance that something like that would happen, Judas would better be as free as possible to take hold of the first opportunity for an arrest, even though it was during the feast days. For the most important thing was that Jesus was cleared away and preferably as soon as possible.[6]

In connection with the critical situation and the relation with the Romans, only one condition remained : no disturbance among the

---

[6] H. N. RIDDERBOS, *Het evangelie naar Mattheüs II*, (KVHS), Kampen 1946, 178, 183.

people. If this stipulation was enforced, one would further pass over every other objection. Now the possibility to arrest Jesus without causing a big sensation happened to occur on the day that one was to eat the Passover meal, according to the law.

It is remarkable how the synoptics, immediately after the information that Judas was looking for a good occasion to deliver Jesus to the chief-priests, link up with the preparation for the Passover. Judas hears how and where the Lord wants to eat the Passover with his disciples, according to the tradition. Peter and John had — as soon as they entered the town — to follow a man bearing a jar. After having inquired they would be brought into a big upper-room, provided with everything. There the Passover had to be arranged (Mt. xxvi 17-19); Mk. xiv 12-16; Lk. xxii 7-13).

This was an important indication that Jesus had the plan to eat the Passover just as before in Jerusalem, notwithstanding the expectations of many people. For the question was frequently discussed in those days : what do you think, will He, or will He not come to the festival (Jn. xi 56)? For it was known how the atmosphere was loaded and how Jesus did not move Himself freely among the crowd, but hided from the people again and again. Often He withdrew from the crowd with his disciples and stayed in desolate regions (Jn. xi 54; xii 36). Judas now heard that the Passover still would be eaten in Jerusalem. But he did not know where. Not he, who held the cash, but Peter and John had to make preparations for the celebration. And it is obvious that Judas only got to know the place where the Passover would be celebrated when he entered the very house. The indications Jesus had given in the circle of his disciples were of such a vagueness for the not-initiated, that it was impossible to say beforehand with certainty where the Lord would be together with his disciples.

At the same time this means that the treacherous assault could not have place during the supper. Judas could indeed report that the Passover would be eaten, but he did not know where. It was "somewhere" in Jerusalem.[7]

Jesus had arranged this all and wanted it, for He ardently desired to eat this last Passover with his disciples before his suffering would begin. He wanted to be undisturbed, and kept all things in

---

[7] Cf. G. RICCIOTTI, *Leven van Jesus*, Utrecht 1949, 611.

His hands, so that the betrayal could only become effective after this Passover (Lk. xxii 15).

Yet an unique opportunity occurred to arrest Jesus. The Lord was close by and one of his disciples who would be brought into acquaintance with the place of meeting, could bring the necessary data to the notice of the conspirators in one way or another. Moreover, the inhabitants of Jerusalem as well as the feasters from outside the town had been occupied by the Passover. Danger for rebellion hardly existed. The people were off the streets and preparing with their families and relatives for the celebration according to a prevailing custom. They were all engaged in performing the extensive Passover ritual for some hours and, within the privacy behind the blind walls to the streetside they would experience little or nothing if something particular would take place outside. If ever a good occasion turned up to arrest Jesus without the people knowing, it would be on that feastday.[8]

There was only one objection, and that was a serious one. The Passover of the members of the court and of their servants suffered. Just because Judas the betrayer could not indicate the place of the meeting beforehand, they had to keep themselves ready a considerable time before the assault. It would be absolutely impossible for them to have the Passover on that evening. That was a hard thing for the gentlemen, a great offering. But they did it. They even brought into danger their own Passover eating. One thing was more important than all considerations. Caiaphas, the high-priest, had put it into words in Jn. xi 50: "You fail to see that it is better for one man to die for the people". Up to two times the evangelist has included this statement. After the arrest of Jesus he falls back on this word (Jn. xviii 14).

This consideration has turned the scale. The decision was taken to postpone the eating of the Passover and to make all preparations for the arrest. And whereas the disciples Peter and John made everything ready for the Passover, and the Lord with his followers appeared later to celebrate the meal according to the law, there was a feverish activity among the members of the Sanhedrin. The temple-guard had to keep itself ready for the assault and Pilate had to be asked to be willing to place at their disposal a cohort of the garrison (Jn. xviii 3). Furthermore one had to wait for a specified report from Judas.

However, Judas could not go any earlier than when Jesus had

---

[8] Cf. GELDENHUYS, o.c., 668, n. 4.

said to him : "What you are going to do, do it quickly" (Jn. xiii 27). Again Jesus Christ, who knew what would happen, kept the leadership in His hands and was going to eat the Passover still one more time with his disciples in order to be able to let pass this celebration of the Old Testament into the institution of the Lord's Supper of the New Testament. Late in the evening Judas goes away to join the betrayersgang and to choose openly their side after a while (Jn. xiii 30). The possibility that the Passover can be eaten that day by the members of the court has disappeared for good. Now they must wait until the next day (Jn. xviii 28). The waiting however would eventually be rewarded. Judas appears and hastily one breaks up, not to the house where the Passover was celebrated in Jerusalem, but to the place where Jesus wandered around often with his disciples, Gethsemane, situated on one of the slopes of the Mount of Olives. Not only the members of the temple-guard and the soldiers provided by Pilate followed Judas, but the members of the Sanhedrin too followed this group on some distance, as Luke observes. Their evening had been spoiled any way! They had not been able to do anything but to be busy for the arrest and to deliberate with each other, what had to happen. They now wanted to see the result of their deliberations (Lk. xxii 52).

Jesus addresses Himself to them : "when I was among you in the temple day after day you never moved to lay hands on me. But this is your hour; this is the reign of darkness" (Lk. xxii 53).

The members of the Sanhedrin and their subordinates postponed the eating of the Passover especially to be able to arrest Jesus without the knowledge of the crowd. There is only one reason that brought them this far : their unlimited hostility and measureless embitterment. If only Jesus is cleared away, all other things are allowed. All considerations have to give way to that.

John points to this. He, who spoke so often about the hostility of the Jews, he does that in this case too, where he draws the attention to the hate that was burning in the hearts of the leaders of the people. They would defile themselves. In this the impiety of the Jews has been demonstrated again. This way of action precisely fits in with the typification Jesus has given in his oration against the scribes and Pharisees : So you too, from the outside like good honest men, but inside you are full of hypocrasy and lawlessness (Mt. xxiii 28).

All this is the more cogent, if we pay attention to the special meaning of Passover. Of the great feasts that Israel celebrated every year, the

Passover certainly should be mentioned first. It is the feast of the birth of the people, of the national independance of Israel : it is the feast that reminds men that Yahweh has brought his people out of the land of Egypt, out of the house of slavery, as the superscription of the law expresses so strikingly (Ex. xx 2).

Therefore it should not surprise us that the Romans were particularly alert at the celebration of this feast, and were watching everything the leaders of the people and the people itself were going to do with the greatest accuracy. Just on this feast the national aspirations of the people could be easily brought into motion. When the deliverance from Egypt was commemorated, would then not be thought of the liberation out of the power of the Romans.[9]

What will happen now? The members of the Sanhedrin get into contact with Pilate, the procurator, and ask from him a detachment of soldiers in order to be able to arrest Jesus of Nazareth. On this great feast, where the people of Israel commemorates how it has been delivered out of the tyrannical grip of the Pharao, in an extraordinary manner, through direct intervention of Yahweh Himself with power and tokens, the leaders of the people make a common affair with Pilate, and go hand in hand with him in order to be able to dispose of the rabbi of Nazareth, deadly hated by them (Mt. xxvii 18). So much the Passover has been deprived of its own meaning to these men!

It is the evangelist John again, who illustrates the point for a moment. The synoptics are only mentioning a gang, breaking up to arrest Jesus (Mt. xxvi 26, 47; Mk. xiv 43; Lk. xxii 47) without indicating how this exactly has been composed in regard to the nationalities, but John adds here that for the composition of this crowd one also had a detachment of soldiers at the disposal (Jn. xviii 57). Now a helping hand is expected from the Romans, and that even on Passover, in order to deliver the people of Him, who brings into danger the existence of the people.

On this point we still have somewhat to go on.

According to the law the Passover had to be eaten with great punctuality. Stipulations had even been taken up into the book of the law, about what had to be done by those who — owing to particular circumstances — were not able to held the Passover on the

---

[9] Cf. J. PICKL, *Messiaskönig Jesus*, München ²1935, 50-52.

day prescribed by the law. They had to eat it on the fourteenth of the second month, i.e. 14 Ziv (later on Ijar) and they had to celebrate the feast then completely according to the ritual, applying 14 Nisan (Num. ix 9-12). This exception did apply in two cases : "If anyone, among you or your descendants, becomes unclean by touching a dead body, or is on a journey abroad, he can still keep a Passover for Yahweh" (Num. ix 10).

In the time of Hezekiah such a second Passover has once been celebrated (2 Chron. xxx). In that case the desire to show the return to Yahweh in the common celebration of the Passover, will have turned the scale. Now as the reformation was powerfully taken up, one wanted to express the joy and thanks, also in celebrating the Passover, in which connection the mighty deeds of Yahweh in the deliverance of his people were commemorated.

It is clear that these conditions for an exception could not be applied for the case suddenly encountered by the members of the Sanhedrin concerning Jesus' arrest. There was no talk of death in the family circle. It is true that they, animated by hatred and thoughts of revenge, were busy pronouncing a deathsentence the same night, but they guarded against touching themselves the sentences to death with their hands. For that purpose they had their men. And certainly they also would like to watch the execution of Jesus and walk out for it to the crosshill of Golgotha, but they would stay at a respectful distance. Just like that, things stood with the second condition. A long journey could not be brought to the fore at all. All members of the court were present in Jerusalem on the time set, and they had done everything to be allowed to eat the Passover on the prescribed hour. There was no reason at all to think that the conditions of exception applied to the situation, encountered by the members of the Sanhedrin.

Even if a postponement of the celebration of the Passover in the sense of a shift to the second month would have been taken into consideration, they still would have to decide to it on completely arbitrary grounds. Facing the question : eat it now or a month later, in this case the solution is chosen that is — in their eyes — the lesser of two evils. The Passover eating is simply postponed for one day, to be hold afterwards with the usual solemnity and respect.

For of course the Paschal lamb has to be eaten. There is a stipulation in the law to see to that: "But if anyone who is clean, or who did not have to go on a journey, fails to keep the Passover, he shall be outlawed from his people. He has not brought offerings to Yahweh

at its appointed time, and he must bear the burden of his sin"
(Num. ix 13).[10]

That is the horrible dilemma the members of the Sanhedrin had
to face in the night of the arrest of Jesus Christ: they had to eat the
Passover and all measures had been taken for that. Woe them if
they did not held it! They would in fact place themselves outside
the community of the people. They would have broken every bond
with their own people and have withdrawn themselves from the
community with Yahweh.

On the other side they were waiting with great suspense for the
coming of Judas so that the planned assault could take place.

In this situation they turn up early in the morning before the
praetorium, where Pilate was. And John describes the horrible impiety
of the members of the Sanhedrin on this point too: they still had to
eat the Passover.

Here the conflict between the leaders of the people on one hand and
Jesus Christ on the other hand reaches a new climax. The only desire
of the members of the Sanhedrin is: Jesus' death. He has to be disposed
of from the community of the people. He does not belong to it. He
is the biggest danger that can be thought of. That is why the case
between the members of the Sanhedrin and Pilate is started at once.
Passing the matters initially mentioned by the synoptics in the lawsuit,
John is speaking at once about the question of Pilate: "What charge
do you bring against this man? (Jn. xviii 29) and the accusation is:
"if he were not a criminal, we should not be handing him over to
you!" (Jn. xviii 30).

The accusation that there is no more place for Jesus in the community and that He has to be brought to death by Pilate, is expressed
by those who have driven their impiety so far, that they have placed
themselves outside the community of the people, because they did
not eat the Passover on the time set! They themselves deserved capital
punishment!

This has to be mentioned by John.

Here the contrast becomes sharp. Jesus has been brought to death
presently. The Jews got what they wanted from Pilate. They have
expelled and banished Him and they have seen how Jesus Christ has
been hung at the cross for dying the death of a damned.

And the members of the Sanhedrin eat their Passover. But it is too

---

[10] W. H. GISPEN, *Het boek Numeri* (COT), Kampen 1959, 144.

late. They loosened themselves from Yahweh and their people. They called the ire of Yahweh over themselves with this deed too, through their sin and unrighteousness.

The structure of the fourth gospel

There is still another particular reason, why exactly John gives this supplementing detail of the Passover that has still to be eaten by the members of the court. This is to be found in the structure of the fourth gospel. It has been pointed out often that the author of this gospel on his turn wants to set the person and work of Jesus Christ into light from an other side.[11] He depicts Jesus as the lamb of God, that takes away the sin of the world (Jn. i 29). For that reason this evangelist lays himself out to record that Jesus visited Jerusalem every Passover, He would be able to go after the beginning of His official discharge of duties (Jn. ii 13; vi 4; xii 1).

The latter can also be described in another way. With respect to the size the fourth gospel is not larger than that of the synoptics. But the classification of this gospel is strikingly different from the classification of the other gospels.

As soon as John spoke of the Lamb of God in the first chapter, one can follow the work of Jesus Christ for some time from day to day. The calling of the first disciples is related, and even the hour in which that happened is noted down (Jn. i 40). Accurately the work of the first days is kept up with (Jn. i 35, 44; ii 1).

But after this the evangelist keeps going with seven miles boots. He arrives into a period that has been depicted broadly by the synoptics and he only mentions what he needs for his own purpose. He never neglects recording that Jesus visited Jerusalem with his disciples in the Passover feasts. And in the last week of the life of the Son of Man in his humiliation, one can follow again events from day till day just as in the beginning. Jesus came into Bethany six days before the Passover (Jn. xii 1) and from that moment on the account is again exhaustive. "The speed", C. BOUMA says, "is curbed now completely and for good, the narrative begins to proceed with hours. From 13:1 onward we are in the last evening before the drama of Golgotha. Seven chapters have been dedicated to the last twenty four hours.

---

[11] H. MULDER, *De eerste hoofdstukken van het evangelie naar Lukas in hun structurele samenhang*, Delft 1948, 9.

The main goal has been reached: to show the Lamb of God on Golgotha taking away the sin of the world (Jn. i 29).[12]

The fact that Jesus is the Paschal Lamb is brought to the fore by this author over and over, in contrast with the synoptics. For that reason he does not only mention the Passovers Jesus visited but further-more talks about all events that can confirm this idea in one way or another.

It is very important that one should keep in mind that Jesus has been appointed as the holy sacrificial lamb by the high-priest (Jn. xi 49-51; xviii 14). Likewise it is of particular significance, that the chief-priests eat the Passover on the day Jesus dies on the cross. This fact has also to be reckoned to the important materials of the fourth gospel.

Against his own intentions, the high-priest has given a prophetic testimony, according to the counsel of Yahweh, that Jesus would die for the people (Jn. xi 51). Against their own intentions, the members of the Sanhedrin too have eaten the Passover on the very day that Jesus died as the Lamb of God (Jn. i 29; xviii 28).

Sofar the report about eating the Passover has been illustrated with the declaration of the high-priest, in the same chapter, (!) that Jesus has to die. Just as the high-priest, in spite of himself, had to appoint Jesus as the holy sacrifice-lamb, the official leaders, in spite of them-selves, ate the Passover when Jesus died.

So the evangelist can hold on to the idea that Jesus has been sacrificed as the Paschal Lamb. What he stated at the beginning: Jesus is the Lamb of God, is going to reach a splendid climax at the end of his description, through the increasing impiety and hardening of the Jews: Jesus dies as the Paschal Lamb. The goal and trail of thoughts of the synoptics is different: that is why they do not need in their description everything that Johns brings to the fore again and again.

They used other materials. But John wanted to bring into a special light events that had been depicted already repeatedly, and with this in mind he collected and elaborated the data that were of a special importance to him. For that reason the evangelist reminds us that after they pronounced the deathsentence, the members of the High court remained standing before the praetorium, so that they did not have to defile themselves. According to the counsel of Yahweh they would eat their Passover when Jesus died.

---

[12] BOUMA, *o.c.*, 18.

Everone who accepts this complex of exegetic considerations, can in principle judge the matter dealt with here as decided : Jesus ate the Passover with his disciples on 14 Nisan and He died on 15 Nisan.

The synoptics and John

There are unmistakable signs that the synoptics were acquainted with the ideas, later developed by John.

First of all we point to the reports concerning Joseph of Arimathaea. All evangelists tell something about the appearance of this disciple at the burial of Jesus. Whereas Matthew and John (!) do not allude to it, Mark and Luke declare emphatically that Joseph of Arimathaea was a member of the court and the latter evangelist adds that he was an upright and virtuous man. He had not consented to what the others had planned and carried out (Mk. xv 42, 43; Lk. xxiii 50, 51).

From this we may conclude that Joseph stayed aloof from the deliberations about a possible arrest of Jesus by order of the highest college of justice of the Jews, but that he also ate the Passover, just as the other Jews, on the set time. But the members of the Sanhedrin were busily occupied and they even had postponed the eating of the Passover because Judas could appear on the scene any moment now, to give the last information about the place where Jesus was staying with his disciples. Joseph has been one of the few exceptions confirming the rule discussed above.

Since he had eaten the Passover on Thursday evening, he could go to Pilate without any objection in the evening and ask for the body of Jesus for a honourable burial (Mk. xv 45).

In connection to this a remark has to be made about the members of the Sanhedrin on Friday-evening. They ate the Passover as was said. The Nazarene was dead, and they could comply with their religious duties. Their planning had shown to be successful. Jesus' death, so important to them, that it had kept themselves busy and had pushed aside everything else, now set them free. When Jesus had been crucified, and the members of the court had convinced themselves that the sentence had been executed wholly according to their wish, they had to make up arrears, and to eat the Passover.

On this Friday evening Joseph of Arimathaea and Nicodemus and the other disciples of Jesus can go their way undisturbedly. They will not be thwarted in the execution of their plans. Neither will they be controlled and they can do everything they want in order to give to their dearly beloved Master the honour they wish for Him (Lk. xxiii 53-55). The members of the High-court are too busy with their own important matters. They do not bother — it seems — about anything anymore!

But they did! On Saturday — when the Passover eating of the official leaders of the people had taken place — the chief-priests and Pharisees came together to Pilate to ask for a favour : they wanted Jesus' grave to be put under guard for some days in order to prevent possible theft of the corpse (Mt. xxvii 62-66). We do not have to assume that an official session of the Sanhedrin preceded this request — it was Sabbath — yet from the formulation given by Matthew it appears that the members deliberated together and afterwards presented a petition to Pilate.[13]

Why the evangelist does not mention the Sabbath, but speaks of : the following day, the day after the preparation, we can leave out of consideration. In any case it is clear that the Sanhedrists did not deal with this request on Friday-evening, but on Saturday morning.[14] When the sun had risen over the new day, and the Passover had been eaten by the members of the Court, they came again to the point where they were before their ceremonial celebration. To their fright they discovered that in the meantime Jesus' friends and disciples had not been inactive, that on this point too arrears had to be made up. Although the Sabbath had begun already, and serious trespassing of the prescriptions for the Sabbath was almost inevitable, all this had to be accepted with the bargain. If they postponed the problem, they might never be able to make up with it again. If Jesus' disciples were going to take possession of his body, and would spread the rumour that Jesus had risen from the dead, the calamity would be incalculable. Who knows, what would happen then, how the people might come into motion and how the passions might flare up.

For that reason the word of the high-priest again had to be taken for guidance. It is better for one man to die for the people (Jn. xviii 14). Therefore the Sabbath had to be violated and a new visit had to be paid to Pilate. The leaders of the people had not been able to come earlier : they had to eat the Passover first! If one surveys the course of events in this way, one comes to this conclusion : "Das ist der Fluch der bösen Tat, dasz sie fortwährend böses musz gebären", and

---

[13] Cf. RIDDERBOS, o.c., 248.
[14] For the chronology : F. W. GROSHEIDE, *Het heilig evangelie volgens Mattheüs* (CNT), Kampen 1954, 443.

he also says that the synoptics were acquainted very well with the fact that the very members of the Court ate the Passover later than it was prescribed by law, although they alluded to that only in passing by, in connection with the different purposes they strove after.

Texts in John linked with John xviii 28

As for the three texts usually mentioned in one and the same time in the gospel according to John, linking up with Jn. xviii 28, we have the conviction that in fact no difficulties would have appeared in the exegesis of these texts, if not Jn. xviii had been there. When the Passover, still to be eaten on the day of the crucifixion, aroused large surprise in the explanation, some other data too appeared to be mentioned by John, being a motive for particular remarks. However, since we gave a satisfactory explanation for Jn. xviii 28, we can be brief about the other texts.

To begin with, there are the texts where the παρασκευὴ τοῦ πάσχα or also only the παρασκευὴ is mentioned (Jn. xix 14 and 31). Preparation Day was the normal name for Friday, the day being a preparation for the Sabbath. This παρασκευὴ fell in the week of the Passover and is typified as such, also by the words later used, since that Sabbath was a day of special solemnity (Jn. xix 31). All other translations, such as preparation to, or preparation for, or something like that, have to be rejected, for they are based upon the incorrect idea that the Passover in general still had to be eaten and that this opinion would be also comprehended in these texts.

Important too is the time indication, following Passover Preparation Day "about the sixth hour", i.e. about noontime. This addition will have to be thus understood, that the proper "preparation" began. The afternoon of the Friday was the "vigil of Sabbath". It was then that all preparations were made with respect to the coming Sabbath. These were very important especially in this case, because Sabbath fell in the feast-week.[15]

So, while the Jews prepared things for the Sabbath, Pilate made himself ready to deliver Jesus to be crucified. (Jn. xix 13, 16).

According to the solution mentioned above, Jesus did not die during the slaughter of the Paschal Lambs, but on the day the members of the Sanhedrin held their postponed Passover. Does not the former opinion agree better with the word of the Scriptures, cited by John:

---

[15] Cf. RICCIOTTI, o.c., 86.

"Not one bone of His will be broken"? (Jn. xix 36). The question is
whether we only have to think of the preparation of the Paschal
Lamb. It is also possible that the writer has let himself be lead by
Ps. xxxiv 20: "Yahweh will not let one bone be broken". In that case
there is a contradiction between what happens to Jesus and what
happens to the murderers : their bones are broken, but Jesus does
not share in that fate. The light of the favour of Yahweh is shining
over the righteous.

However, if one want to continue the line of thought of the Paschal
lamb too, then also the expression: "not one bone will be broken",
does not contradict our opinion. These words refer to the eating at
least as much as to the slaughtering of the lamb.[16]

Texts from the synoptics

Since the solution given here, that Jesus lied down at the Passover
supper on 14 Nisan and died on 15 Nisan on the cross, has been
proposed more than once — although on incorrect grounds and with
insufficient argumentation — a number of texts from the synoptics
have to be discussed, that were brought to the fore against this train
of thought.

Did not Jesus trespass the law himself, because He departed to
the mount of Olives and the law of Passover forbade to leave the town
in Passovernight? (Deut. xvi 7; Ex. xii 22). For in this a particularity
of the first Passover in Egypt had to be kept in honour from generation
to generation : "Let none of you venture out of the house till morning".
It is evident that the objection made here does not make sense anymore if one assumes that the meal described by the synoptics was not
the real Passover.

However, this objection does not prevail in our viewpoint either.
One may keep in mind that it is true that every inhabitant of a house
in Jerusalem had to place at the disposal of the feasters from the
outside his spare room, in order to offer an opportunity for all Israelites
to eat the Passover according to the law. One only has to think about
the meal itself with respect to the difficulties occurring on this point.[17]

The number of feasters was very large, in particular on the Passover,

---

[16] GISPEN, *o.c.*, 144; cf. A. NOORDTZIJ, *Het boek Numeri* (KVHS), Kampen 1941,
103.

[17] H. L. STRACK-P. BILLERBECK, *Kommentar zum Neuen Testament aus Talmud und
Midrasch*, IV, 1, München ²1956, 41, 42; G. DALMAN, *Jesus-Jeschua*, Leipzig 1929,
98 ff.

and therefore specials measures had to be taken. Thousands of people could not sojourn in town. Jesus did indeed teach in the temple in the daytime, but the night He spent on the Mount of Olives, outside the walls of the town (Lk. xxi 37). Thus, the possibility to celebrate Passover in the town was there, but afterwards one went to the Mount of Olives again. The rabbi's had established also that as far as this was concerned, no trespassing was hidden.[18] The immediate surroundings of the town had to be reckoned to the place Yahweh elected. Because of the growth of the population in the own country as well as abroad, there simply was no other solution.

The question whether Judas has gone directly to the garden of Gethsemane with the armed gang, or first of all to the house where the Passover was eaten, has to remain unanswered, for lack of further data. The important point that does matter however, is that Jesus had indeed, against the initial expectations, celebrated the feast according to the law, just as in the previous years, however critical and strained the situation might have been. For that reason the terrible deliberations of Judas and the members of the Sanhedrin were crowned with success. Once it was certain that Jesus came to the feast, Judas knew where to find the master and his disciples (Jn. xviii 2).

It looks a bit exaggerated to us to derive from the use of lanterns and torches by the gang that Judas with his adherents has gone directly to the garden of Gethsemane, since such a cabinet of instruments could also serve well at nightly assaults in Jerusalem. On the ground of the words of John about Gethsemane: "Judas the traitor knew the place well" (Jn. xviii 2) and not "and Judas knew that Jesus was there" one could rather conclude that in the case Judas could not find Jesus in the house in Jerusalem, he was acquainted with it where Jesus would be then. But, as has been said, the number of data is so little, it is hard to make any positive conclusions. This matter may remain undecided upon, as of minor importance.

The question has further been put forward: "Did not, as appears from the gospels, several persons perform duties on the day of Jesus' dying, absolutely contrary to the character of this feastday and even to be considered as a trespassing of the law?"

One reads for example about Simon of Cyrene, that "he came from the field" (Mk. xv 21), and of Joseph of Arimathaea, that he "bought

---

[18] Pes. viii.

a shroud" (Mk. xv 46), and of Nicodemus that he "brought a mixture of myrrh and aloes, weighing about a hundred pounds" (Jn. xix 39).

These cases are not completely comparable. Simon came from Cyrene. In this place in Northern Africa many Jews used to live, for a long time already. Whether he was a Jew or a proselyte, has to remain an open question. Also, whether he came to Jerusalem for this feast, or did live here already for a considerable time (cf. for this matter Acts ii 10; vi 9; xi 20; xiii 1). That he came from the country does not necessarily mean that he was working in the field, and was returning home now. Most probably we should not conclude anything else from this expression than that Simon came from the outskirts of the town and now went to Jerusalem again.[19] We get the impression over and over that the prescriptions for the feastdays in many cases were less stringent now than for the Sabbath, in particular as far as life in — and outside the home was concerned. Since for the Sabbath the possibility of a "Sabbath-journey" was still prevailing, it is not quite clear why Simon of Cyrene would have trespassed against the prescriptions.[20]

As for the buying of the shroud etc. by Joseph of Arimathaea, and Nicodemus, one has to take into consideration that a burial was at issue, even a burial that took place under very special circumstances. The Sabbath was at hand : one should act rapidly (Mk. xv 42). The body of Jesus should not remain hanging on the cross (Deut. xxi 23).

On a feastday preceding a Sabbath, several things were allowed that were usually omitted on a feastday.[21] Moreover, when somebody died, it was permitted to do the necessary things for the burial.[22] Thus looked at, it is not surprising that Joseph of Arimathaea and Nicodemus, who requested and got from Pilate the dead body of their master for a honourable burial, could make the preparations they wanted (Jn. xix 42). So, as far as these texts are concerned, we do not have to face great difficulties.

Compilation

1) Jesus has eaten the Passover with his disciples on the time set by the law, 14 Nisan, just as most of the Jews in Jerusalem (Mt. xxvi 17-29; Mk. xiv 12-25; Lk. xxii 7-23; Jn. xiii 21-30).

---

[19] Cf. Vulg. "de villa".
[20] Cf. C. F. KEIL, *Commentar über das Evangelium des Matthäus*, Leipzig 1877, 518.
[21] Cf. STRACK-BILLERBECK, *o.c.*, II, 829-833.
[22] Shab. xxiii 5.

2) During this Passover the members of the Sanhedrin made their preparations for the arrest of Jesus. They had to wait for indications of Judas in order to be able to catch Jesus without the people knowing (Lk. xxii 6) and consequently they postponed their celebration of the Passover.

3) John mentioned this by saying that the members of the Sanhedrin still had to eat the Passover (Jn. xviii 28), when they appeared before the praetorium to deliver Jesus to Pilate.

4) The motive for this way of acting of the members of the Sanhedrin has been expressed in the statement of Caiaphas: Jn. xi 49-51; c.f. Jn. xviii 14.

5) The data of the evangelist John do not contend with those of the synoptics. They do not give a correction, but an amplification.

6) The fact that John stresses strongly the impiety of the Sanhedrin, is connected with and resulting from the state of affairs that he wrote this gospel when the break between Judaism and Christianism had become definitive.

7) Jesus Christ died the day after eating the Passover, so, on the fifteenth of Nisan. At about the same time the members of the Sanhedrin ate their postponed Passover.[23]

---

[23] This opinion has already been advocated by Eusebius, *De solemnit. Pasch.* 10 (PG. 24, 705, 706) and Chrysostomus, *Hom.* 83, 3 (PG. 59, 452) in a more or less modified form.

SIGNS AND WORKS IN THE FOURTH GOSPEL

M. DE JONGE

Introduction

The purpose of the present paper is to analyze the function of the stories about and comments upon "signs" and "works" within the argument and structure of the Fourth Gospel. Much has been written lately on the existence of a Signs- or Miracles-source or even of a Signs-Gospel,[1] and James M. ROBINSON has argued that "the surprisingly strong survival record of the "miracles-source" (σημεῖα-Quelle) made familiar by BULTMANN is in itself an argument to take this source seriously".[2]

This paper does not intend to analyze or criticize the existing source- and redaction-theories. One cannot exclude the possibility that the Fourth Gospel reflects more than one stage in the development of the theology of the Johannine communities which produced the Gospel and the Epistles of John. In fact a closer analysis of the stage of development of that theology represented by I and II John may help us to discover a later "layer" in the Gospel.[3] It is also likely that the Fourth Gospel incorporates narrative- and discourse-material belonging

---

[1] See the useful survey in G. VAN BELLE, *De Semeia-bron in het vierde evangelie*, Ontstaan en groei van een hypothese, Leuven 1975. R. T. FORTNA's *The Gospel of Signs (MSSNTS* 11), Cambridge 1970 and W. NICOL's *The Sēmeia in the Fourth Gospel* (NT.S 32), Leiden 1972 have drawn much attention lately (see VAN BELLE, *o.c.*, 111-148 on their books and the subsequent discussion). On BULTMANN's earlier theory of a σημεῖα-Quelle see particularly D. M. SMITH, *The Composition and the Order of the Fourth Gospel*, Bultmann's Literary Theory, New Haven and London 1965.

[2] In his article "The Johannine Trajectory" in J. M. ROBINSON and H. KOESTER, *Trajectories through Early Christianity*, Philadelphia 1971, 235.

[3] See some tentative conclusions in my article "Ontwikkelingen binnen de Johanneische Theologie", *VoxTh* 41, 1973, 205-226 and further considerations in "Variety and development in Johannine Christology", chapter VIII in my *Jesus, Stranger from Heaven and Son of God*, Missoula, Mo. 1977. Compare also B. LINDARS, *Behind the Fourth Gospel*, London 1971, esp. chapter 4, and H. THYEN's survey-article "Aus der Literatur zum Johannesevangelium", *ThR* 39, 1974, 1-69, 223-252, 289-329 (not yet finished). Significant is his programmatic statement on page 317: "... das Johannesevangelium aus seinem Entstehungsprozess heraus verständlich zu machen. Wichtig und weiterführend scheint mir vor allem die Einsicht zu sein, das dieser Prozess ein endogenes Phänomen des johanneischen Christentums ist, das seine Traditionen angesichts neuer historischer Herausforderungen jeweils neu auslegt"; see also pp. 328f.

to pre-Johannine stages and non-Johannine strands in the tradition. But the arguments in favour of the existence of a pre-Johannine (or even early Johannine) Signs-source or Signs-Gospel with a clearly defined number of stories and a definite theology of its own, are not conclusive, and the question must be asked whether the distinction between the present Johannine redaction and the supposed presentation in the source really helps to explain the way in which the signs-stories and the statements about Jesus' works function in the present Gospel.

All theories concerning a Signs-source have to assume that "John" criticized his source, and yet incorporated it substantially in his own work. The evangelist is always supposed to have been far more subtle than the people whose work he used; he rewrote considerable parts of the source(s) before him and yet did not do his work thoroughly enough. He left a clear Johannine stamp everywhere and yet we are able to reconstruct the state of his material before it received this stamp.

Now, if it is difficult to believe that the Johannine redaction left sufficient pre-Johannine traces to enable us to explain Johannine theology in terms of an explicit criticism of earlier theological tendencies, we must make an attempt to explain tensions and apparent inconsistencies in John's picture of Jesus' acts first and foremost on the level and within the framework of the very complicated and at the same time carefully balanced theology of the Johannine community as reflected in the Gospel itself. As Barnabas LINDARS put it: "The impression that Jesus is a wonder-worker (the christology commonly attributed to the source, deJ.) is intentional at the stage in the argument to which they belong, i.e. the opening of it. It cannot be taken for granted that, before John rewrote them, they would have given this impression".[4] This paper tries to show that LINDARS' thesis is a useful starting-point for an analysis of the function of "signs" and "works" in the present Gospel. It is worth while to look at the passages concerned from this angle, even if within the compass of one article many aspects cannot be dealt with or can only be mentioned in passing.

John xx 30-31

We should start with xx 30-31, the well-known "first ending" of the Gospel. Here the author makes clear that he described a number of σημεῖα in order to promote and to strengthen faith in Jesus. More

---

[4] *O.c.*, 39.

precisely it is stated that the signs were performed by Jesus ἐνώπιον τῶν μαθητῶν. The Gospel records what these μαθηταί saw, understood and interpreted.

Next, faith in Jesus is faith in Jesus the Christ, the Son of God. *Fides qua* and *fides quae* are closely connected in the Fourth Gospel as the present author has tried to show in a number of earlier studies.[5] Here it may be sufficient to emphasize that Johannine christology centers around the mystery of the unique relationship between the Father and the Son sent by the Father, expressed in various terms and represented by various titles — among these "the Son", "the Son of God", "the Son of Man". These titles indicate, for John, the unique otherness of Jesus, over against designations as prophet, king and also Christ which are expressions of man's highest expectations. They are not entirely discarded; elements of the expectations connected with them are taken up within a larger framework and receive a deeper meaning, and consequently the titles as such are reinterpreted fundamentally. In xx 31 "Son of God" interprets "the Christ". Basic for the σημεῖα is that they lead to faith in Jesus commonly called the Christ as Son of God. In this faith the believers receive true *life* in his name. Signs give *life* to those who are willing and able to believe in Him who presents life through these signs.

John xx 30-31 shows, in connection with the preceding verses 28 and 29, how the disciples believed because they really saw what was revealed to them, but that generations after them are dependent on the word, i.e. on their apostles' testimony. In order to transmit this testimony the Gospel was written (cf. 1 John i 1-4). Thomas, in a way, is a borderline case. He could and should have believed the words of his fellow-disciples, justly commissioned by Jesus through the Spirit (xx 19-23), but he is still in a position in which his request to see and to feel can be granted. He becomes a believer and confesses his faith in words reminiscent of the opening sentences of the Gospel. Those who come after him have to listen to and to rely on the record of the deeds performed by Jesus in the presence of the disciples.[6]

---

[5] See "Nicodemus and Jesus : Some observations on misunderstanding and under standing in the Fourth Gospel", *BJRL* 53, 1970-71, 337-359; "Jesus as Prophet and King in the Fourth Gospel", *EThL* 49, 1973, 160-177; "Jewish Expectations about the "Messiah" according to the Fourth Gospel", *NTS* 19, 1972-73, 246-270, and (earlier) "The Use of the word ΧΡΙΣΤΟΣ in the Johannine Epistles" in *Studies in John* (NT.S 24), Leiden 1970, 66-74.

[6] I hope to show this in more detail elsewhere.

A true understanding of the signs during Jesus' sojourn on earth implies seeing, faith in Jesus sent by God his Father as the giver of Life, and discipleship. The Gospel describes how a number of people received that understanding, and how many people started on their way to Jesus but did not attain that full understanding. It also emphasizes that discipleship means being led to a yet fuller understanding by the Spirit operating within the Christian community after Jesus' departure to the Father.

This, I think, is shown clearly in a number of passages, taken on their own and particularly if considered in their interdependence, within the framework of the entire Gospel.

Two concluding redactional passages comparable to xx 30-31

Two passages which are obviously redactional because they serve as conclusion to larger units of the Gospel call now for some consideration.

The first is x 40-42. Jesus returns to where it all started : the place across Jordan where John had been baptizing earlier. Many come to believe in him there, after having acknowledged that all that John said about this man was true. John's witness in i 19-34 ends with the statement that Jesus is the Son of God. He denies explicitly that he is the Messiah, the Prophet or Elijah (i 21, 25). He is a mere "voice" (i 23).[7] Consequently x 41 states that John did not perform signs but yet spoke the truth. John was a typical witness, a man of *words*. Jesus is a man of words *and signs*; in v 31-36 where Jesus contrasts his own witness to that of John he says: I rely on a testimony higher than John's. There is enough to testify that the Father has sent me, in the works my Father gave me to do and to finish — the very works I have in hand (vs 36).[8]

The second passage is very important for our purpose. At the conclusion of Jesus' public ministry (xii 36), at the transition to the instruction directed to the disciples in chapters xii-xvii, the evangelist states : "In spite of the many signs which Jesus had performed in their presence they would not believe in him" (vs 37). The ἔμπροσθεν αὐτῶν in the present verse stands over against the ἐνώπιον τῶν μαθητῶν of xx 30.[9] The outsiders did not believe and could not believe, as the evangelist assures us with a reference to Is. vi 9, 10.

---

[7] On John the Baptist see "Jewish Expectations ..." (see note 5), 252-256.

[8] On this verse see below p. 122.

[9] As has often been remarked, the word σημεῖον does not occur between xii 37 and xx 30.

I pass over this use of Scripture but want to underline the following comment : "Isaiah said this because he saw his *glory* and spoke about him" (vs 41). Isaiah saw what the unbelieving Jews did not see : the divine glory revealed in Jesus.[10]

In the verses 42-43 the believers among the Jewish leaders appear on the scene — representatives of the many, among the leaders and among the crowds, who believed in Jesus, but not in a way that is acceptable to the Gospel. They cannot be regarded as true believers, because they do not dare to confess Jesus openly for fear of the Pharisees. "They valued τὴν δόξαν τῶν ἀνθρώπων higher than τὴν δόξαν τοῦ θεοῦ (cf. v 44).[11]

The real meaning of Jesus' words and Jesus' signs remained hidden for outsiders. The οὐκ ἐπίστευον εἰς αὐτόν (vs 37), and the οὐκ ἠδύναντο πιστεύειν (vs 39) state the Gospel's position very clearly. The passage xii 36b-43 refers back to ii 23-25, the first passage to speak about signs done by Jesus in Jerusalem. Although Jesus refuses to perform a sign on request, when "the Jews" ask for divine legitimation of his words and action (ii 18, cf. vi 30, vii 31, ix 16, xi 47) and refers to his coming death and resurrection (ii 19; they are *not* explicitly called signs!) he is said to perform signs during the Passover feast in Jerusalem. The result is that many believe in his name. The expression found here is used in i 12 to denote the positive reaction to Jesus of the children of God — yet there is something wrong with the people in Jerusalem : Jesus did not trust himself to them. Why not? The following example of Nicodemus shows, that for all their enthusiasm and sympathy for Jesus, the people in Jerusalem, represented by Nicodemus, did not penetrate into the real secret of Jesus' coming.[12] The σημεῖα are demonstrations of Jesus' special power and authority, but can only be understood and interpreted rightly by people who are initiated in the mystery of the relationship between Son and Father.

There can be no question of legitimation, in the sense that evidence is supplied that will convince any neutral observer. A σημεῖον is a demonstration which asks for reaction. In the case of positive reaction the principal question is, however : What power and authority do you

---

[10] The evangelist means, probably, that Isaiah saw the glory of the preexistent Son, see W. THÜSING, *Die Erhöhung und Verherrlichung Jesu im Johannesevangelium* (NTA XXI 1/2), Münster ²1970, 218f.

[11] On this see "Nicodemus and Jesus" (see note 5), esp. 338f.

[12] See "Nicodemus and Jesus" (see note 5), esp. 339f. and 346-352.

believe to be demonstrated here? Again *fides qua* and *fides quae* are closely related. The inner circle of the disciples receive the true faith; this group of people is commissioned and empowered to hand on the message of life to future generations. All others, including sympathizers and half-believers, are out.[13]

The first two signs

The first two signs, recorded in ii 1-11 and iv 46-54, are both connected with Cana in Galilee. In concluding comments they are called "the beginning of the signs" (ii 11)[14] and "the second sign" (iv 54). They may well have belonged to a pre-Johannine collection of stories. We can easily connect ii 12a with iv 46b, and the enumeration of the signs (which is not continued further in the Gospel) may well stem from the original collection. Moreover there is clearly some discrepancy between ii 11 and the preceding story, if only because the disciples do not really play a part in the story (they are only mentioned in vs 2) and yet occupy a central position in the summing up in vs 11. And, as synoptic parallels to iv 46-54 clearly show, the second story embodies traditional material.[15]

The (probably complicated) prehistory of these two pericopes cannot be discussed here. If we try to define their function within the present Gospel, we may make the following observations:

a) The enumeration of the signs may have been taken over from a source, but why did the evangelist keep it? It is possible that he wanted to connect the two signs in Galilee which lead to true faith — over against the many signs in Jerusalem (ii 23-25, cf. iv 45) which did not.

b) The concluding comment ii 11 connects signs with the revelation of δόξα, leading to belief on the part of Jesus' disciples. The second story centres around the word of Jesus: "Your son will live", spoken

---

[13] The Gospel does not only closely relate *fides qua* and *fides quae*, but takes it for granted that true faith is only possible within the inner circle of those who are instructed by Jesus (particularly in the chapters xiii-xvii where they are prepared for his departure) and who submit themselves to the guidance of the Spirit after Jesus' glorification.

[14] B. OLSSON who in his *Structure and Meaning in the Fourth Gospel*, A textlinguistic analysis of John 2:1-11 and 4:1-42 (*CB.NT* 6), Lund 1974 consistently approaches the Gospel as a structured and meaningful whole, rightly argues that ἀρχή means more than just "first". What happened in Cana is "a primary sign, somehow representation of the creative and transforming work of Jesus" (67-69, see also page 64).

[15] On this see e.g. R. SCHNACKENBURG, *Das Johannesevangelium* I, Freiburg-Basel-Wien 1965, 500-508.

in iv 50, underlined in vs 53 and taken up by the people who meet the father on the way (vs 51). Jesus' word is effective : water is changed into wine, the boy is healed — in his signs Jesus reveals his glory and grants Life. This is in keeping with the Prologue, where the Logos is connected with the Life and the Light (i 4-9). It is accepted by those who receive the ἐξουσία to become children of God (i 11-12). They are able to say : "*we* saw his glory" (i 14), a glory described as a glory which befits the Father's only Son, full of grace and truth.

c) The βασιλικός in the second Cana-story is not explicitly called a disciple, yet he obviously believes in the right way. Vs 48 is commonly thought to be a typically Johannine addition and it no doubt is. It qualifies the belief in Galilean circles (vs 48 uses the second person plural and should be connected with vs 45) as a belief in σημεῖα καὶ τέρατα.[16] Jesus' answer is not so much a reproach as a challenge; it is certainly not a disqualification of signs as such. The man is challenged to believe Jesus as the giver of Life on his word, and he does so (vs 50). The repetition in vs 49 of what was already said in vs 47 is not (or not only) the result of the insertion of vs 48; it makes clear that the man persists in expecting help from Jesus and it places Jesus' promise of life against the dark background of the son's expected imminent death. Faith in Jesus' word is followed by faith on the basis of word plus sign, not only of the man, but also of his whole house; vs 53 serves as a concluding remark to the whole story. The sign follows necessarily, as demonstration of Jesus' life-giving power, after Jesus' word has been accepted. First the word, then the sign — this order is also presupposed in the Thomas-story.

d) ii 11 seems quite straightforward. It emphasizes the central position of the disciples, provides a fitting conclusion to the whole section i 35-ii 11[17] and should certainly be connected with xx 30-31. Yet it becomes clear from the context that even the disciples did not fully understand what they saw until after Jesus' death and resurrection. First, there is the typically Johannine οὔπω ἥκει ἡ ὥρα μου in ii 4. In view of vii 30; viii 20; xii 23, 27; xiii 1; xvii 1 we cannot escape the conclusion that here the hour of Jesus' suffering, death and resurrec-

---

[16] This combination of words is only found here in the Fourth Gospel. It is rather frequently used in Acts and in the Old Testament, particularly in Deuteronomy and other passages influenced by deuteronomistic theology — see K. H. RENGSTORF, σημεῖον, *ThWNT* VII, 199-261, esp. 214f., 219f., 238-241. Here, probably, the addition of καὶ τέρατα emphasizes the miraculous aspect of the signs.

[17] So OLSSON, *o.c.* (see note 14), 77.

tion (seen as a unity) is meant.[18] The evangelist, therefore, in one way or another, views the whole passage ii 1-11, including the reaction of the disciples in ii 11, from a post-resurrectional perspective.

This is also evident in ii 13-21. We have already seen that Jesus refuses a sign which may serve as legitimation for his action in the temple, and refers to his death and resurrection. This interpretation of Jesus' word recorded in vs 19 and significantly misunderstood by the Jews in vs 20, is given in a redactional comment in vs 21. To this is added that the disciples also did not fully understand what Jesus meant until after his resurrection: "After his resurrection his disciples recalled what he had said, and they believed the Scripture and the words that Jesus had spoken" (vs 22).

The statement in ii 11, therefore, stands "between brackets" — the brackets being provided by ii 4 and ii 21. This arrangement is intentional, as will become even clearer as we proceed.

The last sign : The raising of Lazarus in chapter xi

The last sign is appropriately again concerned with the giving of life. John xi is a notorious crux for all scholars who want to distinguish here between the theology of the source and the redaction of the evangelist.[19] Some have thought that in this chapter the signs are reinterpreted so drastically that they are, in fact, disqualified: after the conversation between Jesus and Martha in vss 20-27 the actual raising of Lazarus seems to be superfluous.[20] This interpretation is clearly wrong: here again the word which calls for faith is followed by the sign which demonstrates the truth and the power of the word.

In the context of the present paper we should note in particular vs 4 which speaks of the glory of God, vs 25 which mentions the ἐγώ εἰμι connected with ἀνάστασις and ζωή, and vs 40 which refers back to vs 25 with the words "Did I not tell you that if you have faith you will see the glory of God?" — just before the actual miracle takes place.

---

[18] See, again, OLSSON, o.c. (see note 14), 43-45.

[19] Also FORTNA admits this, quoting words of DODD: "Nowhere in the Gospel have attempts to analyse out a written source, or sources, proved less convincing" (o.c. (see note 1), 74).

[20] So e.g. J. BECKER, Wunder und Christologie, NTS 16, 1969-70, 130-148, esp. 146f.: "Durch seine Stellung degradiert Joh. xi 25f. das eigentliche Wunder zu einer nachhinkenden Sinnlosigkeit" and 147: "Das nämlich ist die Ironie in Joh. xi: Die Ungläubigen denen der Sinn von Joh. xi 25f. verborgen ist, sehen das Äussere und stossen sich am Wundertäter, der diesem Wunder genau zuvor seine theologische Relevanz genommen hatte".

Resurrection and the giving of life are closely connected, here and in v 25-29. In the latter passage it is made clear that giving of life as well as judgment are a divine prerogative granted to the Son by the Father. It is also good to emphasize that both in chapter xi and in chapter v present and future life are mentioned together (cf. vi 39-40, 47-51, 54 and iii 16; viii 51). The risen Lazarus is an example of what was announced in v 25: "A time is coming, indeed is already here, when the dead shall hear the voice of the Son of God, and all who hear shall come to life".[21] We should note that the conversation between Jesus and Martha appropriately ends with a confession by Martha which gives expression to the full Christian faith, in terms reminiscent of xx 31: "I now believe (or: I am convinced, πεπίστευκα) that you are the Messiah, the Son of God, who was to come into the world".

Faith is also mentioned in vs 15 where Jesus says to his disciples: "Lazarus is dead. I am glad not to have been there; it will be for your good and for the good of your faith" (δι' ὑμᾶς, ἵνα πιστεύσητε). Next, there is vs 42 where the prayer (to the Father, vs 41) which accompanies the miracle is said to be spoken for the sake of the ὄχλος standing around, that they may believe that God sent Jesus.

In fact, this story about the final sign shows (again!) that there are three possible reactions to the signs of Jesus: There is, first, the hostile reaction of the Jewish leaders who start planning Jesus' death (xi 47-54, 57; xii 19). Yet, with sublime Johannine irony, the highpriest is portrayed as prophesying unwittingly the meaning of this death (xi 51, 52) and in the discourse immediately following the story of the entry into Jerusalem (xii 20-36) Jesus reveals that the hour of his death is the hour of his glorification (vss 23, 27, 28).

Next, there is the reaction of the sympathizers among the crowd, mentioned in xi 45; xii 9-11, 17-18. Here Jews who come to belief in Jesus because of what they have seen (xi 45; xii 11, 17, cf. also xi 42) acclaim Jesus as the king of Israel (xii 13). This is not, in itself, a wrong designation, but it needs further interpretation — an interpretation in the light of Zech. ix 9 quoted in vs 15, discovered by the disciples, but only "after Jesus had been glorified", as vs 16 tells us.

---

[21] Besides this it is clear that his resurrection, recorded just before the Passion (and, in fact leading up to the Passion) presents to the reader "a preview of the wonder which lies beyond the passion, to hold in his mind as he reads the solemn passion narratives, and so to guide his interpretation of it" (Lindars, o.c. (see note 3), 55).

The sympathizers in the crowd seek in the right direction, but like the people mentioned in ii 23-25 they do not possess the true faith, or real insight.[22]

Full insight is only granted to the disciples, including Martha (even before the sign was performed) who see the glory of God and accept the power of Jesus as Life-giver sent by God, and who express their faith in the appropriate christological terminology. Yet there is the significant proviso in xii 16 which has its parallel in ii 22, a verse already discussed. And Jesus' opening statement in xi 4 "This illness will not end in death; it has come for the glory of God, to bring glory to the Son of God" is at least ambiguous. The ἵνα δοξασθῇ ὁ υἱὸς τοῦ θεοῦ has two aspects — compare xii 23 and, particularly, xii 28 καὶ ἐδόξασα καὶ πάλιν δοξάσω.[23]

In vii 39 we are told that the Spirit could only be given after Jesus' glorification, and according to the Paraclete-passages in the Farewell-discourses it is the Spirit which will teach the disciples everything and will remind them (cf. ii 17, 22; xii 16) of all Jesus has told them (xiv 26, cf. xvi 12-15). Evidently, the disciples occupy a central position in the process of understanding the truth about Jesus during his life on earth. But only after his glorification their understanding will be deepened and strengthened; the Spirit will operate in them and through them and enable them to transmit the message concerning Jesus to following generations.

In connection with this another observation may be pertinent. One of the arguments in favour of the Signs-source hypothesis has always been the isolated position of xx 30, a verse which again characterizes Jesus' deeds as σημεῖα although that word has not been mentioned after xii 37. Moreover καὶ ἄλλα σημεῖα are spoken of, although the resurrection appearances are nowhere classified as signs. The usual explanation is that the evangelist took over the concluding section of the Signs-source with some corrections.

---

[22] See further "Jesus as Prophet and King ..." (see note 5), 168-170.

[23] This subject cannot be treated here; see, particularly, W. THÜSING, Die Erhöhung, (see note 10), 229-30. On pp. 193-198 he includes Jesus' obedience to death in his earthly work and sets it over against the further glorification after his return to the Father; we should speak here of two stages in God's revelation and work of salvation through the Son (and the Paraclete). See, however, also 203: "So ist das verherrlichende Heilswerk in seinen beiden Stadien eine Ganzheit. Das Offenbarungsgeschehen des Erdenlebens Jesu und das des Parakleten sind nicht zwei verschiedene Werke, sondern das Werk Jesu selbst in seinen beiden Verwirklichungsphasen". Compare also R. SCHNACKENBURG, Das Johannesevangelium II, Freiburg-Basel-Wien 1971, 498-512 (Exk. 13 "Erhöhung und Verherrlichung Jesu").

A far more likely theory is, however, that the evangelist could only adequately present the Gospel as a record of signs after he had told how the Risen Lord had given the Spirit to the disciples who had seen the signs. In giving the Spirit Jesus did not only commission them as agents, but he also guaranteed the truth of their message. Moreover, if the δόξα shown forth in the signs has any connection with the δοξασθῆναι of Jesus in his being lifted up from the earth and his return to the Father, it is only to be expected that the revelation of life and glory in the signs is mentioned in retrospect *after* cross and resurrection and the giving of the Spirit — *all* moments in the glorification process — have been recorded.[24]

Short remarks on chapters v, vi, vii and ix

The picture given above may be supplemented by a few remarks on some words and passages in the chapters v, vi, vii and ix.

In chapter v the word σημεῖον is not used, either in the story or in the following discourse which is only loosely connected with it. As by afterthought the healing is set in the context of a sabbath-conflict (vss 9 and 16). Jesus' central answer to the objections of the Jews is found in vs 17: "My Father has never ceased his work and I am working too". The terms used are ἐργάζεσθαι and ἔργα, and these denote the unity of intention and action between Son and Father: this is made very clear in vss 19-20, 30 and 36.[25] The divine actions performed by Jesus are, above all, the giving of life and the exercise of judgment. The real issue at stake in the interpretation of the healing on the sabbath is whether Jesus is a man who wrongly claims equality with God, or whether he is the Son, sent and commissioned by the Father.

This becomes also clear in chapter ix, where the blind man is portrayed as the believing counterpart of the cripple of chapter v. He confesses Jesus as the Son of Man in vss 35-38, after long discussions

---

[24] We are reminded here of ii 18-22; the first time death and resurrection are mentioned explicitly in the Gospel, it is in reply to a request of the Jews to give a sign. They are not, however, themselves called a sign. This may be because, from the evangelist's post-resurrectional viewpoint, the signs bear a preliminary character, whereas death and resurrection mark the beginning of a new period. See R. E. BROWN, *The Gospel according to John (i-xii)*, Garden City, New York, 1966, 530: "Thus, the miracle is a sign, not only qualitatively (a material action pointing toward a spiritual reality), but also temporally (what happens before *the hour* prophesying what will happen after the hour has come). That is why, as we have explained, the signs of Jesus are found only in the first half of the Gospel (chs. i-xii)". Compare also OLSSON, *o.c.* (see note 14), 69.

[25] See further below, page 121 ff.

with the Jews ending in his expulsion from the synagogue : the cripple does not come to any sort of confession (v 10-15). The word σημεῖον occurs only in passing, in vs 16, in a context which is essentially concerned to answer the question whether Jesus is a true prophet or not. Again his relationship to the sabbath law is the main issue (vss 14, 16).[26] The reader of the Gospel who comes to chapter ix after chapter v knows that this question cannot be answered on the level of a discussion about prophecy and obedience to the law of Moses. This is made clear by the evangelist in the beginning and the end of this chapter. Vss 1-5 emphasize that Jesus carries out the work of God who sent him (see especially vss 3-4) and that he does so as the light of the world. The result is that blind people are allowed to see the light, and that others who think they are seeing discover that they are blind (vss 39-41). Light means Life, but at the same time it discloses darkness as darkness — as was already made clear in iii 19-21. Therefore the final discovery of the blind man is that Jesus is the *Son of Man* and he confesses him as such. This discovery is not his own; it comes only after Jesus reveals himself as Son of Man : "Indeed, it is he who is speaking to you" (vs 37). This revelation is given to a man who is truly "a disciple of Jesus" (vs 28) and acts like one, defending Jesus against the disciples of Moses, even to the extent of accepting expulsion from the synagogue.[27]

In chapter vi we have, again, a story — or rather two stories — with a following discourse which gives the Johannine interpretation of the meaning of the event(s) reported in the stories. Again only a few remarks :

First we should note that the people who see the sign interpret it in terms of a reference to the prophet like Moses who is expected to come into the world (vs 14, cf. vs 2). In the discussion at the beginning of the discourse the Jews refer again to what *Moses* did in the desert (vs 30f.). To the evangelist it is self-evident that people with a Jewish background would connect signs with prophecy, particularly with prophecy after the manner of Moses. This is clear here, in ix 13-17 (and 24-34), and particularly in iii 2. Jesus realizes that this is a high-handed attempt to make him king in a human way. He is king according to the Fourth Gospel, but in his own very special, God-orientated

---

[26] Again the fact that the healing was performed on a sabbath is mentioned very late in the story.

[27] See further "Jesus as Prophet and King ..." (see note 5), 170-172.

way (xii 15 and xviii 33-38).[28] Jesus withdraws again to the hills by himself (vs 15).

Before the real meaning of the multiplication of the loaves is disclosed in the discourse, the story of Jesus' walking on the lake is told; in its present not specifically Johannine context it serves a particular Johannine purpose. It is the revelation of Jesus to his disciples, and to his disciples *only*, through the word ἐγώ εἰμι (vss 16-21).

Vss 24-29 serve as a transitional passage to the great homily in vss 32-58.[29] The title Son of Man is substituted for that of prophet (vs 27) and the unity of this Son of Man with God the Father is emphasized. The perishable food is discarded and people are exhorted to work for the food that lasts, the food of eternal life which can only be given by the Son of Man.[30] In the following homily a number of phrases recur repeatedly, underlining the essential points of Johannine christology: The true bread comes from heaven (vss 32 and 33 as interpretation of vs 31), Jesus is the bread descended from heaven (vss 41, 50, 51, 58) because he may say that he has descended from heaven (vss 38, 42). He is the living bread (vs 51), that is: the bread of life (vss 35, 48, cf. vs 33). To accept Jesus as the bread of life is to receive the true life (vss 50, 51b-58, cf. vss 40, 47). Several times the unity of intention and action between the Father and the Son is emphasized with different expressions (vss 38, 40, 44, 45, 46, 57); see particularly vs 38: καταβέβηκα ἀπὸ τοῦ οὐρανοῦ οὐχ ἵνα ποιῶ τὸ θέλημα τὸ ἐμὸν ἀλλὰ τὸ θέλημα τοῦ πέμψαντός με. The essential difficulty for the Jews is their conviction that Jesus is a man whose father and mother they know and who, therefore, cannot claim to have come from heaven (vs 42, cf. 52). In the last part of the chapter, vss 60-65) we hear that the difficulty of the Jews is also the difficulty of the great majority of Jesus' disciples.[31] In the end only "the twelve" are left; on their behalf Peter testifies that Jesus' words are "words

---

[28] See "Jesus as Prophet and King ..." (see note 5), *passim*, esp. 167f.

[29] On the following see particularly PEDER BORGEN, *Bread from Heaven* (NT.S 10), Leiden 1965.

[30] See vss 26f. and also 31, 49. In vs 26 Jesus even denies that his interlocutors have seen signs (notwithstanding vss 2, 14). These who do not relate the signs to the gift of the true life have not really seen anything — compare here the same tension and ambiguity in the notion of faith elsewhere in the Gospel!

[31] Probably vss 51b-58 (and also vss 60-65) belong to an antidocetic stage in the composition of the Gospel. See "Ontwikkelingen in de Johanneische theologie" (see note 3), 220.

of eternal life" and he calls him "the Holy One of God". Again the disciples, this time the inner circle of the disciples (those who were present when Jesus walked on the lake and addressed his disciples),[32] are the only true believers.

On chapter vii two remarks should be made. The first is on the introductory passage vss 1-9. Here the unbelieving brothers of Jesus advise him to seek publicity in Jerusalem in order that his disciples may see his "works" (vs 3). They are right about the relation between seeing, disciples, and "works" (evidently identical with the signs in xx 30, 31); they are wrong, however, in connecting this with a revelation to *the world* (vs 4). The world hates Jesus who unmasks the works of the world as evil (vs 7). Moreover Jesus' time has not yet come (vs 6, 8, cf. ii 4). If he goes to Jerusalem it is οὐ φανερῶς ἀλλὰ ὡς ἐν κρυπτῷ (vs 10).

The second comment is on vii 31, where believers in the crowd ask: "When the Messiah comes, is it likely that he will perform more signs than this man?" The connection between "signs" and the title "Messiah" is only found in Christian writings. John does not comment on this statement directly, but in other places, notably in xi 27 and xx 31, passages we have already discussed, he clearly supplements and corrects the statement of these believers by adding the phrase "the Son of God" — and this is entirely in keeping with the main line of the christological argumentation in the present chapter.[33]

Signs and works

Looking back upon the passages in the Fourth Gospel where σημεῖον is used we may recapitulate as follows:

a) Seven times the word is used by Jews, either belonging to the crowd or to the authorities. Twice a sign is asked for legitimation (ii 18; vi 30); Jesus refuses because he does not accept the frame of reference presupposed by the question. Also in the five other cases the word is used without a full understanding of Jesus' real being (iii 2; vii 31; ix 16; x 41; xi 47).

b) The same is true in four cases where the evangelist describes reactions of Jews: ii 23; vi 2, 12; xii 18. Yet

---

[32] The designation "the Twelve" is used only here and in xx 24, and is obviously regarded as known to the readers; it is not used in vss 16-21 but occurs in vs 67 to distinguish the faithful few from the many who have gone away.

[33] See "Jewish Expectations ..." (see note 5), 257-260.

c) the Gospel wants to make clear that Jesus' signs could elicit true faith, and in fact did so in the case of the disciples, and the βασιλικός not explicitly called a disciple (ii 11; iv 54; xii 37; xx 30).

d) Only twice do we find the word on the lips of Jesus himself, and both times with a critical connotation with regard to the reaction of people in Galilee (iv 48; vi 26).

The signs point to Jesus' special power and authority, but by no means unequivocally. They may lead to faith, but also to rejection; often they lead to an imperfect understanding which is, in fact misunderstanding. The evangelist, writing from the perspective of a Christian community relying on the word of the disciples/apostles, is quite clear and adamant about that.

If we now turn to the word ἔργον to which we had occasion to refer a few times already,[34] we notice that in two texts it is certainly used on the same level and with practically the same meaning as σημεῖον. In vii 3 the use of τὰ ἔργα σου is parallel to that of σημεῖα in xx 30. In vi 30 the expression τί ποιεῖς σὺ σημεῖον is used besides τί ἐργάζῃ (following on a discussion on τὸ ἔργον/τὰ ἔργα τοῦ θεοῦ). In vii 3 the word ἔργα is used in antithesis to the "works of the world" in vii 7. In the second case mentioned it is used in order to connect the works wrought and inspired by God in men with the works worked by God in and through Jesus (vi 27f.; iii 19-21; cf. viii 39-41).

With the exception of the texts just mentioned the word ἔργον is only used in connection with Jesus by Jesus himself.[35] In all cases Jesus uses it in order to give expression to his unity in intention and action with God. The words "Son" and "Father" occur in this context and the term ἔργα is clearly regarded as more suitable to denote the inner meaning of Jesus' actions than the word σημεῖα. Jesus' works are God's works performed by and through Jesus. Once that is clear,

---

[34] On this word see now the monograph by J. RIEDL, "Das Heilswerk Jesu nach Johannes, (FThSt 93), Freiburg-Basel-Wien 1973. In Zeichen und Werke, Ein Beitrag zur Theologie des 4. Evangeliums in Erzählungs- und Redestoff (AThANT 55), Zürich 1969, W. WILKENS has tried to explain the differences between signs and works by means of the theory of two forms of the Gospel, both written by the same author. A signs-gospel would have been expanded with discourse material and redacted; characteristic for the second stage is the use of the word "works". WILKENS finds it difficult to explain why the word "sign" does not occur in chapter v, and only once in chapter ix. He also tends to maximize the differences in use and meaning between the two central words.

[35] In x 33 it is used by the Jews, because they pick up the word used by Jesus in vs 32.

all ambiguity is removed and only one reaction is possible; study of the ἔργα-passages leads us to the heart of the matter and the centre of Johannine christology and theology. We may, very briefly, point to the following aspects of the use of ἔργον.

First, there is the use of ἔργον in the singular in iv 34 and xvii 4, the first and the last text where the word is used in connection with Jesus. The terminology is very similar; in iv 34 we read: "It is meat and drink for me to do the will of him who sent me until I have finished his work", and in xvii 4: "I have glorified thee on earth by completing the work which thou gavest me to do". Essentially the works are one work, done on the initiative of God and in obedience to the Father. The work comprises more than just a number of acts which can be described as σημεῖα; it is all Jesus did (and said) on earth.

God's initiative is expressed in the terms ὁ πέμψας με (iv 34) and ὃ δέδωκάς μοι (xvii 4). Both expressions recur in similar contexts (resp. in vi 38f.; ix 4; cf. xvii 3 just before vs 4; and in v 36). Jesus' works are also said to be performed "in the name of the Father" (x 25); therefore they may also be called God's works (ix 3; x 37f.).

Jesus' obedience is expressed by ποιεῖν τὸ θέλημα τοῦ πέμψαντός με (iv 34; v 30; vi 38f.). In v 30 this presupposes a continuous listening to the Father (καθὼς ἀκούω κρίνω) which is, again, parallel to "looking to the Father" in v 19. Jesus' work can only be God's work in a *continuous* unity of intention and action between Son and Father (v 17, 19f., 20 (!), 30). If in this context also a perfect is used (as in vs 22 τὴν κρίσιν πᾶσαν δέδωκεν τῷ υἱῷ, cf. v 36; xvii 4 and xii 50), or in similar passages an aorist (viii 26 ἃ ἤκουσα παρ' αὐτοῦ, cf. viii 40; xv 15; viii 28 καθὼς ἐδίδαξέν με), this serves to emphasize that God took the initiative for this continuous "cooperation". The Son is completely and uniquely dependent on the Father.[36] Besides in the expressions just mentioned this is brought out in the ἐν ἐμοὶ ὁ πατὴρ κἀγὼ ἐν τῷ πατρί of x 38, and the ὁ πατὴρ ἐν ἐμοὶ μένων ποιεῖ τὰ ἔργα αὐτοῦ in xiv 10, connected with the ἐγὼ ἐν τῷ πατρὶ καὶ ὁ πατὴρ ἐν ἐμοί of vs 11.

Thirdly, because Jesus' works are the works of the Father they can be said to provide convincing evidence with regard to Jesus' relation to God (v 36; x 25, cf. x 37; xiv 11; xv 24). We cannot discuss

---

[36] On this and related aspects of the relation between Jesus and God, see also my "Gods Zoon en Gods kinderen", *Rondom het Woord* 18, 1976, 57-73.

this in detail,[37] but it should be remarked that the whole question of legitimation returns here. Once one accepts that Jesus has the right to claim that his works are those of the Father, one should believe in his unique mission; no other reaction is possible. But in order to accept this, one needs faith. The identification of Jesus' ἔργα with God's ἔργα is only possible and convincing within the circle of the believers : to outsiders it remains an impossible conclusion, as v 18; viii 13-19, 26-29, 40-42; x 31-39 show clearly.

Fourthly it should be remarked that Jesus' work, although said to be completed at his return to the Father (xvii 4; iv 34), is continued. The programmatic μείζω τούτων ὄψῃ in i 50 probably refers to all the Son of God/Son of Man will do from that moment onwards, during his sojourn on earth and later. In v 20 the present healing points to future μείζονα ἔργα, in the context : the giving of life and the final judgment. Clearly all activity of the Son in unity with the Father is meant, from the present moment till the last judgment and the raising of the dead inclusive — before and after his return to the Father. In xiv 12-14 Jesus tells his disciples that he who has faith in him, because of the works done by the Father in and through Jesus, "will do what I am doing; and he will do greater things still because I am going to the Father". In fact the Son will do these greater things himself, "so that the Father may be glorified in the Son".[38]

Nowhere do we hear that the disciples perform signs; clearly the word most suited to denote their activity, and their Master's continuing activity, is ἔργα. What they do he does, just as their word is his word (xvii 8, 14, 17, 18, 20 and xx 21, 24-31).

This brings us to a last point. All Jesus did *and said* on earth is summed up in the word ἔργον, and in the instances ἔργα is used, the word refers, in all likelihood, not only to the σημεῖα proper, but also to a wide range of activities, just because God is active in the Son, and the Son completely obedient to the Father. If this is so, what, then, is the relation between "works" and "words"? Two things should be emphasized here :

---

[37] See J. BEUTLER, *Martyria*. Traditionsgeschichtliche Untersuchungen zum Zeugnisthema bei Johannes (FTS 10) Frankfurt 1972, esp. 259f., 272f. and 293-298.

[38] Because of iv 34; xvii 4, and also ix 4 it is clear that there is not only continuity, but also discontinuity between the works of the earthly Jesus and the exalted Son; one may compare here the two stages observed in connection with glory and glorification. See, again, W. Thüsing, *Die Erhöhung*. (see note 10), esp. 58-63.

There is a clear parallelism between seeing and hearing, works and words, and, to some extent, also interchangeability. As to the relation between Son and Father, v 19 with its emphasis on βλέπειν and ποιεῖν, is followed by v 30 with its emphasis on ἀκούειν and κρίνειν as an illustration of this ποιεῖν.[39] The same applies *mutatis mutandis* to v 37, 38 after v 36 and viii 28. The very use of the term τὰ ἔργα ... μαρτυρεῖ περὶ ἐμοῦ in v 36 (cf. x 25) shows how closely works and words are related; the same is clear in the passing remark in x 21. Yet works and words are never identified. xv 24 stands parallel to xv 22; after the temporarily concluding passage xii 37-43 dealing with the impact of Jesus' signs, we get a new concluding reference to Jesus' witness in complete unity with the Father in vss 44-50, ending with the statement "What the Father has said to me, therefore — that is what I speak". Vss 44-50 come unexpected after vs 36b and have no organic link with the preceding chapters. They consist of a number of statements which, in other forms, already occurred in other contexts; these verses add nothing new and they are not meant to add anything new. In the present composition of the Gospel they give a summing up of the real intention of Jesus' preaching, after the preceding verses 37-43 which look back on Jesus' signs.

Secondly, we have already noticed that the Gospel has a preference for belief in Jesus' word preceding belief in him on the strength of his signs. This is clear in the case of the βασιλικός in chapter iv, and in that of Martha in chapter xi, while the Thomas-story in chapter xx points in the same direction. The demonstrative character of the signs is apt to be misinterpreted; but nowhere does the Gospel disqualify the signs as superfluous or "second best". R. BULTMANN's often quoted word: "Die Werke Jesu — als Ganzes gesehen: sein Werk — sind seine Worte" (occurring in § 48 "Die Offenbarung als das Wort" of his *Theologie des Neuen Testaments*)[40] is one-sided and wrong.

The passages just mentioned link up with x 32-38 and xiv 8-12 which, while underlining the unity between Father and Son, connect and distinguish what Jesus speaks and does. Jesus' acts are essential; x 37 referring back to v 36 gives the word of Jesus "If I am not acting as my Father would, do not believe me". To this vs 38 adds: "But if I am, accept the evidence of my deeds, even if you do not believe

---

[39] See also iii 32: "He who comes from heaven bears witness to what he has seen and heard".

[40] Tübingen 1953, 407; ²1958, 413.

me". Jesus' words could and should be convincing; his works irrefutably demonstrate his unity with the Father. This is said to non-believing Jews. Their misunderstanding and rejection of Jesus may, in the last resort, be attributed to God's initiative (xii 37-43! just like the faith of the believers), yet they have no excuse (xv 22-25, cf. ix 40f).

This passage, like the next, clearly does not aim at discrediting the value of Jesus' deeds. xiv 10 is usually adduced as the final proof-text for the identification of ἔργα and ῥήματα; it cannot be used as such, because in vs 11 these two are again distinguished, and related to one another in the same way as in x 32-38. Moreover the verse should be seen against the background of the discourse on the unity of the Father and the Son in chapter v where there is no identification but thoroughgoing parallelism. In vs 11 we find "believe me" beside "accept the evidence of the deeds themselves", this time not as an argument for Jewish outsiders but as one directed to disciples. Again the deeds are not mentioned as "second best", but as finally convincing evidence. Jesus' words are effective, and his ἔργα give a reliable testimony. For those who are able to believe in it, there is a surprising unity of event and proclamation in all that God works in and through Jesus — but no identity.

THE PERSPECTIVE OF ROMANS VII

TH. DE KRUYF

It is a well-known fact that the interpretation of many texts and passages is not only dependent on a correct exegesis of the various linguistic elements of the text itself, but also on the perspective in which the text is seen. However banal, this statement contains a great number of difficulties, both on the level of theoretical analysis and of practical application. Without going into too many details on a theoretical level, one should at least make a distinction between the perspective which is the result of a certain way of viewing the text under consideration in its (complete) context, which we might call the "literary perspective", and the perspective which is created by the interpreter looking at the text from his particular point of view, which could be called the "hermeneutical perspective".[1] Apart from more subjective factors, the point of view of an interpreter of the NT is necessarily affected by his position in the midst of the cross-currents created by the various disciplines, particularly in the fields of literature, history and theology, each with its own methods and presuppositions, which together form, at least to a large extent, NT scholarship. So, practically speaking, a text like Rom. vii will be viewed in a rather different way by experts (not all of them NT scholars) in the fields of philology, philosophy, Jewish law, Roman law,[2] psychology, comparative religion, dogmatic theology.[3] The history of the interpretation of Rom. vii is an outstanding example of the fact that the interpretation and evaluation of linguistic data are influenced, to a noticeable degree, by the perspective and the point of view of the interpreter.[4]

---

[1] In German one could use the words *Gesamtanschauung* and *Grundanschauung* in order to express this distinction. The latter word is used by E. GIESE, *Römer 7, neu gesehen im Zusammenhang des gesamten Briefes*, Marburg 1959, 1; the perspective of the *Gesamtanschauung* is contained in the subtitle.

[2] Including Hellenistic law.

[3] In this connection, from my own point of view and from personal experience, I am still wondering whether a small theological college or seminary is a better place to discuss these problems than a modern university.

[4] For literature consult: W. G. KÜMMEL, *Römer 7 und die Bekehrung des Paulus*, Leipzig 1929; B. M. METZGER, *Index to Periodical Literature on the Apostle Paul*, Leiden 1960 (till 1957); E. GIESE, *o.c.*; G. WAGNER, *An Exegetical Bibliography on*

In 1971 a group of French(-speaking) scholars published the results
of a conference on "Exegesis and Hermeneutics"[5] in which we find a
remarkable contribution by A. VERGOTE[6] on the connection between
exegesis and psychoanalysis in the interpretation of Rom.[7] VERGOTE's
point of departure is the fact that Paul uses anthropological terms
which ought to be explained by an informed psychology.[8] This is to
say that psychoanalysis (referred to by VERGOTE as the most systematic
analysis of psychological concepts) ought to support exegetes when
they try to translate Paul's anthropological terms, especially his use
of the pronoun ἐγώ, into modern categories.[9] Why did Paul use the
pronoun ἐγώ in this way? It is not sufficient to say that this was a
rhetorical way of speaking, because then the question remains why
Paul did use this particular way of speaking in this context.[10] VERGOTE's
answer is: Paul uses this pronoun precisely when he begins to write

Paul's Letter to the Romans (Bibl. Aids 3), Rüschlikon-Zürich 1973 (till 1972); even
apart from the commentaries one finds nearly all the great names in these lists, which,
despite every effort, are still incomplete: ALTHAUS, BÉNOIT, BORNKAMM, H. BRAUN,
F. F. BRUCE, BULTMANN, CERFAUX, CONZELMANN, W. D. DAVIES, VON DOBSCHÜTZ,
FEUILLET, FITZMYER, FRIEDLÄNDER, FUCHS, GOGARTEN, JEWETT, KÄSEMANN, KERTEL-
GE, KÜMMEL, KUSS, LOHMEYER, LYONNET, T. W. MANSON, MEEKS, MOULE, REICKE,
RIGAUX, SCHELKE, SCHLIER, TOUSSAINT, to name but a few. The SNTC seems to
distinguish itself by a marked abstinence in the field of Rom vii: so far I have discovered
only W. GROSSOUW, De verscheurde mens van Romeinen zeven, in: Vriendengave
B. Kard. Alfrink, Utrecht (1964), 68-80, and W. C. VAN UNNIK, Enige aspekten van
de anthropologie bij Paulus, in: Festschrift J. Severijn, Kampen (1966), 37-46. This
is not to say that the Dutch scene is empty: there is at least also A. LEKKERKERKER,
Röm 7 und 9 bei Augustin, Amsterdam 1942; H. F. KOHLBRUGGE, Das siebente Kapitel
des Briefes Pauli an die Römer in ausführlicher Umschreibung, Elberfeld 1839; O.
NOORDMANS, Psychologie en Evangelie, in: Zoeklichten, Amsterdam (1949), 59-82
(considered by Lekkerkerker in his Commentary as the most original interpretation,
with Kohlbrugge's, of the last 150 years); H. S. PRETORIUS, Bijdrage tot de exegese en
de geschiedenis der exegese van Romeinen vii, 1915; H. RIDDERBOS, Paulus, Kampen
[3]1973; G. DE RU, Betekenis en functie van de wet bij Paulus, KeTh 17 (1966), 143-160.
    [5] R. BARTHES, P. BEAUCHAMP, H. BOUILLARD, J. COURTÈS, E. HAULOTTE, X. LÉON-
DUFOUR, L. MARIN, P. RICŒUR, A. VERGOTE, Exégèse et Herméneutique, Paris 1971.
    [6] Of the Centre de psychologie de la religion at the Catholic University of Louvain.
    [7] Apport des données psychanalytiques à l'exégèse. Vie, loi et clivage du Moi aux
Romains 7, o.c., 109-147; there is also an introduction with a summary of exegetical
positions (99-108) and a "round table" in which the exegetes A. DUPREZ, P. GRELOT,
S. LÉGASSE et X. LÉON-DUFOUR contribute some very pertinent questions. On psychoanalysis and exegesis in general see Y. SPIEGEL, Psychoanalytische Interpretationen
biblischer Texte, München 1972.
    [8] O.c., 113.
    [9] O.c., 116-118. To be quite clear: in no way does VERGOTE try to analyze Paul's
own psychology.
    [10] On the use of τόποι see e.g. W. C. VAN UNNIK, Once more St. Luke's Prologue,
in: Neotestamentica VII (1973) (= Essays on the Gospel of Luke and Acts), 7-26.

about the Law: "the ἐγώ is used precisely as an answer to the Law which pronounces a sentence in the second person singular of the prohibiting mood:[11] 'Thou shalt not covet'". The usual classification of interpretations as "psychological" or "historico-theological" is completely wrong, because it presupposes the ἐγώ as a fixed subject of experiences. This is exactly where psychoanalysis is able to help the exegetes: the ἐγώ is not the fixed subject of experience, it is not simply a *datum*, but it grows out of a process of digestion of all sorts of cultural matters, of speech, of law, of institutions, of rites. Symbols and language create a human being, the ἐγώ, not the other way round.[12] This fundamental insight is necessary for the understanding of Paul's description of the ἐγώ in confrontation with the Law. The Law with its commandment "Thou shalt not covet" (Rom. vii 7) is like the Father-figure in the Oedipus tragedy. The "unconscious" child, the child that has not yet an ἐγώ, needs the father's prohibitive commandment "thou shalt not covet ... (your mother)" in order to have the possibility to develop its ἐγώ, its own human personality. The human being becomes a human person through the process of the confrontation of commandment and desire. Knowing these elementary data of psychoanalysis, it is more easy to follow Paul's thought in Rom. vii. Paul does not speak about the ἐγώ in a dualistic way, but he describes the struggle of the emerging ἐγώ through the conflict between the commandment and the desire; he does not think about the psychology of an individual but of the history of mankind. "In the perspective of Rom. vii the Law is a clear, personal appeal, which is received with a lucid awareness of a more superior promise. Its command precedes both bad conscience and hardened legalism. Yet, it inaugurates a tragic existence because its fatal powerlessness is in an obscure way resented but not yet understood. It polarizes the subject in a hopeful but impossible struggle.[13] In effect, according to VERGOTE, Paul describes the transient role of Judaism and its Law. The solution of the conflict can only be given by God who is the Author of the promise.[14]

---

[11] "Du mode interdictif" (p. 123).

[12] "Le moi, n'est pas une donnée première; il se constitue par l'intériorisation des données culturelles, des discours, de la loi, des institutions, des rites. Ce sont d'abord les symboles et le langage qui font l'homme, le moi, et non pas l'inverse", *o.c.*, 135.

[13] *O.c.*, 133.

[14] "Le juif, en effet, ne voit pas encore que seul l'Auteur de la loi peut répondre de la promesse qu'elle contient ... Le cœur du judaïsme est fait de la polarité entre

Of course, this short summary does less than justice to Vergote's contribution to the exegesis of Rom. vii.[15] However, it may serve as an illustration of the problems of perspective as a major factor in the interpretation of a certain text or passage, problems which are connected with the interdependence of various disciplines and methods in the practise of NT exegesis, problems which are beyond the limits of this article, but which one ought to keep in mind. On the other hand, and this may be easily overlooked, VERGOTE's paper is also an example of the influence of what we have called the literary perspective, which is the result of a certain way of viewing the text in its context. Depending, no doubt, on exegetes, VERGOTE states the principles of his interpretation in a paragraph entitled "Chapter vii within the structure of the Letter to the Romans".[16] In his view, chapters vi, vii and viii are closely connected : the main theme of Rom. vi, i.e. that the christian died with Christ in order to live with him (vi 8-14), is developed in Rom. viii, and Rom. vii is the essential link because it explains the connection between the four elements that are mentioned in Rom. vi, i.e. flesh, sin, law and death.[17] Chapter vii, therefore, is not a digression, but has to be explained within the opposition between the (former) existence, dominated by sin, law, death on the one side, and the (present) christian life, defined by the Spirit, the Father and hope on the other side. It seems fairly obvious that it would have been difficult, not to say impossible, to develop VERGOTE's interpretation within a perspective that sees Rom. vii 7-25 as an excursus containing an apology of the Law.[18]

Hidden within the problems of the literary perspective there is yet another question : that of the perspective in which the author himself, from his point of view, saw the subject which he treated in a particular passage. One might call this the "historical perspective".[19] Although

---

promesse et loi. ... C'est que le judaïsme n'est qu'un moment dans le devenir religieux de l'humanité ..." (133).

[15] It is interesting to note that VERGOTE received his license in theology for an exegetical study on "L'exaltation du Christ en croix selon le IVe évangile", EThL 28 (1952), 5-23.

[16] O.c., 119-125.

[17] O.c., 119-120; this view, of course, is not presented as original, see the references on p. 120, note 2. In fact, the position of VERGOTE is not quite clear, because he accepts the model of the three stages of the history of salvation (Adam-Torah; Torah-Christ; Christ-), though this model depends largely on chapter v.

[18] See the references in E. KÄSEMANN, An die Römer (HNT 8a), Tübingen (1973), 182.

[19] One could argue that the historical perspective is to be considered in its own

nearly all modern scholars agree that Rom. vii is not autobiographical in the strict sense, the question crops up again and again. Once more, VERGOTE may be cited. He distinguishes between the historical experience about which Paul speaks in the past tense (Rom. vii 7-13), and the present (christian) interpretation of a past experience, about which Paul speaks in the present tense (Rom. vii 14ff). Having established this distinction, VERGOTE proceeds : "We do not dispute the possibility that Paul as a Jew has ever experienced the contradiction which he now reflects upon. But our text gives us to understand that before he became a christian Paul was not able to conceptualize the conflict as a universal religious law".[20] At this point, clearly, the question of Paul's perspective in dealing with the matter of Rom. vii is at issue.[21]

The preceding example has been discussed at great length in order to show that a methodical limitation to the problems of any one of the different perspectives in which a text or passage can be viewed, can only be fictitious, because the influence of other ways of looking at a text will certainly appear more or less clearly at some stage of the investigation. While limiting myself in this article to the question of the literary perspective of Rom. vii within its context, I shall try to be aware of this fact.

Twenty years after I started my studies in Romans, under the direction of S. LYONNET, the problems of Paul's "presentation of christian doctrine"[22] do not seem to have come much nearer to their solution.[23] A look at the Introduction and the first Chapter of R. RUIJS' dissertation on the Structure of the Letter to the Romans will convince anyone of the complexity of the question and even of

---

right and that it ought to be distinguished from both the literary and the hermeneutical perspective. Although I find myself in complete disagreement with those who consider all the historical material (or scholarly hypotheses) pertaining to the situation of the author as irrelevant to the interpretation of a text, in this case I can see the question of the historical perspective only as part of the problems of the literary perspective, because, with the possible, but theoretical, exception of explicitly autobiographical texts, we do not have direct access to the author's actual point of view at the moment of his writing a particular passage.

[20] "... le conflit en loi religieuse universelle", o.c., 124.

[21] Vergote himself rejects autobiographical interpretations, o.c., 122.

[22] "Doctrinae christianae compendium", *Melanchthons Werke* II/1, Gütersloh (1952), 7; about his disposition see Römerbriefkommentar 1532, WERKE V (1965) Beilage 373 ff.

[23] "Eine eindeutige Lösung drängt sich aus dem Studium der Sekundärliteratur nicht auf. Die Vielfalt der Lösungsversuche zeigt, wie komplex die Frage ist." U. LUZ, Zum Aufbau von Röm 1-8, *ThZ* 25 (1969), 165.

its bibliographical difficulties.[24] If we leave apart the introduction
i 1-15 and the parenetical chapters xii-xv (xvi) (and for the moment
also ix-xi which seems to be more or less self-contained) the problem
of the structure of Romans appears to be centred in Rom. v: there
we find, according to nearly all the authors, the transition from the
first to the second part of the Letter.[25] Whereas it is also generally
accepted that the first part contains at least i 18-iv 25 and deals
with the theme of the justification of all people, Jews and Greeks,
through faith, the interpreters disagree widely on two points: where
does the second part begin, at the beginning, in the middle or at the
end of chapter v, and: what is the main theme of this second part?
Parallel with this divergence of opinions we find a great variety of
criteria, proposed in order to establish structures of form and thought
in Romans.[26]

What is really astonishing in this, is the fact that, apparently, Paul
has succeeded in expressing his thoughts adequately in the first part
of his letter, and has failed to do so in the second part. Exegetes
generally do not ask questions about this surprising fact, perhaps
because, from their perspective as interpreters, difficulties of interpretation are considered as normal rather than exceptional. There
remains, nonetheless, a question, and if one tries to answer this
question, one can choose between at least three avenues: one leading
to Paul himself as the cause of the difficulties, one leading to the
subject Paul is dealing with, and one leading to the interpreters. If we
go directly to Paul, we are confronted with the supposition of a rather
radical change of Paul's personal situation sometime when he was
writing (or dictating) chapter v, a supposition which is highly unlikely
and in any case merely speculative. A similar supposition, when
applied to a great number of independent scholars, is simply absurd.
The only avenue open to us is, therefore, the one leading to the
subject Paul is dealing with in the second part. There must be some
special difficulty inherent in this subject, which is not contained in
the subject of the first part, and which explains the fact that in the

---

[24] R. RUIJS, *De struktuur van de brief aan de Romeinen*, Een stilistische, vorm-
historische en thematische analyse van Rom 1, 16-3, 23 Utrecht/Nijmegen 1964. In more
recent years the attention seems to have wandered elsewhere, compare the literature
in E. KÄSEMANN's Commentary.

[25] See the summaries in e.g. E. GIESE, *o.c.*, 8-18; R. RUIJS, *o.c.*, 1-16; U. LUZ,
o.c., 163-165.

[26] See the survey in R. RUIJS, *o.c.*, 16-33; of special interest is the analysis of
Paul's "thought-structures" by U. LUZ, *o.c.*, 165-175.

second part Paul does express himself in such a way that there is room for a number of interpretations. What kind of special difficulty could this be?

Instead of trying to answer this new question directly, I want to draw attention to another, though perhaps less obvious, conclusion from the fact that the problem of the structure of Romans appears to be centred in Rom. v: the very fact that there is a difference of opinion as to where the second part begins — whereas there is a general agreement about the main disposition of i 16-iv 25[27] — implies that the second part begins where our difficulties begin, that is to say, not in the middle or at the end of chapter v, but at the beginning, with v 1 where we read a variant which shows that the difficulties of interpretation go back to the oldest textual transmission known to us: δικαιωθέντες οὖν ἐκ πίστεως εἰρήνην ἔχομεν/ἔχωμεν πρὸς τὸν θεὸν διὰ τοῦ κυρίου ἡμῶν Ἰησοῦ Χριστοῦ.[28] In the case of the interpretation (and even the reading!) of this verse, what has been said about the influence of both the literary and the hermeneutical perspective becomes obvious. Only a limited number of scholars seem to have an open mind.[29] The opinion of the majority is summarized by T. W. MANSON: "The authorities are divided between 'we are at peace' and 'let us continue at peace': the former gives the better sense".[30] The main argument is expressed in the most positive way by H. LIETZMANN, certainly not an uncritical scholar: the first verses of chapter v are so imbued with the certainty of our salvation that this in itself makes it clear that in v. 1 ἔχομεν must be read: the exhortation to "keep peace with God", contained in ἔχωμεν, does not make sense in this context.[31] If one accepts this argument as valid

---

[27] The only major problem is in chapter 2: where does Paul pass from the judgment of all people to the judgment of the Jews?

[28] ἔχομεν: א[a] B[3] G[gr] P Ψ etc.; ἔχωμεν: א* A B* C D K 33 etc.; see GNT (1966). According to H. LIETZMANN, An die Römer (HNT 8), Tübingen [4]1933, 58 and W. FOERSTER, ThWNT II, 414 the difference between indicative and subjunctive could not be heard in dictation.

[29] "Das Urteil über die glänzend bezeugte und (Lietzmann) uralte Leseart ἔχωμεν fällt schwer und sie wird immer noch stark verteidigt (Sanday-Headlam: Lagrange; Kuss; J. Knox, Life 17; Neugebauer, In Christus 61; Dinkler RAC VIII, 463f.; erwägenswert: Bardenhewer; Murray). Gleichwohl spricht der Kontext mit seinen indikativischen Feststellungen wie der Skopus des Abschnittes gegen sie." (E. KÄSEMANN, o.c., 123).

[30] Romans (PCB), London 1962, 944.

[31] "Das Thema von 1, 17 ist erwiesen. Es folgt die Weiterführung des Gedankens: Auf Grund der im Evangelium offenbarten Gottesgerechtigkeit haben wir die Gewissheit des künftigen Heiles; das wird in c. 5 dargelegt. Von dieser Stimmung der Sicher-

(and with it a variant which is inferior from the point of view of
textual criticism, on account of external evidence and of the — in this
case sadly neglected — principle of internal evidence : *lectio difficilior
praeferenda*), there is no answer to the question why Paul did not
express the main theme and the disposition of the second part in a
more clear way. But, if we take the question why Paul expressed
himself more clearly in the first than in the second part of Romans
seriously, if we also accept v 1 as the beginning of the second part of the
letter and if, moreover, we read the subjunctive ἔχωμεν instead of
the indicative ἔχομεν, in short : if we are looking at this verse from
such a perspective, what do we find?

a) It is obvious that we should start with the meaning of the subjunctive ἔχωμεν. As W. SANDAY-A. HEADLAM point out, the meaning
of ἔχωμεν is "not : = 'make peace' (which would be σχῶμεν) but
rather 'keep' or 'enjoy peace'", with a reference to Acts ix 31.[32]
But what is the meaning of the subjunctive mood in itself? Is the
meaning of an exhortation (Aufforderung) the only alternative to the
indicative? F. BLASS is rather careful in his description : the subjunctive
has, it seems, the basic meaning of that what ought to be (from the
point of view of the speaker), but it is also related to the future
tense; in fact, the subjunctive is used in a broader sense than the one
contained in the basic meaning : it expresses the realisation of what
is developing from the present situation in certain circumstances.[33]
G. MUSSIES, in a much more recent investigation on the morphology of
koine Greek[34] also recognizes this broader meaning, but under the
heading "dependent use"; however, the description he gives in his
conclusion, "the value of the subjunctive implies an urging-expecting
attitude on the side of the speaker or the subject of the sentence with
regard to the relation person — action" comes very near to the one
given by F. BLASS. It seems, therefore, that there is no obligation

---

heit sind gleich die folgenden Sätze so stark durchdrungen, dass dadurch allein schon
klargestellt ist, dass in v. 1 ἔχομεν zu lesen ist; die in ἔχωμεν liegende Aufforderung,
mit Gott 'Frieden zu halten' ist in diesem Zusammenhang völlig sinnlos." (*o.c.*, 58).
He even goes so far as to say : even if Tertius would have understood and written
ἔχωμεν, "Der Sinn muss auch hier über den Buchstaben siegen : ἔχομεν gibt allein den
echten paulinischen Sinn." (*ibidem*).

[32] W. SANDAY-A. HEADLAM, *The Epistle to the Romans* (ICC), Edinburgh ⁵1902,
120.

[33] F. BLASS, *Grammatik des Neutestamentlichen Griechisch*, Göttingen ²1902, 212-
213.

[34] *The Morphology of Koine Greek, as used in the Apocalypse of St. John*. Leiden
1971, 244-246.

to read the subjunctive as an exhortation "let us have (keep) peace with God" — and certainly not in an ethical sense —; the subjunctive can also be understood as expressing an urgent expectation, oriented towards the future, and perhaps with an implied question.[35]

b) It will not be necessary to explain that εἰρήνη is not to be taken in the strictly Greek sense, namely as opposed to πόλεμος, ἔρις etc., but in the full sense of the OT שָׁלוֹם,[36] with its eschatological dimension.

c) I think that we now have enough indications to explain the difference between the first and the second part of Romans, which seems to confuse so many commentators. In the first part Paul is speaking about what he has experienced as the apostle of the gentiles : the revelation of the wrath of God (i 18) has made way for the manifestation of the saving justice of God, apart from the Law, through faith in Jesus Christ (iii 21-22).[37] This part covers the past and the present, both for the Jews and for the Gentiles, at least for those "who believe in him that raised from the dead Jesus our Lord, who was put to death for our trespasses and raised for our justification" (iv 24-25). Paul is sure of this, not only because of his faith, but also because he has experienced the "revelation of the justice of God" in the gospel (i 17). But, as U. Luz has pointed out, one of the most typical characteristics of Paul's way of thinking and writing is the "verification of theological pronouncements in reality".[38] Paul himself, when writing this letter, is not a prisoner of the past (although the past is following him, Acts xx 3) or sitting idly in the present. He is looking forward to the future.[39] Paul is sure in his faith : δικαιω-θέντες οὖν ἐκ πίστεως ..., but at the same time there is the uncertainty of what is not yet reality; there are questions, expectations, concern about a future that is hidden in the present. Why, otherwise, does he ask all those (rhetorical?) questions at the end of chapter viii? In fact, I think that these questions are the explicitation of what Paul has in mind when writing v 1 : "having been justified through faith, I expect

---

[35] See G. MUSSIES, o.c., 244.

[36] Th. C. DE KRUIJF, Justice and Peace in the New Testament, Bijdr. 32 (1971), 377-381.

[37] About the justice of God as iustitia salvifica, not distributiva, see S. LYONNET, Les étapes du mystère du Salut selon l'épitre aux Romains, Paris 1969.

[38] "Verifikation theologischer Aussagen an der Wirklichkeit", o.c., 173.

[39] It is probable that Paul wrote the letter to the Romans in Corinth and a reconstruction of Paul's situation at that time, based upon 1 and 2 Corinthians, Romans xv (xvi?) and Acts xx, though necessarily hypothetical, may give some indication of Paul's "historical" perspective at that critical moment of his life.

urgently that we have (or : we may have also/we will have surely —
with a tiny question-mark) the (full) peace towards God through
our Lord Jesus Christ —, (vs 2) the same through whom we have
obtained access to this grace in which we stand (have been placed)".[40]

d) Looking back to Rom. i 16-17, where Paul first states his theme,
we also find elements which are easy to understand as expressing
Paul's experience : "For I am not ashamed of the gospel, it is the
power of God for salvation to everyone who has faith, to the Jew
first and also to the Greek. For in it (in the gospel) the justice of
God has been revealed through faith ..."; and elements about which
there is some discussion :[41] εἰς σωτηρίαν, with an eschatological
connotation, especially in connection with the δύναμις θεοῦ; the
expression ἐκ πίστεως εἰς πίστιν, together with the quotation (Heb. ii
4), in which faith equals faithfulness. I am inclined to think that Paul
had a rather clear idea of what he was going to say in the first part of
his letter when he wrote i 16-17, whereas the contents of what we read
in v-viii and even in v-xi was at the back of his mind.

e) What has been said so far does not clarify the structure of Rom.
v-viii (xi); on the contrary, it shows that we can not expect a really
transparant structure, because Paul is constantly wrestling with his
subject, with questions and partial answers, new questions and new
answers. πίστις as a key-word has been supplanted by ἐλπὶς/ἐλπίζειν
(in the first part only iv 18; then : v 2.4.5; viii 20.24; viii 25) and
ἀγάπη/ἀγαπᾶν (v 5.8; viii 35; viii 28.37). The beginning of chapter v
does not show a "mood of certainty"[42] but Paul's pride (perhaps even
arrogance) based on hope (v 2).

More important, therefore, than the disposition of the second part
is, I think, the *movement* of Paul's argumentation. This is constantly,
from chapter v through xi, an argumentation *a minori ad maiorem*, not
unlike the קל וחומר of Hillel's hermeneutic system,[43] eminently suited
for questions of the relation between the present and the future.
Introduced by the formula οὐ μόνον δέ, ἀλλὰ καὶ, the chain : ἐλπὶς —

---

[40] There is no reason why the perfect ἐσχήκαμεν should not be taken seriously, as
H. LIETZMANN suggests (*o.c.*, 58).

[41] Parallel with the discussion about whether i 16-17 states the main theme of the
whole letter (e.g. W. G. KÜMMEL, *Einleitung in das Neue Testament*, Heidelberg ([16] 1969),
218 : "das Briefthema") or only of the first part (e.g. S. LYONNET, *Quaestiones in epistu-
lam ad Romanos II*, Roma 1956, 9, to be compared with v 1-11 as the theme of 5-8).
See also U. LUZ, *o.c.*, 166.

[42] H. LIETZMANN (see note 31).

[43] H. MÜLLER, *ZNW* 58 (1967), 73-92.

θλίψεις — ὑπομονή — δοκιμή — ἐλπὶς — ἀγάπη, is a first example
(v 3-5); v 9 contains the typical expression πολλῷ μᾶλλον (v 10.15.17;
xi 12: πόσῳ μᾶλλον) and the basis of the argument: πολλῷ οὖν
μᾶλλον δικαιωθέντες νῦν ἐν τῷ αἵματι αὐτοῦ σωθησόμεθα δι᾽ αὐτοῦ
ἀπὸ τῆς ὀργῆς (note the contrast between δικαιωθέντες νῦν and the
future σωθησόμεθα). The whole of the difficult passage v 12-21 is
then, as I see it, an involved explicitation and development of this
basic argument, which at the end of chapter viii comes again to the
fore in force, after another chain-argumentation (viii 28-30), comparable
to the one in v 3-5, and culminating in: εἰ ὁ θεὸς ὑπερ ἡμῶν, τίς
καθ᾽ ἡμῶν; (viii 31).[44]

All this should be analyzed in greater detail, but what has been
said so far may suffice for the purpose of relating the interpretation
of a certain passage, Rom. vii, to a particular way of viewing its
context, Rom. v-viii (xi).

From the point of view that has been presented, it is impossible
to accept all those interpretations of Rom. vii in which not the whole
of chapter v is considered as part of the context of chapter vii:[45]
those who put the division between ch. v and vi (BONNARD: classic)
or between v 11 and v 12 (FEUILLET); those who take ch. vii together
with ch. viii (CAMBIER, KÄSEMANN); finally those who see vii 7-25 as an
excursus (LUTHER, BULTMANN). On the other hand, a structure like the
one proposed by LYONNET, BRUNOT, GIESE[46] corresponds well with
the literary perspective presented so far.

If we consider the place and the function of ch. vi and vii in the unit
ch. v-viii, our point of departure should be once more the main
argument Paul is using throughout this part and which he has formulated again at the end of ch. v: "as Sin reigned in Death, likewise
also Grace will reign through justice to eternal life through Jesus Christ
our Lord". The question with which ch. vi begins is directly connected
with this argumentation a minori ad maiorem: "What then shall we
say: are we to continue in Sin that Grace may abound? By no
means!" (vi 1). Paul, having used a theological argumentation, is

---

[44] I am convinced that the argumentation is carried on in 9-11 (xi 12: πόσῳ
μᾶλλον): for Paul who wants to verify his theology in reality the situation of Israel
is the ultimate "test-case" to see whether really ἡ ἐλπὶς (δὲ) οὐ καταισχύνει (v 5).

[45] In the following only a few authors are mentioned in parenthesis as an example.

[46] These authors also give a number of arguments, independent from what has
been brought forward in this article, which I can not discuss but which generally can
be taken as confirmation.

concerned with the verification of his argument in reality, that is, in christian experience, his own and that of all christians; that is, not just any experience, but an informed experience : "We, who have died to Sin, how can we still live in it? Do you not know ...?" (vi 2-3). The christian experience itself describes the limits of the type of theological argument Paul has been using in ch. v and is still using now : "For if we have been united with him in a death like his, we shall certainly be united with him in a resurrection like his" (vi 5).

In this way I see ch. vi and vii as dominated by two factors : the underlying argumentation, carried on from ch. v, as in vi 5, and the concern to verify this argumentation in the reality of an informed christian experience, expressed particularly in the type of question formulated in vi 1, together with an appeal to christian knowledge, as in vi 3. In fact, this seems to be a formal element in the structure of ch. vi-vii : τί οὖν ἐροῦμεν; ... μὴ γένοιτο. ... ἢ ἀγνοεῖτε ... (vi 1-3); τί οὖν; ... μὴ γένοιτο. οὐκ οἴδατε ... (vi 15-16); ἢ ἀγνοεῖτε, ἀδελφοί, ... (vii 1); τί οὖν ἐροῦμεν; ... μὴ γένοιτο· ἀλλὰ ... οὐκ ἔγνων ... (vii 7); only in vii 13 the form is different : "did that which is good, then, bring death to me? μὴ γένοιτο· ἀλλὰ ...[47] These two factors, therefore, dominate the literary structure of ch. vi-vii, but they do not produce a logical disposition of the contents. Rather, they give a certain literary rhythm to the flow of Paul's thoughts which, as to their contents, still circle around the themes of the three major obstacles to the full realisation of God's love in us : sin, death and law, mentioned in v 12-21.[48] It now remains to be seen whether a distinction between the character of Paul's argumentation, the literary structure of ch. vi-vii, and the themes about which Paul is thinking, may contribute to the interpretation of chapter vii.

It is usual to speak about "the problem of Romans vii", but it is not quite clear whether the problem concerns the whole chapter or the passage vii 7-25. From the point of view of the main theme the problem concerns the whole chapter, because the theme-word, νόμος, is mentioned in vii 1. From the point of view of the literary structure, however, the problem begins in vii 7 : there we have a formal parallel to vi 1; and also, perhaps even more important, in vii 7 Paul starts speaking in the first person singular, introducing an element which dominates the discussion about this part of Romans : the famous ἐγώ,

---

[47] We find the same type of question and appeal also in xi 1.7.11 and, in a somewhat different form, in iii 1-20, see E. GIESE, o.c., 8-9.

[48] In this I agree with A. BRUNOT and S. LYONNET.

which has been anticipated only lightly in iii 7. There is also a
secondary problem of structure in the transition between vii 12 and
vii 13 :[49] in vii 13 we have once more the question (and in vii 14a the
appeal in the plural!), and between vii 12 and vii 15 we find also a
transition from the past to the present tense. We are, therefore,
confronted with three problems : that of the transition from the theme
of sin to the theme of law; that of the transition from the normal
plural "we" to the exceptional singular ἐγώ; and that of the transition
from the past to the present tense within this passage.

The problem of the transition from the theme of sin to the theme
of law is not a difficult one if one keeps in mind that for the Pharisee
Paul the concept of sin is naturally linked with "the Law".[50] Sin
and "the Law", as concepts, are related; moreover, the link between
the two themes has already been laid in iii 1-20, "since through the
law comes knowledge of sin" (iii 20); and the transition has been
prepared in vi 14.15. The real problem is, how they can be related in
reality, as the Law comes from God and sin is against God and his
Law, and, from a theological point of view, this problem remains
in force, even for Paul who is convinced that justification has come,
finally, apart from law, through faith. So, one can say that the
thematic transition is made in vii 1, but the real problem is stated
in vii 7 and developed in the following passage.

How is it possible that the Law is connected with sin? A great
number of explanations has been offered why Paul at this point
changes from the usual plural to the singular.[51] At the moment,
as far as I can see, any psychological interpretation, and certainly the
supposition that Paul wrote about himself, is frowned upon, though
all theological and theologico-historical interpretations are still having
difficulties with Paul's "remarkable anthropology".[52] This preference

---

[49] Between vii 13 and vii 14 according to E. KÄSEMANN, o.c., 176; 182; 188,
but he does not seem to pay much attention to literary structure.

[50] The first time Paul mentions the concept of sin in this letter, he does so using
the word ἀδικία (i 18 : twice); the first time he uses the verb ἁμαρτάνειν, it is in
company with the adverb ἄνομος and the first time he uses the word νόμος coincides
with the second mentioning of ἁμαρτάνειν (both in the same verse, ii 12); finally, the
first time he uses the substantive ἁμαρτία, this happens in a very Jewish context (iii 9-19).

[51] See the "panorama des exégèses" in Exégèse et herméneutique (see note 5), 105-
106 : I. psychological interpretation : 1. autobiographical : a. christian experience, shared
by Paul; b. Paul's experience before his conversion; 2. universal : the experience of
mankind before Christ; II. theologico-historical : 1. the stages of Heilsgeschichte; 2. the
experience of "Adam".

[52] E. KÄSEMANN, o.c., 196.

for a theological interpretation and rejection of a psychological-auto-biographical interpretation is understandable from a theological point of view, that is to say, if one is interested primarily in *what* Paul has to say about ... (himself and the law; the Jew and the law; any christian and the law etc.). From a literary point of view, that is to say, if one is interested in the question *why* Paul (suddenly) writes in such a way, the question might not be why Paul writes about himself (etc.), but rather why he uses the first person singular. And for this question there is a very simple answer, provided one accepts what has been said about Paul wanting to verify theological statements in reality, that is, in informed christian experience (including certainly his own). The answer then might very well be that Paul uses the first person singular when it comes to the matter of the Law, simply because he himself has much more experience on this point than anyone else in christianity, and he knows it, although *what* he is writing *about* is indeed a (historico-) theological problem that concerns us all : witness the fact that Paul, after the question in vii 13, makes his appeal to christian knowledge in the first person plural (vii 14). In other words : Paul does not describe a personal experience of "*simul iustus et peccator*", nor a personal situation before his conversion, as a number of older explanations has it, but he writes about a theological problem — the relation of law and sin — from his own experience, or, let us say, rather, *on his own authority*. This explanation, of course, does not solve all the details of the problem of Paul's use of anthropologi-cal terms, but these problems become of secondary importance.

There remains the question of the transition from the past to the present tense between vii 12 and vii 15. Here also everything depends on how one puts the question. Does Paul really want to speak first about the past and then about the present? Or is this too a matter of literary expression? Experience can be seen as something of the past (logically) but also as something of the present (emotionally) : it depends. Now, there is again a rather simple literary explanation for the change from the past to the present tense, from one way of presenting experience to another : the question in vii 13, following the preceding, is still in the past tense; but the appeal to the knowledge of the christian readers in vii 14 is, quasi necessarily (that is, since Paul wants to use the formula οἴδαμεν γὰρ) in the present tense. Why not suppose that Paul, having made the change, goes on in the present tense, perhaps without even being aware of the switch? It is, after all, the experience that counts, whether seen as past or as present, and then only as a verification of Paul's theological argumentation. I must concede that this argumentation is less apparent in vii 7-25 than in the other parts of Romans v-xi. In fact, I think that it is present at all only if one takes viii 1-4 as belonging to ch. vii as well as to ch. viii. But for this there is a classical explanation : vii 7-25 is indeed, among other things, an apology of the Thora,[53] which Paul seems to have understood in a way no christian in his time or since could value.

This article contains a double focus : that of the relation between a certain perspective and its relation to the interpretation of a certain passage, and the interpretation of that passage itself. They come together in a particularly difficult *crux interpretum* : the end of chapter vii, to be exact, vii 24-25. This difficulty is mirrored in the translation of ταλαίπωρος in vs. 24, which is generally rendered by "wretched" or an equivalent,[54] whereas the first meaning given by dictionaries seems to come nearer to "suffering", even "tormented".[55]

The best explanation I can think of at this moment is the one in which the three perspectives, mentioned at the beginning of this article and developed in the following discussion, meet : from the literary point of view as discussed in the part about chapter v and about the literary structure of ch. vi-vii, Paul is, indeed, speaking from his own experience; from the (hypothetical) historical point of view I do not know whether Paul was "wretched" or "miserable", but he certainly was suffering or, even more, made to suffer; and from the hermeneutical point of view I simply want to say that this is the way I understand Romans vii in its context at this moment.

---

[53] See E. KÄSEMANN, *o.c.*, 182.

[54] "wretched" : RSV; "miserable" : NEB; "malheureux" : Crampon; "unglückli-cher" : V. Schweitzer, Stuttgarter Kepplerbibel 1935; "ellendig" : Statenvertaling, NBG; "rampzalig" : Willibrord; "ongelukkige" : Het NT voor deze tijd; אוֹי : Delitzsch.

[55] LIDDELL-SCOTT (about the verb): do hard work, endure hardship, distress; the adjective (first meaning given) : "suffering"; W. BAUER : "elend, geplagt". I hope that some colleagues, more learned than I am, will take this up and see whether the nearest rendering fitting into the text and context of Rom vii 24 could not be "ge-pijnigd".

THE FRAGMENT 2 COR VI 14-VII 1

A Plea for its Authenticity

J. LAMBRECHT

In the last twenty five years — since the discovery of the Dead Sea Scrolls — an increasing number of exegetes have dealt with the "puzzling passage"[1] 2 Cor vi 14-vii 1. W. Grossouw (1951) concludes his short study with this statement about the non-Pauline origin of the passage: "I see no other viable explanation. One can speak here of the cumulative force of the arguments".[2] J. A. Fitzmyer (1961) formulates his opinion as follows: "The evidence seems to total up to the admission of a Christian reworking of an Essene paragraph which has been introduced into the Pauline letter".[3] For J. Gnilka (1963) 2 Cor vi 14-vii 1 is not the Christian reworking of an Essene paragraph, but rather a fragment written by an unknown Christian who was undoubtedly influenced by traditions such as were circulating at Qumran and are expressed in the Testament of the Twelve Patri-

---

[1] J. A. Fitzmyer, Qumran and the Interpolated Paragraph in 2 Cor vi 14-vii 1, in: Fitzmyer, *Essays on the Semitic Background of the New Testament*, London 1971, 205-217 (205). This study was first published in *CBQ* 23 (1961), 271-280. Cf. L. R. Stacho-wiak, Die Antithese Licht-Finsternis — ein Thema der Paulinischen Paränese, *ThQ* 143 (1963), 385-421: "Es ist vielleicht der eigenartigste Abschnitt des ganzen Briefs, sowohl in formeller wie in inhaltlicher Hinsicht" (399).

[2] Over de echtheid van 2 Cor 6, 14-7, 1, *StC* 26 (1951), 203-206 (p. 206). Cf. W. Gros-souw, The Dead Sea Scrolls and the New Testament. A Preliminary Survey, *StC* 26 (1951), 289-299; 27 (1952), 1-8: "I can hardly believe that St. Paul should consciously have 'quoted' this passage, which breaks up so disturbingly the context" (p. 3, note 100). Grossouw is here criticizing K. G. Kuhn's opinion, Die Schriftrollen vom Toten Meer. Zum heutigen Stand ihrer Veröffentlichung, *EvTh* 11 (1951-52), 72-75: "Der Abschnitt II Kor. 6, 14 bis 7, 1, der ein nicht von Paulus verfasstes, sondern von ihm nur zitiertes Stück ist, erweist sich nun als völlig in die Terminologie, Denkweise und Sprechweise dieser Texte gehörig".

[3] *O.c.*, 217. Cf. P. Benoit, Qumrân et le Nouveau Testament, *NTS* 7 (1960-61), 276-296: "un passage aussi qumrânien de pensée et de style que 2 Cor 6:14-7:1, sorte d'aérolithe tombé du ciel de Qumrân dans une épître de Paul" (279). H. Braun, *Qumran und das Neue Testament I*, Tübingen 1966, 201-204, already listed some twenty authors who had dealt with the question of the relation between 2 Cor vi 14-vii 1 and the Qumran documents. Braun's own opinion is: "... der für II. Kor 6, 14-7, 1 besonders enge Qumranbezug ... fällt gegen die Echtheit von II. Kor 6, 14-7, 1 eben doch ins Gewicht" (203).

archs.[4] Thus, for these three authors the passage is a post-Pauline interpolation. G. KLINZING (1971) distinguishes two layers: a pre-Christian Essene document and its Christian reworking. But, contrary to FITZMYER,[5] he does not exclude the possibility that Paul himself inserted the fragment into his writings.[6] This last hypothesis is also put forward by J.-F. COLLANGE (1972), who maintains that 2 Cor vi 14-vii 1 represents a Judean-Christian document. According to Collange Paul himself incorporated this text into the second edition of his apology: ii 14-vi 2 + vi 14-vii 1 + vii 2-4 (+ chap. ix).[7] H. D. BETZ (1973)[8] and J. J. GUNTHER (1973)[9] propose, once again, a post-Pauline insertion. Both authors, moreover, believe that 2 Cor vi 14-vii 1 betrays ideas which must have been propounded by Paul's opponents. Betz even states: "The conclusion is unavoidable that the *theology* of 2 Cor vi 14-vii 1 is not only non-Pauline, but anti-Pauline".[10]

---

[4] 2 Cor 6: 14-7: 1 in the Light of the Qumran texts and the Testaments of the Twelve Patriarchs, in: *Paul and Qumran. Studies in New Testament Exegesis* (ed. J. MURPHY-O'CONNOR), London 1968, 48-68. This is the English translation of: 2 Kor 6, 14-7,1 im Lichte der Qumranschriften und der Zwölf-Patriarchen-Testamente, in: *Neutestamentliche Aufsätze*. Festschrift J. Schmid (ed. J. BLINZLER, O. KUSS, F. MUSSNER), Regensburg 1963, 86-99.

[5] *O.c.*, 217: To "label this heavily Qumran passage as a Pauline 'quotation' of an Essene paragraph ... is no solution ...".

[6] G. KLINZING, *Die Umdeutung des Kultus in der Qumrangemeinde und im Neuen Testament* (StUNT 7), Göttingen 1971, 167-184.

[7] J.-F. COLLANGE, *Énigmes de la deuxième épître aux Corinthiens*, Étude exégétique de 2 Cor. 2:14-7:4 (MSSNTS 18), Cambridge 1972, 281-317 (see also 6-14). This second edition may have been sent to "the saints who are in the whole of Achaia" (2 Cor i 1). In the light of the "doublets" vi 11-13//vii 2-4 and chap. 8//chap. 9 COLLANGE postulates two editions of the apology-section. The first contained ii 14-vi 13 (+ chap. 8) and was addressed to the Corinthians (cf. vi 11 and i 1). On COLLANGE's theory, see the clear-cut judgment of C. K. BARRETT, *The Second Epistle to the Corinthians* (BNTC), London 1973, 194-195: "Collange's suggestion ... is not convincing.".

[8] 2 Cor 6:14-7:1: An Anti-Pauline Fragment? *JBL* 92 (1973), 88-108.

[9] *St. Paul's Opponents and their Background*, A Study of Apocalyptic and Jewish Sectarian Teaching (NT.S 35), Leiden 1973, 308-313: 2 Corinthians 6:14-7:1. "... nothing in it (= 2 Cor vi 14-vii 1) is incompatible with the teachings and language of Paul's opponents. If it was not written by them, at least its teachings provide illustrative contemporary parallels to the thought of the Apostle's antagonists" (313).

[10] BETZ, *a.c.*, 108. "The fragment addresses Jewish Christians" (99). "One can say ... that incidents like that at Antioch (Gal. 2:11-14) must have been the cause of 2 Cor 6:14-7:1" (100). Also M. A. CHEVALLIER, *L'Esprit et le Messie dans le Bas-Judaïsme et le Nouveau Testament* (EHPhR), Paris 1958, 138-139, relates 2 Cor vi 14-vii 1 to Paul's Jewish-Christian opponents: "Peut-être est-ce pour souligner à quel point Paul 'ouvre son cœur' tout grand à ses correspondants qui le suspectaient (6:11-13) que l'apôtre ou un copiste aurait introduit une exhortation rédigée dans leur propre style"

The arguments against the authenticity of 2 Cor vi 14-vii 1 can be brought together under five headings : (1) disruption of the context, (2) *hapaxlegomena*, (3) peculiarities in the chain of quotations (vi 16b-18c), (4) points of contact with the Essene writings, and (5) un-Pauline theology. This short study is not a complete treatment of the authenticity problem. By analyzing context, structure and line of thought of the passage it will deal mainly with the first, third and fifth arguments.

1.   The Context

The passage 2 Cor vi 14-vii 1 stands at the end of the long section ii 14-vii 4 which is often called Paul's apology and can easily be detached from the surrounding verses. The data concerning Paul's journey break off at ii 13 and are resumed and continued in vii 5.

a) For our purposes, attention should be given, within the apology ii 14-vii 4, to vi 3-10, a list of hardships by means of which Paul defends himself : "We put no obstacle in any one's way, so that no fault may be found with our ministry" (vi 3). Thereafter, vi 11-13 represents a new start and is a highly emotional, apologetical and even reproachful confession which ends with an appeal. It should be noted, however, that vi 11-13 presupposes the preceding paragraph, since the catalogue of hardships is designed to prove that Paul has indeed "opened his mouth" to the Corinthians (cf. vi 11a), that "his heart is wide open" for them (cf. vi 11b) and that they are "not restricted" by him (cf. vi 12a). The same can be said of vii 2-4, the paragraph which follows vi 14-vii 1. The hardships are the evidence that the Corinthians are in his heart "to die together and to live together" (vii 3).[11] Moreover, in vii 2 ("We have wronged no one ...") Paul defends himself just as he did in vi 3, and by means of the expression "with all our affliction" in vii 4 he certainly refers back to the painful circumstances depicted in vi 4-10.

b) But what about the relation of these small pericopes, vi 11-13 and vii 2-4, to vi 14-vii 1? Already a first reading reveals that within vi 11-13 and vii 2-4 there are several subtle shifts in the train of thought, whereas the central paragraph, vi 14-vii 1, seems to be more dominated by a single idea which holds it together.

---

(139). Cf. also L. CERFAUX, *Le chrétien dans la théologie paulinienne* (LeDiv 33), Paris 1962, 264, and *La théologie de l'Église suivant saint Paul* (UnSa 54), Paris 1965, 130; COLLANGE, *o.c.*, 317.

[11] On this expression see J. LAMBRECHT, "Om samen te sterven en samen te leven". Uitleg van 2 Kor. 7,3, *Bijdr* 37 (1976), 234-251.

Initially, one has the impression that v. 11a and v. 11b are perfect parallels : our mouth is open, and : our heart is wide (open). However, we note that v. 11b must be read together with v. 12a which explains and completes its sense : our heart is wide open, i.e. for you; there is in us no lack of space for you! Thus, v. 11b represents the first shift in Paul's line of thought; it moves from the statement of his openness or frankness in speech (v. 11a, see the catalogue of vi 4-10) to an affirmation of his loving relations and affection *vis-à-vis* the Corinthians. Then in v. 12b Paul rebukes his addressees (second shift!) : there is a lack of space within them. The meaning of this antithetical clause is not immediately evident : lack of space for the Corinthians or for us (= Paul)? The expression at the beginning of v. 13 ("in return, in fair understanding, as a recompense of like kind") suggests that the latter understanding, i.e. "for us (Paul)" is to be preferred, and this inter-pretation is subsequentally confirmed by the explicit appeal in vii 2a : "do make a place for us (in your hearts)". The third shift in thought occurs in v. 13 : after the rebuke of v. 12b Paul formulates an appeal : "do you also be wide open".

vii 2a ("Make room for us") repeats and re-inforces the appeal of vi 13. Verse 2b then gives the motive for this appeal : the Corinthians should make place for Paul since he has wronged none (of them). We note that this motivation differs from that suggested in vi 12-13 where the reason was that the Corinthians should act toward Paul as he had acted toward them. In v. 3a Paul expresses his realization that his self-defense might seem offensive to his readers : "Not to condemn". Whom? The meaning of this phrase in v. 3a would remain unclear without the help of v. 3b wherein Paul affirms in a positive and explicit fashion ("I said before that you are in our hearts ...") what he had already stated negatively in vi 13 and rather vaguely in vi 12b. Because of the union between Paul and the Corinthians there can be no question of his condemning them. In v. 4 Paul explicates what this union means for him concretely : it enables him to be frank with them and to boast about them, and further : to be full of consola-tion and overflowing with joy, notwithstanding all his affliction. Once again, there are shifts in Paul's reasoning in this second section : from appeal to motivation (self-defense) to excuse (loving union with the Corinthians) to a depiction of his way of acting and feeling.

c) It should by now be evident that vi 11-13 and vii 2-4 are closely related to one another. 2 Cor. vi 14-vii 1, on the other hand, is different. The tone of this unit is parenetical. The author calls for separation from unbelievers (see vi 14, 17 and vii 1) and, in a more positive way, for holiness (cf. vii 1). The fact that "they" (the author and the adressees : "we") are God's temple (vi 16b) and God's people (vi 16def) entails that there cannot be any fellowship between light and darkness (vi 14b-16a).

It has become apparent that vi 11-vii 4 contains three sub-units : vi 11-13; vi 14-vii 1 and vii 2-4, and that the central unit looks like a sudden interjection between vi 11-13 and vii 2-4. The structure of these three units is concentric : a b a'. The following considerations may help to confirm the presence of a cyclic composition. Both vi 11-13 and vii 2-4 are characterized by their strikingly emotional and personal appeal. There are many asyndeta. Paul stresses his openness and frankness; he emphasizes that from his side the relation between him and his readers is as intimate as possible (they are present in his heart); he pleads that they should act in fair exchange towards him. This emotional quality of Paul's language may have caused the different shifts in his train of thought. That beginning (vi 11-13) and end (vii 2-4) are so similar in tone proves their inclusive function. Of course, if vi 14-vii 1 is a later insertion, then these two frame units would originally have been a single text unit. But this question must be considered in more detail below.

There is not only similarity in tone and style; ideas and, to some extent, wording are also strikingly parallel in vi 11-13 and vii 2-4. We list four correspondences :

Compare :	*with* :
χωρήσατε ἡμᾶς (vii 2a; appeal)	πλατύνθητε καὶ ὑμεῖς (vi 13; appeal)
πρὸς κατάκρισιν οὐ λέγω (vii 3a; excuse)	στενοχωρεῖσθε δὲ ἐν τοῖς σπλά-γχνοις ὑμῶν (vi 12b; rebuke)
	ὡς τέκνοις λέγω (vi 13; softening)
ὅτι ἐν ταῖς καρδίαις ἡμῶν ἐστε (vii 3b; union)	ἡ καρδία ἡμῶν πεπλάτυνται οὐ στενοχωρεῖσθε ἐν ἡμῖν (vi 11b and 12a; union)
πολλή μοι παρρησία πρὸς ὑμᾶς (vii 4a; frankness)	τὸ στόμα ἡμῶν ἀνέῳγεν πρὸς ὑμᾶς (vi 11a; frankness)

So the question is : Does 2 Cor vi 14-vii 1 as a self-contained parenetical paragraph violently disrupt the connection between the two other sub-units within the section vi 11-vii 4?

2. The Text

Before answering this question let us first examine the text of vi 14-vii 1.

a) The appeal in vi 14a is different from that in vi 13. In vi 13 Paul asks for a reciprocal affection on the part of the Corinthians; in vi 14a, on the contrary, the imperative is purely parenetical. The whole passage vi 14-vii 1 is admonition, moral exhortation; separation from unbelievers is the dominant idea. The closing verse vii 1 takes up, by means of its subjunctive καθαρίσωμεν, the idea implied in the negative imperative of vi 14a : μὴ γίνεσθε ἑτεροζυγοῦντες.

b) The structural qualities of the vigorous admonition vi 14-vii 1 are such that they are worth presenting in a somewhat detailed way :

A vi 14a   μὴ γίνεσθε ἑτεροζυγοῦντες ἀπίστοις·

B   14b a τίς γὰρ μετοχὴ δικαιοσύνῃ καὶ ἀνομίᾳ,
       14c b   ἢ τίς κοινωνία φωτὶ πρὸς σκότος;
   vi 15a a' τίς δὲ συμφώνησις Χριστοῦ πρὸς Βελιάρ,
       15b b'   ἢ τίς μέρις πιστῷ μετὰ ἀπίστου;
   vi 16a c   τίς δὲ συγκατάθεσις ναῷ θεοῦ μετὰ εἰδώλων;

C   16b   ἡμεῖς γὰρ ναὸς θεοῦ ἐσμεν ζῶντος·
       16c – καθὼς εἶπεν ὁ θεὸς ὅτι
       16d a 1 ἐνοικήσω ἐν αὐτοῖς καὶ ἐμπεριπατήσω,
       16e   2 καὶ ἔσομαι αὐτῶν θεός,
       16f   3 καὶ αὐτοὶ ἔσονταί μου λαός.

   vi 17a b   διὸ ἐξέλθατε ἐκ μέσου αὐτῶν καὶ ἀφορίσθητε,
       17b – λέγει κύριος,
       17c b'   καὶ ἀκαθάρτου μὴ ἅπτεσθε·
       17d a' 1' κἀγὼ εἰσδέξομαι ὑμᾶς,
   vi 18a   2' καὶ ἔσομαι ὑμῖν εἰς πατέρα,
       18b   3' καὶ ὑμεῖς ἔσεσθέ μοι εἰς υἱοὺς καὶ θυγατέρας,
       18c – λέγει κύριος παντοκράτωρ.

D vii 1a a ταύτας οὖν ἔχοντες τὰς ἐπαγγελίας, ἀγαπητοί,
       1b b καθαρίσωμεν ἑαυτοὺς ἀπὸ παντὸς μολυσμοῦ σαρκὸς
                                               καὶ πνεύματος,
       1c c ἐπιτελοῦντες ἁγιωσύνην ἐν φόβῳ θεοῦ.

We distinguish, in spite of their unequal length, four parts : A B C D.[12] A is the introductory clause which formulates in metaphorical

---

[12] Cf. BETZ, a.c., 89-99 : "Analysis reveals at once that the parenesis which we have before us is very carefully constructed" (89). The following elements are listed :
(1) A Concrete Parenesis (6:14a).

language the main prohibition: "Do not become unequally yoked with unbelievers". B contains five parallel questions which all begin with τίς. Because of their rhetorical character they resemble exclamations which point to an evident opposition between righteousness and inequity, light and darkness, Christ and Beliar, believer and unbeliever, God's temple and idols. Do the first four of these questions constitute a chiastic structure: a b b' a'? The term μέρις (v. 15b) may point back to μετοχή (v. 14b), and συμφώνησις (v. 15a) to κοινωνία (v. 14c).[13] But the repetition of τίς (γάρ|δέ) ... ἢ τίς in verses 14bc and 15ab does not recommend this view. In the light of this grammatical construction, an a b a' b' symmetry seems to be preferable, although a parallelism of content can hardly be found in the four clauses which appear to be meant as simple variations on the same theme. Perhaps, then, in spite of its τίς δέ, the more ecclesiological fifth question (c = v. 16a), which is taken up by v. 16b ("temple of God"), stands somewhat apart.[14] Part B is connected with A by the motivating γάρ: because the Corinthians are righteous believers, they should no longer mismate themselves with unbelievers.

Part C, also linked with the preceding section by a motivating γάρ, stresses that the believers ("we")[15] are indeed the temple of the living God, the phrase "temple of God" being an element of the final opposition in B. This affirmation is proved by citations from the O.T. First, by means of Lev xxvi 12 — the Covenant formula —, it is pointed out that the promise of God's presence with his people is realized now for believers. From this state of affairs it follows (cf. διό

---

(2) The Theological Foundations (6:14b-7:1).
    a. An Ontological Orientation (6:14b-16a).
    b. A Confessional Self-definition of the Congregation (6:16b).
    c. A Quotation of the Divine Promise (6:16c-18).
    d. A General Parenesis (7:1).

[13] Cf. ibid., 91.

[14] Cf. A. PLUMMER, A Critical and Exegetical Commentary on the Second Epistle of St. Paul to the Corinthians (ICC), Edinburgh 1915, 207: "The first four questions are in pairs; the last being a conclusion to the series and a premise for what follows ... We have four different constructions in the five sentences, all for the sake of variety; two datives, dat. followed by πρός, gen. followed by πρός, dat. followed by μετά".

[15] "The reading ἡμεῖς ... ἐσμεν, strongly supported by both Alexandrian and Western witnesses (ℵ* B D* 33 81* it^d cop^en, bo al), is to be preferred to ὑμεῖς ... ἐστε (P46 C D^c G K Ψ 614 Byz Lect it^g, 61 vg syr^p, h goth arm al), since the latter reading was very naturally suggested by the recollection of 1 Cor 3.16 as well as by the context (verses 14 and 17), while there was no reason for putting ἡμεῖς ... ἐσμεν in its stead" (B. M. METZGER, A Textual Commentary on the Greek New Testament, London-New York 1971, 580).

which introduces the second citation, taken from Is lii 11) that believers
should leave the Gentiles, be separated from them and stop touching
unclean things. If this is done, God will receive them. He will be a
father to them and they will be God's sons and daughters — the
third quotation, the well-known promise to David, from 2 Sam vii 14.
The structure of this *catena* of quotations is striking. Note should be
taken of the symmetrical placing of the quotation formulae : at the
beginning and at the end of the unit, and in the middle of the second
citation. The central position of b is by no means accidental : between
the Covenant formula which depicts an already existing reality, the
basis of a new ethical life, and the promise to David which refers
to God's future gift, a gift that depends upon the believer's moral
attitude. Attention should also be given to the structural symmetry
and to the similarity in content of both promises, that of the Covenant
and that to David (a and a').[16]

Part D is clearly a conclusion : see the consecutive οὖν. The promises
of vii 1a refer back to Ca and a' : because we have these promises we
should cleanse ourselves from every pollution of flesh and spirit. Db
resumes the exhortation which is present also in A and Cbb'. Dc,
finally, is the positive complement of Db : purification is not the
whole matter; we must achieve a perfect holiness. By means of the
stereotyped expression ἐν φόβῳ θεοῦ God's future judgment is referred
to in a rather indirect way. As conclusion, part D is decidedly something more than merely a framing counterpart of part A.

c) By now the chain of thought should be apparent. The author
motivates his exhortation in A by reminding the believers of what
they are. Five terms explain their identity and, by opposing these
terms to their contraries, its implications. There can be no question
of an agreement between Christ and Beliar. In C that identity,
referred to by the expression "temple of the living God", is once
more stressed and now proved by O.T. citations which depict the
relation between God and his people and family. In the middle of
this part there is again an exhortation : come out, be separated, no
longer touch. The long sentence of D resumes for the last time the
whole admonition. The first participial clause ἔχοντες τὰς ἐπαγγελίας
(a) indicates why cleansing is required, while the second ἐπιτελοῦντες
ἁγιωσύνην (c) complements the rather negative καθαρίσωμεν (b).

---

[16] Cf. CERFAUX, *Le chrétien*, 263.

3. *The Argument from the Context*

a) In order to appreciate the force of the argument from the context one has to consider together several facts. 2 Cor vi 14-vii 1 unexpectedly interrupts the chain of thought present in vi 11-13. That chain of thought continues in vii 2-4. It is possible to read vii 2 after vi 13 without any sense of a break in the train of thought. vii 2-4 not only resumes the ideas of vi 11-13, but does so by using the same images of heart and space. The (interpolated) fragment vi 14-vii 1 is a self-contained unit which as such can easily be removed from the context of the letter. Moreover, the parenetical content of the fragment in no way coheres with that of the framing passages. It appears unexpectedly.

b) Familiarity with Paul's way of writing should, however, lead us to consider the foregoing argument from context as not very strong. Paul often interrupts himself. "Paul not infrequently allows himself to wander from his point, and then brings himself back to it with something of a jerk".[17] Although the admonition to moral purity contained in this passage breaks the chain of thought, and as such is indeed rather unexpected, can we be certain that Paul himself could not have made this interruption? In this connection we might refer to a study of C. K. BARRETT where some attention is given to 2 Cor ii 12-13 and vii 5.[18] Verses vii 5ff. resume the autobiographical report which was broken off after ii 13. The apology of ii 14-vii 4 presents itself as a long insertion which radically differs from its framing context and is therefore often seen as an independent letter. BARRETT, however, points out that, among other things, precisely the manner in which vii 5 takes up the thread, shows that Paul himself was responsible for the interruption, the long digression and the resumption.

Are there also within the text and context of 2 Cor vi 14-vii 1 data which would suggest that Paul himself made the insertion? Some scholars do detect a certain connection between 2 Cor vi 14-vii 1 and the context. Thus, they refer to the exhortation in v 20 and vi 1-2

---

[17] BARRETT, *o.c.*, 194.

[18] Titus, in: *Neotestamentica et Semitica. Studies in Honour of M. Black* (ed. E. E. ELLIS and M. WILCOX), Edinburgh 1969, 1-14 (see 8-9). BARRETT refers only to the change from first person singular to first person plural which "furnishes an argument against the view that 2:13 and 7:5 were originally continuous, 2:14-7:4 being an interpolation from another letter" (n. 25 on page 9). One could also mention, however, in this connection, the change from "spirit" to "flesh" and, further, the repetition of "to come" and "to have rest" in vii 5 which in ii 12 and 13 are applied to Troas whereas in vii 5 they refer to Macedonia.

and affirm that the appearance of parenesis in vi 14-vii 1 is not so unexpected after all (cf. the verb παρακαλέω in v 20 and vi 1).[19] Others discern a logical connection between our text and vi 11-13 : Open wide your hearts to us in return (vi 13) and, therefore, do what we ask (vi 14-vii 1); or : Open wide your hearts, but avoid libertinism![20]

It must be admitted that the mere possibility of a logical connection between text and context can hardly be taken as a satisfactory explanation. But these considerations should be envisaged together with a number of further details. (1) Both vi 13 and vi 14a have verbs in the second person plural imperative (πλατύνθητε, v. 13; and γίνεσθε, v. 14a) : the transition between them is not so abrupt after all. (2) vii 2-4 is not only the continuation, but also the resumption of vi 11-13. Compare vii 2a with vi 13; vii 2b with vi 12; and, less strictly, vii 3b with vi 11b; and vii 4a with vi 11a. This seems to indicate that there was always an interruption after vi 13. (3) If we admit that it was Paul himself who was responsible for the interruption vi 14-vii 1, then the clause προείρηκα ὅτι ἐν ταῖς καρδίαις ἡμῶν ἐστε ... in vii 3b, which refers back to vi 11-12, becomes perfectly understandable, whereas on the hypothesis that originally vii 2-4 followed immediately after vi 11-13, the expression "I have said before" seems a bit strange.[21] (4) It is well-known that an author, not always consciously, takes up (sometimes in a different meaning) words and phrases which he had used not long before : what had been used remains, as it were, at the writer's disposition. So the presence of θλιβόμενοι in vii 5 can

---

[19] Among others H. WINDISCH, Der zweite Korintherbrief (KEK; Neudruck der Auflage 1924; ed. G. STRECKER), Göttingen 1970, 212, 220, conjectures that originally vi 14-vii 1 stood after vi 1-2. On this hypothesis see the discussion of É.-B. ALLO, Seconde Epître aux Corinthiens (EtB), Paris ²1956, 192. It will be remembered that COLLANGE's theory leads to the same order (second edition of the apology).

[20] On these context considerations see the survey of COLLANGE, o.c., 303-304. Cf. also P. E. HUGHES, Paul's Second Epistle to the Corinthians (NLC), London ⁴1973, 243-244. HUGHES concludes his discussion : "Seen in its setting (= 6:13 and 7:2-4), then, the section 6:14-7:1, with its plainly worded warning against the danger of compromise is most skilfully and graciously enshrined by the loving passages on either side of it, while at the same time it itself is prompted by this same spirit of affection" (244). K. PRÜMM, Diakonia Pneumatos. I : Theologische Auslegung des zweiten Korintherbriefes, Rom-Freiburg-Wien 1967, 379-381, is a fervent defender of the passage's authenticity as well as of its original position in 2 Cor.

[21] Cf. R. V. G. TASKER, The Second Epistle of Paul to the Corinthians (Tyndale), London 1958, 101-102 : "It is worth noticing that the words I have said before may be taken to imply that Paul is deliberately making a reference back to 6:11-13 after what he is conscious has been an abrupt diversion. If this deduction is legitimate, it is an argument against the view that 6:14-7:1 is an interpolation from another letter".

probably be (partly) explained by the θλίψει of vii 4. More important for our purposes is the consideration that the use of the terms σάρξ (not in the typically Pauline sense!)[22] and φόβος in vii 5 may indeed suggest that, regarding the wording, Paul was influenced by what he himself had just written in vii 1. Cf. also the use of δικαιοσύνη (moral meaning!) in both vi 7 and vi 14, and compare φόβος κυρίου in v 11 with φόβος θεοῦ in vii 1c. Are context and text not composed then by the same person?

In view of all these observations one remains rather hesitant about the so-called argument from the context.

4.   The Chain of Quotations

It is generally claimed that notwithstanding the presence of three introductory formulae more than three quotations are linked and fused together in order to form a concatenation in our passage. The following references have been proposed:

Ezek xxxvii 27 for vi 16def;
Lev xxvi 12 for vi 16def;
Is lii 11 for vi 17ac;
Ezek xx 34 (or xi 17 or Zeph iii 20) for vi 17d;
2 Sam vii 14 for vi 18ab;
Is xliii 6 for vi 18b (end);
2 Sam vii 8 or 27 for vi 18c.

a) Chains of quotations are not infrequent elsewhere in Paul's letters. According to some critics, however, there are five features of this chain which evidence or suggest its un-Pauline character. (1) The introductory formula καθὼς εἶπεν ὁ θεός (vi 16c)[23] is not found elsewhere in Paul. (2) The quotations are combined in a peculiar way. Normally, at least, Paul "takes care to distinguish the individual quotations from one another and to identify the author (Rom ix 25-29; x 18-20; xv 9-12)".[24] (3) The biblical texts used here are not found elsewhere

---

[22] The "un-Pauline" use of flesh as "reinigungsfähig" (used in this sense in some Qumran texts) is very much stressed by H. BRAUN, o.c., 202-203. Flesh and spirit are used in ii 13; vii 5 and vii 1b in their normal Hebrew sense according to which "flesh" and "spirit" are almost equivalents and can both stand for the whole person (so in ii 13 and vii 5). In vii 1b, however, "since they can hardly be identical, they will refer to the inner and outer aspects of the self" (BARRETT, Second Epistle, 202).

[23] The formula "has its Qumran counterpart in CD 6:13; 8:9 ('šr 'mr 'l), but is found neither in the Old Testament nor the Mishnah" (FITZMYER, o.c., 216).

[24] GNILKA, a.c., 59. Cf. L. GASTON, No Stone on Another. Studies in the Significance of the Fall of Jerusalem in the Synoptic Gospels (NT.S 23), Leiden 1970, 177: "The

in Paul. (4) A Qumran text (4QFlor i 10-12) also cites 2 Sam vii 14.
(5) There is, finally, the likelihood, supported by the discovery of the
Dead Sea Scrolls, that such combinations of biblical texts, the so-called
testimonia, were already existent in pre-Christian times. This probability
may somewhat facilitate the assumption of an un-Pauline origin of
the chain.[25]

b) A comparison of 2 Cor vi 16b-18c with e.g. Rom iii 10-18
(a pre-Pauline Testimony?) shows that in Paul concatenations are
possible in which the O.T. authors are not identified nor the individual
citations distinguished (note, however, that in our opinion a clear
distinction is in fact made within the three quotations of 2 Cor vi
16b-18c). An introductory formula such as καθὼς εἶπεν ὁ θεὸς ὅτι
(vi 16c) can hardly be qualified as un-Pauline. Admittedly, it is a
hapax in Paul, but one should take into account the variation of
Paul's formulae and the fact that ὅτι ὁ θεὸς ὁ εἰπών of 2 Cor iv 6
represents a quite similar expression.

A. PLUMMER notes concerning vi 14b-16a (= B): "The great variety
of expression is no doubt studied, and it is effective".[26] One may ask
whether vi 16b-18c (= C) is not to an even greater extent the result
of extremely careful editorial activity. It would seem that the author
intended to present three (and no more) citations, namely Lev xxvi
12; Is lii 11 and 2 Sam vii 14. The three formulae in vv. 16c, 17b and
18c strongly suggest this view. Although, of course, the author could
have felt free to conflate two or more O.T. passages into one citation,
we prefer not to consider the first citation (vi 16def) as a combination
of Lev xxvi 12 and (because of ἐνοικήσω) Ezek xxxvii 27[27] nor the
third (vi 17d-18b) as a conflation of 2 Sam vii 14 with Ezek xx 34

---

chain of Old Testament texts, which are not quoted exactly but according to the
meaning desired in their present context, is a common Qumran phenomenon". This
phenomenon, however, can hardly be restricted to Qumran!

[25] Cf. FITZMYER, *o.c.*, 215-216.

[26] *O.c.*, 207.

[27] Ezek xxxvii 27: καὶ ἔσται ἡ κατασκήνωσίς μου ἐν αὐτοῖς καὶ ἔσομαι αὐτοῖς
θεός, καὶ αὐτοί μου ἔσονται λαός. FITZMYER, speaks of a "conflated quotation of
Lev 26:12 and Ez 37:27" (*o.c.*, 215). Despite the idea of dwelling and the third
person plural found in Ezek xxxvii 27, it would seem that one OT text is sufficient
and that because of its use of the verb ἐμπεριπατήσω Lev xxvi 12 is to be preferred.
Or have we to assume, as does e.g. G. KLINZING, *o.c.*, 178, that ἐνοικήσω ἐν αὐτοῖς
is "eine freie Übersetzung" of Ezek xxxvii 27 (Hebr. or LXX)? Both words, ἐνοικήσω
(2 Cor vi 16d) and κατασκήνωσις (Ezek. xxxvii 27 LXX), could be translations of
the Hebrew root *škn*. — Rev xxi 3 (σκήνη and σκηνόω) seems to be a quotation from
Ezek xxxvii 27, not from Lev xxvi 12. Note that in Rev xxi 7 the promise 2 Sam vii 14
is quoted.

(or xi 17 or Zeph iii 20; because of εἰσδέχομαι)²⁸ and Is xliii 6 (because of the expression "sons and daughters"). We should bear in mind, however, that more of less vague reminiscences of several passages cannot be excluded and that both the Covenant formula and the promise to David appear in many variants in the O.T. and later Jewish literature.

Can we explain the way in which the author uses, adapts and rewrites his O.T. texts? Lev xxvi 12 reads : καὶ ἐμπεριπατήσω ἐν ὑμῖν καὶ ἔσομαι ὑμῶν θεός, καὶ ὑμεῖς ἔσεσθέ μου λαός. The author of the fragment changed the second person into the third; the clause ἐνοικήσω ἐν αὐτοῖς is to be seen as an anticipatory interpretation of the phrase ἐμπεριπατήσω ἐν ὑμῖν, by which God's presence in the temple-community is made explicit. One may call this anticipation a necessary addition since through it the nexus with vi 16b ("we are the temple of the living God") is effected. The author does not hesitate to present this addition as part of the citation.

In Is lii 11 we read : ἀπόστητε, ἀπόστητε, ἐξέλθατε ἐκεῖθεν καὶ ἀκαθάρτου μὴ ἅπτεσθε, ἐξέλθατε ἐκ μέσου αὐτῆς ἀφορίσθητε, οἱ φέροντες τὰ σκεύη κυρίου. The author of 2 Cor vi 17 abbreviates the text; he inverts the order : καὶ ἀκαθάρτου ... comes at the end, after an inserted λέγει κύριος. In the new context "Babylon" is absent and a real departure is no longer intended.

The third citation is a free adaptation of 2 Sam vii 14 : ἐγὼ ἔσομαι αὐτῷ εἰς πατέρα καὶ αὐτὸς ἔσται μοι εἰς υἱόν. The third person singular (αὐτῷ, αὐτός) which points to the son of David, has, in vi 18, become an ecclesiological plural (second person). "Son" had consequently also to be put in the plural and "and daughters" is added.²⁹ As in the first citation there is also a short expansion at the beginning (κἀγὼ εἰσδέξομαι ὑμᾶς) which the author integrates into the citation. Note, however, that here, in opposition to vi 16def, the image of the temple is no longer present; εἰσδέξομαι points already to the adoption language of vi 18ab. — The closing formula λέγει κύριος παντοκράτωρ (vi 18c) is probably taken from 2 Sam vii 8 (cf. vii 27).

---

²⁸ Cf. BETZ, a.c., 97 : "One can never be certain whether two words are in fact a quotation".

²⁹ No conscious reference to Is xliii 6 ("... bring my *sons* from afar and my *daughters* from the end of the earth") is to be assumed here. We may also quote the comment of BARRETT, o.c., 201 : "It is significant that Paul, whose attitude to women has often been misrepresented, should modify his Old Testament quotation so as to include God's daughters as well as his sons".

This short discussion of the *catena* of quotations confirms the impression left by the analysis of vi 14b-16a : here too the author redacted carefully and the result of his editorial care is a remarkable structure. Given the expansions and the rewriting in this concatenation — all this in view of adaptation to the new context — it is preferable, it would seem, not to speak here of a Testimony or to suppose its preexistence.

To be sure, structure and rewriting by themselves do not prove a Pauline origin and, moreover, there remains the fact that Paul does not quote Lev xx 12; Is lii 11 and 2 Sam vii 14[30] elsewhere in his letters. Neither Covenant nor promise to David are characteristically Pauline themes. Yet, as can be seen in Rom i 3 (a pre-Pauline tradition?) and xv 12 (cf. Is xi 1) the David tradition was known to Paul[31] and in 2 Cor iii 7-18 he deals, be it in a polemical way, with Moses and the Covenant. We would be over-systematizing Paul's theology if we were to maintain that, because of the non-Pauline character of Covenant and promise to David, Paul could not accidentally have referred to traditions which belonged to the current and cherished patrimony of his people. But this brings us to the problem of content.

Pauline origin, however, could be presumed if the language of the *catena* and of the rest of the passage is thoroughly that of Paul. Therefore, before examining the content, due attention should be given now to the presence of Pauline style within vi 14-vii 1, and this despite

---

[30] In 4QFlor i 10-12 the 2 Sam vii 14 quotation is understood in a Messianic, not in an ecclesiological sense. On 4QFlor i see the excursus "Das Verhältnis von 2 Kor 6, 14ff. zu 4 QFl 1 und die Tradition vom eschatologischen Tempel", in : G. KLINZING, *o.c.*, 175-179, where he strongly criticizes B. GÄRTNER, *The Temple and the Community in Qumran and the New Testament. A Comparative Study in the Temple Symbolism of the Qumran Texts and the New Testament* (MSSNTS 1), Cambridge 1965, 49-56, who claimed that there are several parallels between the two texts. But, with regard to the transferal of the concept of the temple to the community, KLINZING himself may be too apodictic when he writes, *o.c.*, 167-168 : "Die christliche Umdeutung des Tempels (temple-community) wurde jedoch nicht aufs Neue und selbständig aus der jüdischen Hoffnung entwickelt, sondern als bereits geprägte Vorstellung aus der Qumrangemeinde übernommen". See the judicious remarks of E. SCHÜSSLER FIORENZA, Cultic Language in Qumran and in the New Testament, *CBQ* 38 (1976), 159-177 : "in order to specify the distinctive usage of cultic language in Qumran and in the NT" (159). Cf. also M. FRAEYMAN, La spiritualisation de l'idée du temple dans les épîtres pauliniennes, *EThL* 23 (1947), 378-422 (esp. 390-392); R. J. McKELVEY, *The New Temple. The Church in the New Testament*, Oxford 1969 (see esp. 93-98); J. COPPENS, The Spiritual Temple in Pauline Letters and its Background, *Studia Evangelica*. Vol. VI (ed. E. A. Livingstone; TU 112), Berlin 1973, 53-66.

[31] Cf. D. C. DULING, The Promises to David and their Entrance into Christianity-Nailing down a Likely Hypothesis, *NTS* 20 (1973-74), 55-77 (esp. 72).

the fact that the brevity of the passage and the number of O.T.-citations it contains do not provide much occasion for Paul's redactional activity. Yet, we can note that the change from second person to first person plural (vi 16b and vii 1) is typical of Pauline parenesis.[32] Paul adds λέγει· κύριος also in Rom xii 19[33]; he is the only N.T. author to use ἁγιωσύνη (see Rom i 4 and 1 Thess iii 13); he uses in the same context κοινωνία and μετέχω (1 Cor x 16-17; cf. μετοχή and κοινωνία in 2 Cor vi 14bc). Constructions such as μὴ γίνεσθε (vi 14a),[34] ὑμεῖς γάρ ... (vi 16b)[35] and ταύτας οὖν ἔχοντες (vii 1a)[36] are in keeping with his way of writing. Paul likes to use ἄπιστος, θεοῦ ζῶντος (in the genitive: cf. 1 Thess i 9; Rom ix 26; 2 Cor iii 3), ἐπιτελέω and ἀγαπητός, this last word also in addresses as in vii 1a.[37]

---

[32] We may refer e.g. to Rom xiv-xv; 1 Cor v 6-8.

[33] The quotation in Rom xii 19 is taken from Dt xxxii 35. The same quotation is also found in Hebr x 30 (without λέγει κύριος!) and the text of both Rom xii 19 and Hebr. x 30 differ in the same way from the LXX. Had this phrase concerning God's vengeance become a proverbial saying at this time? In Rom xiv 11 (a combination of Is xlviii 18 and xlv 23), where the formula also appears, the formula is taken over from Is xlviii 18. On λέγει κύριος see also E. E. ELLIS, *Paul's Use of the Old Testament*, Edinburgh-London 1957, 107-112.

[34] Cf. Rom xii 16 and 1 Cor vii 24. In Rom xii 16 Paul rewrites Prov iii 7 which has μὴ ἴσθι ...

[35] Cf. ἡμεῖς γάρ ... in Phil iii 3 and Gal v 5.

[36] Cf. the variations of this construction with ἔχω e.g. in 2 Cor iii 12; iv 1, 13.

[37] On Pauline style see i.a. KLINZING, *o.c.*, 182; COLLANGE, *o.c.*, 312 and especially A. SCHLATTER, *Paulus der Bote Jesu. Eine Deutung seiner Briefe an die Korinther*, Stuttgart ⁴1969, 580-581 · "Die Sprache dieser Sätze umfasst nichts, was auf eine fremde Hand hindeutete" (581). And what about the *hapaxlegomena*? We can distinguish between *hapaxlegomena* in the strict sense and those terms which, although they do appear elsewhere in Paul's letters, are taken in another sense than Paul normally uses them. Due attention should be given to the large number of words in our passage which fall into one or the other of these categories, and thus to the cumulative force of this argument :
a) Four words do not occur anywhere else in the entire Greek Bible: ἑτεροζυγέω, συμφώνησις, συγκατάθεσις, Βελιάρ (cf. Βελιάλ in Ms. A of Jg xx 13). Four words are *hapaxlegomena* in the whole N.T. : μετοχή (the only other occurrence of this term in the Greek Bible is in Ps cxxi 3), ἐμπεριπατέομαι, εἰσδέχομαι, μολυσμός (only three occurrences of this last term in the LXX). καθαρίζω (see Eph v 26 and Tit ii 14) and παντοκράτωρ do not appear elsewhere in the authentic Pauline letters. Col i 12 is the only other occurrence of the term μέρις in Paul.
We should, however, take into consideration the fact that Paul does use cognates of some of these terms : the verbs μετέχω (frequently), μολύνομαι (1 Cor viii 7) and ἐκκαθαρίζω (1 Cor v 7), and the adjective σύμφωνος (1 Cor vii 5). Moreover, it should be recalled that the Pauline *hapaxlegomena* ἐμπεριπατέομαι and παντοκράτωρ (and possibly also εἰσδέχομαι) are taken over from the LXX. Finally, the verb ἑτεροζυγέω may have been suggested by the adjective ἑτερόζυγος of Lev xix 19. We may also quote ALLO, *o.c.*, 190: "La multiplication des questions oratoires (vv. 14b-16a),

5. *The Argument from Content*

a) The so-called un-Pauline theology within vi 14-vii 1 can be illustrated by three complementary statements. (1) The author of 2 Cor vi 14-vii 1 employs the Covenant formula (vi 16) in order to characterize the situation of believers. (2) At the end of the fragment the author stresses the necessity of "perfecting holiness in the fear of God" (vii 1). (3) This goal of holiness can only be attained by means of purification and strict segregation, i.e., rigorous withdrawal from the heathen world. BETZ argues that these features are not only un-Pauline but even anti-Pauline. In his view, Paul, in contrast to the three foregoing conceptions, (1) represents the Christian situation by referring to God's promise to Abraham, and to Abraham's salvation through faith, not to Covenant, Moses and Torah, (2) combats every form of confidence in personal achievement of perfection by means of the "works of the Law" and (3) rejects (cf. 1 Cor v 9-10) the radical separation which was required by the Jewish way of life. A Christian, according to Paul, practices "freedom in Christ". Paul is not interested in purification.[38]

b) First of all, there is a danger that Paul is seen in too monolithic and one-sided a way when attention is payed exclusively to the central, yet polemical affirmation of righteousness apart from works of the Law, through faith and grace alone. Such a presentation of Paul's theological position has to play down or even reject a number of texts which are most probably written by Paul. If, moreover, as BETZ does, a forced, biased explanation is given of 2 Cor vi 14-vii 1,[39]

---

qui reviennent toutes au même, portait l'Apôtre à chercher des synonymes variés dans son riche vocabulaire". Cf. also CERFAUX, *Le chrétien*, 261.

b) Paul never uses πιστός is an absolute way to denote a "believer" (in Christ). The combination of the terms ἐπιτελέω and ἁγιωσύνη into the expression ἐπιτελοῦντες ἁγιωσύνην (vii 1), the use of δικαιοσύνη (vi 14) in the sense of ethical uprightness, the neutral "anthropological" meaning of "flesh-spirit" (vii 1) and the exhortation "to cleanse oneself from every defilement of flesh and spirit" are, to say the least, not typically Pauline.

On the sense of δικαιοσύνη see page 153; on "flesh-spirit" see note 22. In connection with πιστός cf. the observation of BARRETT, *o.c.*, 199: "the semi-technical use of *believer* was bound to develop sooner or later out of the description of Christians as faithful, and there is no reason why Paul should not himself have been responsible for the development". For the remaining expressions, we refer to our discussion of the argument from content.

[38] Cf. BETZ, *a.c.*, 99-107.

[39] We may refer here, e.g., to his discussion of ἑτεροζυγέω, *a.c.*, 89-90. Is it so certain that the figurative use of this verb rests on the author's conscious association of the current Jewish equation "yoke-Torah"? Is it to be accepted that "the terminology

it is not surprising that a radical opposition will be detected between this passage and the Pauline message as it appears e.g. in a very clear way from Gal. It should be asked, however, whether the real Paul was not more many-sided and, now and then, less systematic or polemical than this.

It is important, further, to note that the purity which in vi 14-vii 1 is required is moral, not ritual,[40] as is apparent from a right understanding of the antitheses in vi 14b-16a. The O.T. expressions in vi 14a, 17ac and the cultic terms elsewhere in the pericope are used in a figurative sense. The antithetical way of speaking is decidedly paradoxical and should not be taken as literal speech demanding a strict and "bodily" separation.

Moreover, the pericope, we think, contains the very Pauline "already-not yet" tension, the presence of both the indicative and imperative (cf. e.g. Gal v 25). In 2 Cor vi 16b (and also in the first term of each opposition in the five parallel questions; vi 14b-16a) there is a conviction of redemption, reconciliation or righteousness as an already present reality. The future tenses of the Covenant formula (vi 16def) are, in light of vi 16b, most probably to be understood as fulfilled promises. All this is the indicative which allows and asks for (διό) the imperative : see vi 17ac (cf. vii 1b). In vi 17d-18b, however, the future tenses still point to a future reality which is a yet unfulfilled promise. These subtle time distinctions should not surprise us, certainly not in Paul who e.g. deals in Rom v 9-11 with both justification or reconciliation as already present and a still future salvation. Again, in view of 2 Cor vi 14-17 it would be wrong to over-emphasize the future character of the promises mentioned in vi 18ab and vii 1a. The final reality is already present in a certain, anticipatory way. Further, the positive expression ἐπιτελέω ἁγιωσύνην,[41] by means of which Paul points to human ethical involvement, must not be explained as "right-

---

πιστός/ἄπιστος cannot be taken in the Pauline sense" (90), that " 'faith' in the Pauline sense plays no role in the fragment" (ibid.), that "the Christians whose theology is contained in it are in fundamental agreement with Judaism that whether one is a 'believer' or a 'non-believer' is determined by whether or not one is under the yoke of the Torah" (100)?

[40] It would seem that this point is not sufficiently stressed by FITZMYER, o.c., 215, where he deals with "separation from all impurity".

[41] Cf. J. M. S. BALJON, Geschiedenis van de boeken des Nieuwen Verbonds, Groningen 1901, 68, who changed his opinion on this point (see his earlier De tekst der brieven van Paulus aan de Romeinen, de Corinthiërs en de Galatiërs ..., Utrecht 1884, 147-150) : "Het bezwaar, dat men wel eens aan 7:1 (ἐπιτελεῖν ἁγιωσύνην) ontleend heeft, is wellicht wat ver gezocht".

eousness out of works", any more than a sound exegesis explains in this way e.g. the ἐργαζώμεθα τὸ ἀγαθόν of Gal vi 10. The judgment idea suggested by the phrase ἐν φόβῳ θεοῦ occurs frequently in Paul, e.g. in Rom v 9-11, to which we have already referred : σωθησόμεθα δι᾿ αὐτοῦ ἀπὸ τῆς ὀργῆς (v. 9; see also 2 Cor v 10!).

In this context, one should also bear in mind that in 2 Cor vi 14-vii 1 Paul does not address himself in a polemical way to his opponents. The passage is rather a piece of "common" parenesis meant for Christians who live in the midst of manifold dangers in a Gentile world.[42] And therefore, one should not expect a conscious reflection on the problem of justification here.

Neither the argument from context nor that from content provides sufficient ground for rejecting the Pauline authorship of 2 Cor vi 14-vii 1. Little or nothing against the authenticity of this passage can be derived from the high-quality literary structure of the chain of quotations and of the whole text. It would seem that the arguments which are based on the number of *hapaxlegomena* or on the parallels with the Essene writings[43] are also not very persuasive. Of course, to say

---

[42] The remark of PLUMMER, *o.c.*, 205-206 is to the point here : "... this is one of the many places in 2 Cor. in which our ignorance of the state of things at Corinth renders certainty unattainable. We do not know to what kind of intimacy with heathen acquaintances and customs the Apostle is alluding".

[43] On the *hapaxlegomena* see note 37. On the points of contact with the Essene writings cf. K. G. KUHN, Les rouleaux de cuivre de Qumrân, *RB* 61 (1954), 193-205 (see notes 1 and 2 on page 203) and the studies of FITZMYER and GNILKA referred to in this article. The latter author distinguishes several basic theological thought-patterns which are present both in our fragment and in the Essene documents : (1) The application of the metaphor of the temple to a community; (2) the idea of separation from impurity and the godless environment, from iniquity and idols; (3) the ethically dualistic thought. Although the dualism Christ-Belial "does not seem to have originated in Jewish but in Christian circles" (*o.c.*, 56), "the opposition God-Belial (or Beliar) is older and typical of the Qumran texts and of the *Test. XII Patriarchs*" (*o.c.*, 66). This older Jewish dualism influenced the later Christian version. Moreover, "the antitheses light-darkness, and justice-injustice, do not in themselves enable us to mark off a narrowly defined area of tradition, but the association of the two pairs light-darkness and God-Belial (or Beliar) indicates the Jewish circles to which exegetes have constantly had recourse for parallels ... The conjunction of the contrasting pairs light-darkness, Christ-Belial, believer-unbeliever, which sounds the main theme of 2 Cor 6:14-7:1 points clearly to a traditional association also found in the Qumran texts" (*o.c.*, 66).

It should also be recalled in this context that the introductory formula of vi 16c appears in CD (see note 23), that the notion of a 'lot' is typical for the Qumran-community (but we would expect κλῆρος instead of μέρις), that 2 Sam vii 14 (cf. 2 Cor vi 18) is utilized in 4QFlor i 10-12 (but see note 30).

One simply cannot deny the affinities between 2 Cor vi 14-vii 1 and the Qumran documents. Still, we could ask : must we therefore reject the authenticity of the passage? If in any case we must accept that the author was a Christian, why, in light of context,

that there exists little against its originality or to affirm that Paul could have composed a text such as we find in 2 Cor vi 14-vii 1 is hardly a positive and cogent proof. But given — this should be remembered — the complete manuscript support for the passage *and* the characteristics of Pauline style, a rather conservative [44] attitude in this matter is certainly to be preferred. [45]

---

structure and content of the passage, could we not further accept that the Christian author was Paul himself? And in this connection we should not forget that "Beliar" seems to have become a vogue word in the first century, nor lose sight of the strong O.T. flavor of the passage. See also note 24.

[44] Cf. the majority of the commentators, e.g. ALLO, BARRETT, BRUCE, GROSHEIDE, HÉRING, HUGHES, KEULERS, LIETZMANN-KÜMMEL, PLUMMER, PRÜMM, SCHLATTER, WINDISCH.

E. DINKLER, the editor of R. BULTMANN, Der zweite Brief an die Korinther (KEK, Sonderband), Göttingen 1976 (= notes which BULTMANN used for his lectures between 1940 and 1952), discusses *o.c.*, 181-182 the passage vi 14-vii 1 which BULTMANN does not deal with. He calls it "typisch jüdische Paränese", perhaps "christlich bearbeitet" and suggests : "Möglich, dass Paulus selbst ein solches Stück zitierte; dann wohl Fragment aus dem verlorenen ersten Brief; es könnte der Mahnung μὴ συναναμίγνυσθαι πόρνοις (1 Kor 5:9-11!) vorangegangen sein, denn diese Mahnung würde sich gut an 7:1 anschliessen" (p. 182). Others before DINKLER defended the view that 1 Cor v 9 refers to our passage, a fragment then from the so-called Previous Letter. Cf. e.g. J. C. HURD, *The Origin of I Corinthians*, London 1965, 235-237. HUGHES, *o.c.*, 242, comments : "The attractiveness of this hypothesis is understandable, but as it belongs entirely to the realm of conjecture, it is lacking in corroboration of any kind".

[45] Since the conclusion of this paper (September 1976) two more studies have appeared which, independently, deal with our passage: G. D. FEE, II Corinthians vi 14-vii 1 and Food Offered to Idols, *NTS* 23 (1976-77), 140-161; and M. E. THRALL, The Problem of II Cor. vi 14-vii 1 in some Recent Discussion, *NTS* 24 (1977-78), 132-148. Both accept the passage as Pauline.

IS WITTINESS UNCHRISTIAN?

A Note on εὐτραπελία in Eph. v 4

P. W. VAN DER HORST

In order to know why the author of the Epistle to the Ephesians says (v 4) that there is no room for εὐτραπελία in the Christian community, one should try to determine the meaning and semantic associations of that word on a broader basis than is commonly done in the commentaries. Most of them say that the word meant "wittiness, facetiousness" in Greek authors. Very often they confine themselves to a reference to two passages in Aristotle (see below), where it is said that the meaning of εὐτραπελία (pleasantry, urbanity) lies somewhere between βωμολοχία (buffoonery) on the one hand, and ἀγροικία (boorishness) on the other hand; and that εὐτραπελία is πεπαιδευμένη ὕβρις (cultivated insolence). Neither of the two statements, which seem to be contradictory, suffices to clarify why εὐτραπελία is forbidden in Eph. v 4. Some commentators say that, whereas in general εὐτραπελία is positively regarded in Greek literature, it is sometimes spoken about there in a bad sense. But these remarks are either not supported by citations from the Greek authors or are illustrated by wrong or dubious instances. Therefore we will try to trace the history of its usage by listing chronologically (as far as possible) a number of texts where εὐτραπελία and the related εὐτράπελος and εὐτραπελεύομαι occur.[1] An English translation of the texts is given in the footnotes.[2]

---

[1] There are some books and articles, though not many, dealing with humour in antiquity, e.g. W. SÜSS, Das Problem des Komischen im Altertum, NJKA 23 (1920), 28-45 (discussing ancient theories of what is comical); L. RADERMACHER, Weinen und Lachen, Studien über antikes Lebensgefühl, Wien 1947; G. SOYTER, Griechischer Humor von Homers Zeiten bis heute, Berlin 1961[2] (an anthology of texts with notes); E. DE SAINT-DENIS, Essais sur le rire et le sourire des Latins (PUD 32), Paris 1965; W. SÜSS, Lachen, Komik und Witz in der Antike, Zürich 1969; U. REINHARDT-K. SALLMANN (edd.), Musa Jocosa, Arbeiten über Humor und Witz, Komik und Komödie der Antike (Andreas Thierfelder zum 70. Geburtstag), Hildesheim 1974 (studies of details in individual authors); G. GIANGRANDE, L'humour des Alexandrins, Amsterdam 1975 (was inaccesible to me; it had not yet been published when this article was completed). Unfortunately, all these writings do not help us in determining the exact meaning of εὐτραπελία; only SAINT-DENIS' discussion of the semantic evolution of urbanitas (o.c.,

Pindar, *Pyth.* I 92 μὴ δολωθῇς, ὦ φίλε, κέρδεσιν εὐτραπέλοις.[3]

Pyth. IV 104f. εἴκοσι δ᾽ ἐκτελέσαις ἐνιαυτοὺς οὔτε ἔργον οὔτ᾽ ἔπος εὐτράπελον κείνοισιν εἰπών.[4] The first instance is not wholly beyond doubt; some mss. read ἐντραπέλοις (shameful). The second is extremely uncertain; most mss. read ἐντράπελον; a scholion reads ἐκτράπελον (odious; perverse), adopted by some editors; only one ms. has εὐτράπελον, which at least must have had a very negative sense in the eyes of the copyist.[5]

Aristophanes, *Vesp.* 467-470 τῶν νόμων ἡμᾶς ἀπείργεις ὧν ἔθηκεν ἡ πόλις, οὔτε τιν᾽ ἔχων πρόφασιν οὔτε λόγον εὐτράπελον, αὐτὸς ἄρχων μόνος.[6]

Thucydides II 41, 1 ξυνελών τε λέγω τήν τε πᾶσαν πόλιν τῆς Ἑλλάδος παίδευσιν εἶναι καὶ καθ᾽ ἕκαστον δοκεῖν ἄν μοι τὸν αὐτὸν ἄνδρα παρ᾽ ἡμῶν ἐπὶ πλεῖστ᾽ ἂν εἴδη καὶ μετὰ χαρίτων μάλιστ᾽ ἂν εὐτραπέλως τὸ σῶμα αὔταρκες παρέχεσθαι.[7]

Plato, *Resp.* VIII 563a (speaking about the symptoms accompanying the change from democracy to tyranny) καὶ ὅλως οἱ μὲν νέοι πρεσβυτέροις ἀπεικάζονται καὶ διαμιλλῶνται καὶ ἐν λόγοις καὶ ἐν ἔργοις, οἱ δὲ γέροντες συγκαθιέντες τοῖς νέοις εὐτραπελίας τε καὶ χαριεν-

---

145-161) is of some use for us, since that problem is partly parallel to ours. Eph. v 4 is not discussed by Hans VON CAMPENHAUSEN in his essays "Ein Witz des Apostels Paulus und die Anfänge des christlichen Humors" and "Christentum und Humor", in his *Aus der Frühzeit des Christentums*, Tübingen 1963, 102-108 and 308-330, neither by W. F. STINESPRING, "Humor", *IDB* II (1962), 660-662. All kinds of terms for a joke, wit, wittiness, jest etc. are treated by J. H. H. SCHMIDT, *Synonymik der griechischen Sprache* III, Leipzig 1879 (repr. Amsterdam 1969), 447-456. SCHMIDT's discussion of εὐτραπελία needs correcting, as also that of R. C. TRENCH, *Synonyms of the New Testament*, London 1894[12], 121-125. Matthew ARNOLD's remarks on εὐτραπελία in his "Speech at Eton" (printed in his *Irish Essays and Others*, London 1882, 181-207; see esp. 187 ff.) are highly speculative. N.B. εὐτραπελία does not occur in the LXX.

[2] If available, the translations in the Loeb Classical Library are used, sometimes slightly modified or corrected.

[3] "Be not allured, my friend, by cunning gains".

[4] "I have brought twenty years to an end, and in them have done, nor said, nothing perfidious".

[5] Unfortunately, T. K. ABBOT, *The Epistles to the Ephesians and to the Collosians*, Edinburgh 1897, 149, bases his otherwise rather good treatment of εὐτραπελία in Eph. v 4 on these two texts from Pindar (and, of course, the two hackneyed quotations from Aristotle, dealt with below).

[6] "You debar us from the laws, which the city has enacted, having no pretext, nor any dexterous argument, you solitary aristocrat".

[7] "In a word, then, I say that our city (sc. Athens) as a whole is the school of Hellas, and that, as it seems to me, each individual amongst us could in his own person, with the utmost grace and versatility, prove himself self-sufficient in the most varied forms of activity."

τισμοῦ ἐμπίμπλανται, μιμούμενοι τοὺς νέους, ἵνα δὴ μὴ δοκῶσιν ἀηδεῖς εἶναι μηδὲ δεσποτικοί.[8]

Isocrates, *Areop.* 49 (speaking on the Athenians in earlier times) σεμνύνεσθαι γὰρ ἐμελέτων, ἀλλ' οὐ βωμολοχεύεσθαι· καὶ τοὺς εὐτραπέλους δὲ καὶ τοὺς σκώπτειν δυναμένους, οὓς νῦν εὐφυεῖς προσαγορεύουσιν, ἐκεῖνοι δυστυχεῖς ἐνόμιζον.[9] (Cf. *Antid.* 284). *Antid.* 296 πρὸς δὲ τούτοις καὶ τὴν τῆς φωνῆς κοινότητα καὶ μετριότητα καὶ τὴν ἄλλην εὐτραπελίαν καὶ φιλολογίαν οὐ μικρὸν ἡγοῦνται συμβαλέσθαι μέρος πρὸς τὴν τῶν λόγων παιδείαν.[10]

Aristotle,[11] *Eth. Nic.* IV 8, 1127b34-1128b4 : "Life also includes relaxation and one form of relaxation is playful conversation. Here, too, we feel that there is a certain standard of good taste in social behaviour, and a certain propriety in the sort of things we say and in our manner of saying them, and also in the sort of things we allow to be said to us; and it will also concern us whether those in whose company we speak or to whom we listen conform to the same rules of propriety. And it is clear that in these matters too, it, is possible either to exceed or to fall short of the mean.

Those then who go to excess in ridicule are thought to be buffoons and vulgar fellows (βωμολόχοι καὶ φορτικοί), who itch to have their joke at all costs, and are more concerned to raise a laugh than to keep within the bounds of decorum and avoid giving pain to the object of their raillery. Those on the other hand who never by any chance say anything funny themselves and take offence at those who do, are considered boorish and morose (ἄγροικοι καὶ σκληροί). Those who jest with good taste are called witty or versatile — that is to say, full of good turns (οἱ δ' ἐμμελῶς παίζοντες εὐτράπελοι προσαγορεύονται, οἷον εὔτροποι); for such sallies seem to spring from the character, and we judge man's characters, like their bodies, by their movements.

---

[8] "And in general the young ape their elders and vie with them in speech and action, while the old, accommodating themselves to the young, are full of pleasantry and graciousness, imitating the young for fear they may be thought disagreeable and authoritative."

[9] "For they cultivated the manners of a gentleman, not those of a buffoon; and as for those who had a turn for jesting and playing the clown, whom we to-day speak of as clever wits, they were then looked upon as sorry fools."

[10] "And, in addition to these advantages, they consider that the catholicity and moderation of our speech (sc. of the Athenians), as well as our flexibility of mind and love of letters, contribute in no small degree to the education of the orator."

[11] Because of the great length of some passages we will not give the Greek text of these in full, but a translation with the relevant Greek words and phrases between brackets.

But as matter for ridicule is always ready at hand, and as most men are only too fond of jokes and raillery, even buffoons are called witty and pass for clever fellows (καὶ οἱ βωμολόχοι εὐτράπελοι προσαγορεύονται ὡς χαρίεντες); though it is clear from what has been said that wit is different, and widely different, from buffoonery. The middle disposition is further characterized by the quality of tact (ἐπιδεξιότης), the possessor of which will say, and allow to be said to him, only the sort of things that are suitable to a virtuous man and a gentleman : since there is a certain propriety in what such a man will say and hear in jest, and the jesting of a gentleman differs from that of a person of servile nature, as does that of an educated from that of an uneducated man. The difference may be seen by comparing the old and the modern comedies; the earlier dramatists found their fun in obscenity (αἰσχρολογία), the moderns prefer innuendo (ὑπόνοια), which marks a great advance in decorum. Can we then define proper raillery by saying that its jests are never unbecoming to gentlemen, or that it avoids giving pain or indeed actually gives pleasure to its object? Or is it impossible to define anything so elusive? For tastes differ as to what is offensive and what amusing.

Whatever rule we lay down, the same will apply to the things that a man should allow to be said to him, since we feel that deeds which a man permits to be ascribed to him he would not stop at actually doing. Hence a man will draw the line at some jokes; for raillery is a sort of vilification (τὸ γὰρ σκῶμμα λοιδόρημά τί ἐστιν), and some forms of vilification are forbidden by law; perhaps some forms of raillery ought to be prohibited also. The cultivated gentleman will therefore regulate his wit, and will be as it were a law to himself.

Such then is the middle character, whether he be called "tactful" or "witty" (εἴτ᾽ ἐπιδέξιος εἴτ᾽ εὐτράπελος λέγεται). The buffoon is one who cannot resist a joke (ὁ δὲ βωμολόχος ἥττων ἐστὶ τοῦ γελοίου); he will not keep his tongue of himself or anyone else, if he can raise a laugh, and will say things which a man of refinement would never say, and some of which he would not even allow to be said to him. The boor is of no use in playful conversation (ὁ δ᾽ ἄγροικος εἰς τὰς τοιαύτας ὁμιλίας ἀχρεῖος); he contributes nothing and takes offence at everything; yet relaxation and amusement seem to be a necessary element in life".[12]

---

[12] Cf. Eth. Nic. II 7, 1108a23-26 περὶ δὲ τὸ ἡδὺ τὸ μὲν ἐν παιδιᾷ ὁ μὲν μέσος εὐτράπελος καὶ ἡ διάθεσις εὐτραπελία, ἡ δ᾽ ὑπερβολὴ βωμολοχία καὶ ὁ ἔχων αὐτὴν βωμολόχος, ὁ δ᾽ ἐλλείπων ἄγροικός τις καὶ ἡ ἕξις ἀγροικία. "In respect of pleasant-

Eth. Nic. VIII 3, 1156a13-14 οὐ ... τῷ ποιούς τινας εἶναι ἀγαπῶσι τοὺς εὐτραπέλους, ἀλλ᾽ ὅτι ἡδεῖς αὐτοῖς.[13]

Eth. Nic. VIII 4, 1157a3-6 μάλιστα δὲ καὶ ἐν τούτοις αἱ φιλίαι μένουσιν ὅταν τὸ αὐτὸ γίγνηται παρ᾽ ἀλλήλων, οἷον ἡδονή, καὶ μὴ μόνον οὕτως ἀλλὰ καὶ ἀπὸ τοῦ αὐτοῦ, οἷον τοῖς εὐτραπέλοις, καὶ μὴ ὡς ἐραστῇ καὶ ἐρωμένῳ.[14]

Eth. Nic. VIII 6, 1158a30-33 οὔτε γὰρ ἡδεῖς μετ᾽ ἀρετῆς ζητοῦσιν οὔτε χρησίμους εἰς τὰ καλά, ἀλλὰ τοὺς μὲν εὐτραπέλους τοῦ ἡδέος ἐφιέμενοι, τοὺς δὲ δεινοὺς πρᾶξαι τὸ ἐπιταχθέν· ταῦτα δ᾽ οὐ πάνυ γίνεται ἐν τῷ αὐτῷ.[15]

Eth. Eud. III 7, 1234a4-23 : "Wittiness (εὐτραπελία) also is a middle state (μεσότης), and the witty man is midway between the boorish or stiff man and the buffoon (ὁ εὐτράπελος μέσος τοῦ ἀγροίκου καὶ δυστραπέλου καὶ τοῦ βωμολόχου). For just as in the matter of food the squeamish man differs from the omnivorous in that the former takes nothing or little, and that reluctantly, and the latter accepts everything readily, so the boor stands in relation to the vulgar man or buffoon — the former takes no joke except with difficulty, the latter accepts everything easily and with pleasure. Neither course is right : one should allow some things and not others, and on principle — that constitutes the witty man (εὐτράπελος). The proof of the formula is the same as in other cases : wittiness of this kind (not the quality to which we apply the term in a transferred sense)[16] is a very becoming sort of character (ἥ τε γὰρ εὐτραπελία ἡ τοιαύτη, καὶ μὴ ἣν μεταφέροντες λέγομεν, ἐπιεικεστάτη ἕξις), and also a middle state is praiseworthy, whereas extremes are blameworthy. But as there are two kinds of wit (one consisting in liking a joke, even one that tells against oneself if it is funny, for instance a jeer, the other in the ability to

---

ness in social amusement, the middle character is witty and the middle disposition wittiness; the excess is buffoonery and its possessor a buffoon; the deficient man may be called boorish, and his disposition boorishness."

[13] "We enjoy the society of witty people not because of what they are in themselves, but because they are agreeable to us."

[14] "In these cases also the friendship is most lasting when each friend derives the same benefit, for instance pleasure, from the other, and not only so, but derives it from the same thing, as in a friendship between two witty people, and not as in one between a lover and his beloved."

[15] "For they (sc. rulers) do not seek for friends who are pleasant because they are good, or useful for noble purposes, but look for witty people when they desire pleasure, and for the other sort seek men who are clever at executing their commissions; and these two qualities are rarely found in the same person."

[16] Sc. buffoonery.

produce things of this sort), these kinds of wit differ from one another, but both are middle states; for a man who can produce jokes of a sort that will give pleasure to a person of good judgement even though the laugh is against himself will be midway between the vulgar man and the frigid (μέσος ἔσται τοῦ φορτικοῦ καὶ τοῦ ψυχροῦ). This is a better definition than that the thing said must not be painful to the victim whatever sort of man he may be — rather, it must give pleasure to the man in the middle position, since his judgement is good".[17]

Eth. Eud. VII 5, 1240a2-3 διὸ ἐνίοτε ἀνομοίοις χαίρουσιν, οἷον αὐστηροὶ εὐτραπέλοις καὶ ὀξεῖς ῥᾳθύμοις· εἰς τὸ μέσον γὰρ καθίστανται ὑπ' ἀλλήλων.[18]

Rhet. II 12, 1389b10-12 (this paragraph on the character of the young begins, 1389b2-3, with ἅπαντα ἐπὶ τὸ μᾶλλον καὶ σφοδρότερον ἁμαρτάνουσι, "all their errors are due to excess and vehemence". In this context it is said that they are :) καὶ φιλογέλωτες, διὸ καὶ εὐτράπελοι· ἡ γὰρ εὐτραπελία πεπαιδευμένη ὕβρις ἐστίν.[19]

Rhet. II 13, 1390a21-23 (on old men) ὀδυρτικοί εἰσι, καὶ οὐκ εὐτράπελοι οὐδὲ φιλογέλοιοι· ἐναντίον γὰρ τὸ ὀδυρτικὸν τῷ φιλογέλωτι.[20]

Hippocrates :[21] *Dec.* 7 χρὴ τὸν ἰατρὸν ἔχειν τινὰ εὐτραπελίην παρακειμένην· τὸ γὰρ αὐστηρὸν δυσπρόσιτον καὶ τοῖσιν ὑγιαίνουσι καὶ τοῖσι νοσέουσιν.[22]

Demetrius, *Eloc.* III 177 (the Dorians are accustomed to broaden all their words, e.g. by saying βροντά instead of βροντή. This is the reason why comedies were not written in Doric, but in the pungent

---

[17] Cf. *Magna Mor.* I 30, 1193a11-19 εὐτραπελία δ' ἐστὶ μεσότης βωμολοχίας καὶ ἀγροικίας, ἔστιν δὲ περὶ σκώμματα. ὅ τε γὰρ βωμολόχος ἐστὶν ὁ πάντα καὶ πᾶν οἰόμενος δεῖν σκώπτειν, ὅ τε ἄγροικος ὁ μήτε σκώπτειν βουλόμενος δεῖν μήτε σκωφθῆναι, ἀλλ' ὀργιζόμενος. ὁ δ' εὐτράπελος ἀνὰ μέσον τούτων, ὁ μήτε πάντας καὶ πάντως σκώπτων μήτ' αὖ ἄγροικος ὤν. ἔσται δὲ ὁ εὐτράπελος διττῶς πως λεγόμενος· καὶ γὰρ ὁ δυνάμενος σκῶψαι ἐμμελῶς, καὶ ὃς ἂν ὑπομείνη σκωπτόμενος, εὐτράπελος· καὶ ἡ εὐτραπελία τοιαύτη.

[18] "Hence sometimes people take delight in persons unlike themselves, the stiff for instance in the witty and the active in the lazy, for they are brought by one another into the middle state."

[19] "And they are fond of laughter, and therefore witty; for wit is cultured insolence."

[20] "They are querulous, and neither witty nor fond of laughter; for a querulous disposition is the opposite of a love of laughter."

[21] This text is placed after Aristotle, since it is probably spurious and dates from the Hellenistic period.

[22] "The physician must have at his command a certain ready wit, as dourness is repulsive both to the healthy and to the sick."

Attic) ἡ γὰρ ᾿Αττικὴ γλῶσσα συνεστραμμένον τι ἔχει καὶ δημοτικὸν καὶ ταῖς τοιαύταις εὐτραπελίαις πρέπον.²³

Posidippus, fr. 28, 4f. (he blames the Athenians for saying that their particular speech is Greek) τί προσδιατρίβων συλλαβαῖς καὶ γράμμασιν τὴν εὐτραπελίαν εἰς ἀηδίαν ἄγεις;²⁴

Polybius IX 23, 3 Κλεομένης ὁ Σπαρτιάτης οὐ χρηστότατος μὲν βασιλεύς, πικρότατος δὲ τύραννος, εὐτραπελώτατος δὲ πάλιν ἰδιώτης καὶ φιλανθρωπότατος;²⁵

XII 16, 14 (a young man makes a witty plea for himself in a lawcourt) ὁ μὲν οὖν νεανίσκος οὕτως εὐτραπελευσάμενος ἐξέλυσε τὴν σπουδήν, οἱ δ᾿ ἄρχοντες...²⁶

XXIII 5, 7 (on a smart, impressive high-society personage) ὁμοίως δὲ καὶ κατὰ τὴν ἄλλην διάθεσιν ἐν μὲν ταῖς ὁμιλίαις εὔχαρις καὶ πρόχειρος ἦν, παρά τε τὰς συνουσίας εὐτράπελος καὶ πολιτικός, ἅμα δὲ τούτοις φιλέραστος.²⁷

Cicero, *Ep. ad Fam.* VII 32, 1 "Quod sine praenomine familiariter... ad me epistolam misisti, primum addubitavi, num a Volumnio senatore esset, quocum mihi est magnus usus; deinde εὐτραπελία litterarum fecit, ut intellegerem tuas esse. Quibus in litteris omnia mihi periucunda fuerunt".²⁸

Diodorus Siculus XV 6, 4 τότε μὲν οὖν διὰ τὴν εὐτραπελίαν τῶν λόγων μειδιάσας ὁ Διονύσιος ἤνεγκε τὴν παρρησίαν, τοῦ γέλωτος τὴν μέμψιν ἀμβλύνοντος.²⁹

XX 63, 3 οὐ μὴν ἀλλὰ διὰ τὴν ἐν τοῖς πότοις εὐτραπελίαν κατα-

---

²³ "For the Attic dialect has about it something terse and popular, and so lends itself naturally to the witticisms of the stage." In III 172 Demetrius says that there may be a witty play on words in nicknames, when a sort comparison is implied in them : ἡ γὰρ ἀντίθεσις εὐτράπελος.

²⁴ "Why be so much concerned with how you speak, syllables, letters, and the rest of it, that you make other folks dislike your wit?"

²⁵ "Was not Cleomenes of Sparta at once a most excellent king and a most cruel tyrant, and then again in private intercourse most urbane and courteous?"

²⁶ "Thus the young man's ready wit relaxed the gravity of the court, but the magistrates ..."

²⁷ "And similarly, as regards his other qualities, his conversation was charming and unembarrassed, and in convivial society he was versatile and urbane and also fond of love-making."

²⁸ "When you sent me a letter in familiar style ... without giving your *praenomen* I was inclined to doubt at first whether it was not from Volumnius the senator, with whom I am in constant touch; but as I read on, the graceful badinage of the letter convinced me that it was from you. Everything in it gave me the greatest pleasure."

²⁹ "Now at the time Dionysius, smiling at the ready wit of the words, tolerated the freedom of speech, since the joke took the edge of the censure."

νοήσας τῶν μεθυόντων τοὺς ἀλλοτρίως τὰ πρὸς τὴν δυναστείαν ἔχοντας παρέλαβεν αὐτούς ποτε κατ᾽ ἰδίαν.[30]

XXXVIII/XXXIX 7 (on Sulla who robbed many temples) εὐτραπελευόμενος δὲ ἀπεφαίνετο κρατεῖν τῷ πολέμῳ πάντως διὰ τὸ τοὺς θεοὺς αὐτῷ συνεργεῖν, εἰσενηνοχότας χρημάτων πολύ τι πλῆθος αὐτῷ.[31]

Philo, *Leg. ad Gaium* 361 : "Gaius (the emperor) asked us an important and solemn question : "Why do you not eat pork?" At this inquiry our opponents again burst into such violent peals of laughter, partly because they were really amused and partly because they made it their business as flatterers to let this remark seem witty and entertaining (ὑπὲρ τοῦ τὸ λεχθὲν δοκεῖν σὺν εὐτραπελίᾳ καὶ χάριτι εἰρῆσθαι)".

Josephus, *Ant.* XII 170-173 "When he (sc. Joseph the Tobiad) arrived at Alexandria, he heard that Ptolemy was in Memphis, and so he met him there and presented himself to him. Now the king was sitting in a chariot with his wife and with his friend Athenion — this was the man who had been an envoy to Jerusalem and had been entertained by Joseph —, and as soon as Athenion caught sight of him, he introduced him to the king, saying that this was the person whom he had described to him, when he returned from Jerusalem, as an excellent and liberal young man. Ptolemy, therefore, first greeted him and even invited him to come up into his chariot, and when he was seated, began to complain about the actions of Onias. Then Joseph said, "Pardon him because of his age; for surely you are not unaware that old people and infants are likely to have the same level of intelligence. But from us who are young you will obtain everything so as to find no fault". Thereupon Ptolemy, being pleased with the charm and ready wit of the young man (τῇ χάριτι καὶ τῇ εὐτραπελίᾳ νεανίσκου), began to be still fonder of him as though he were an old and tried friend, so much so that he told him to take up his residence in the palace and had him as a guest at his own table every day."

Ant. XII 210-214 "Once when he (sc. Hyrcanus) was invited together with the leading men of the country to feast with the king (Ptolemy), he was placed at the foot of the table, being slighted as still a youth

---

[30] "None the less, however, when through the jesting at the drinking bouts he (Agathocles) had discovered which of those who were flushed with wine were hostile to his tyranny he invited them individually."

[31] "He would say in jest that his supremacy in battle was assured, since the gods, by their large contributions to his war chest, were aiding his cause."

by those who assigned the places according to rank. And all those who reclined at table with Hyrcanus piled up before him the bones of their portions — from which they themselves had removed the meat —, so as to cover the part of the table where he reclined, whereupon Tryphon, who was the king's jester and was appointed to make jokes and raise laughter when there was drinking, with the encouragement of those who reclined at the table, stood up before the king and said, "My lord, do you see the bones lying before Hyrcanus? From this you may guess that his father has stripped all Syria in the same way as Hyrcanus has left these bones bare of meat". The king then laughed at Tryphon's words, and asked Hyrcanus why there were so many bones lying before him, and he replied, "It is natural, my lord; for dogs eat the bones together with the meat, as these men do" — and he looked toward those who reclined there, indicating that there was nothing lying before them —, "but men eat the meat and throw the bones away, which is just what I, being a man, have now done." Thereupon the king, who admired his reply for being so clever and to show approval of his wit, ordered all to applaud (ὁ δὲ βασιλεὺς θαυμάσας τὴν ἀπόκρισιν αὐτοῦ σοφὴν οὕτως γενομένην, πάντας ἐκέλευσεν ἀνακροτῆσαι, τῆς εὐτραπελίας ἀποδεχόμενος αὐτόν)".

Dio Chrysostom, Or. XXXIII 3 (Dio apologizes for his lack of eloquence) τί οὖν ἡμᾶς ἐλπίζετε ἐρεῖν; ἢ τί μάλιστα ἀκοῦσαι σπεύδετε παρὰ ἀνδρῶν οὐκ εὐτραπέλων; [32]

Or. LXVI 19 οὐκοῦν ἀνάγκη τὸν ὑπὸ τῆς νόσου ταύτης ἐχόμενον ὑπεύθυνον περιέρχεσθαι καὶ προσέχειν ἑκάστῳ καὶ δεδοικέναι μή τινα ἑκὼν ἢ ἄκων λυπήσῃ, μάλιστα τῶν ἑτοίμων τινὰ καὶ τῶν εὐτραπέλων. [33]

Plutarch, Antonius 43, 3 (the soldiers were very fond of Antonius) τούτου δὲ αἰτίαι πλείονες ἦσαν, ὡς προειρήκαμεν· εὐγένεια, λόγου δύναμις, ἁπλότης, τὸ φιλόδωρον καὶ μεγαλόδωρον, ἡ περὶ τὰς παιδιὰς καὶ τὰς ὁμιλίας εὐτραπελία. [34]

---

[32] "What, then, do you expect us to say? Or what above all are you eager to hear from men who are not of nimble wit?"

[33] "Accordingly, whoever is the victim of this malady of courting popularity is bound to be subject to criticism as he walks about, to pay heed to everyone, and to fear lest wittingly or unwittingly he give offence to somebody, but particularly to one of those who are bold and of ready wit."

[34] "And the reasons for this were many, as I have said before: his high birth, his eloquence, his simplicity of manners, his love of giving, his complaisance in affairs of pleasure or social intercourse."

Rect. rat. aud. 16, 46D (one should not be indifferent towards admonitions and reproofs) σκῶμμα μὲν γὰρ ἀνύβριστον ἐν παιδιᾷ τινι μετ᾽ εὐτραπελίας ἀφείμενον ἐνεγκεῖν ἀλύπως καὶ ἱλαρῶς οὐκ ἀγεννὲς οὐδ᾽ ἀπαίδευτον ἀλλ᾽ ἐλευθέριον πάνυ καὶ Λακωνικόν ἐστιν.[35]

Quom. adul. ab am. internosc. 7, 52E (Alcibiades is mentioned as an example of a flatterer who manages to get into a person's good graces) Ἀθήνησι μὲν σκώπτων καὶ ἱπποτροφῶν καὶ μετ᾽ εὐτραπελίας ζῶν καὶ χάριτος.[36]

Quaest. Rom. 40, 274D (the Greeks become effeminate) ἔλαθον ἐκρυέντες τῶν ὅπλων καὶ ἀγαπήσαντες ἀνθ᾽ ὁπλιτῶν καὶ ἱππέων ἀγαθῶν εὐτράπελοι καὶ παλαιστρῖται καλοὶ λέγεσθαι.[37]

Virt. Mor. 2, 441B (Chrysippus has called too many things virtues, e.g. ἐσθλότης, μεγαλότης, καλότης :) ἑτέρας τε τοιαύτας ἐπιδεξιότητας, εὐαπαντησίας, εὐτραπελίας ἀρετὰς τιθέμενος, πολλῶν καὶ ἀτόπων ὀνομάτων οὐδὲν δεομένην ἐμπέπληκε τὴν φιλοσοφίαν.[38]

Quaest. Conv. II 1, 629E-F (the Persians joked with each other on matters about which it was more agreeable to be teased than not) εἰ γὰρ ἐπαινοῦντες ἕτεροι πολλάκις λυποῦσι καὶ προσίστανται, πῶς οὐκ ἄξιον ἦν ἄγασθαι τὴν εὐτραπελίαν ἐκείνων καὶ τὴν σύνεσιν, ὧν καὶ τὰ σκώμματα τοῖς σκωπτομένοις ἡδονὴν καὶ χάριν παρεῖχεν;[39]

Cic. V 4 (on Cicero's speeches) ἡ δὲ περὶ τὰ σκώμματα καὶ τὴν παιδιὰν ταύτην εὐτραπελίαν δικανικὸν μὲν ἐδόκει καὶ γλαφυρόν, χρώμενος δ᾽ αὐτῇ κατακόρως πολλοὺς ἐλύπει καὶ κακοηθείας ἐλάμβανε δόξαν.[40]

---

[35] "As for a pleasant scoff, wittily delevered and in pure fun, if a man know how to take it cheerfully and without offence, his conduct argues no ignoble or uncultured mind, but one altogether generous and Spartan." (The text goes on: "On the other hand, to hear a reprehension or admonition to reform character, delivered in words that penetrate like a biting drug, and not to be humbled at hearing it ... is a notable sign of an illiberal nature.")

[36] "At Athens he indulged in frivolous jesting, kept a racing stable, and led a life full of urbanity and agreeable enjoyment."

[37] "They have unconsciously lapsed from the practice of arms, and have become content to be termed nimble athletes and handsome wrestlers rather than excellent men-at-arms and horsemen."

[38] "He postulated also the other qualities of the same sort, dexterousnesses, approachablenesses, adroitnesses, as virtues, and thus filled philosophy, which needed nothing of the sort, with many uncouth names."

[39] "For if other men often vex and annoy by their praise, as they do, surely it was right to admire the urbanity and understanding of men whose very jokes offered pleasure and gratification to those who were the butts?"

[40] "His readiness to indulge in such jests and pleasantry was thought indeed to be a pleasant characteristic of a pleader; but he carried it to excess and so annoyed many and got the reputation of being malicious." Other passages in Plutarch with εὐτραπελία : *Ag. et Cleom.* XII 3, *Comm. not.* 9, 1062B.

Aelian, *Nat. Anim.* V 26 (one can teach a monkey everything) οὕτως ἄρα ἡ φύσις ποικίλον τε καὶ εὐτράπελόν ἐστιν.[41]

Var. Hist. V 13 ἦσαν δὲ ἄρα Ἀθηναῖοι δεινῶς ἐς τὰς πολιτείας εὐτράπελοι καὶ ἐπιτήδειοι πρὸς τὰς μεταβολὰς παντὸς μᾶλλον.[42]

Pollux, *Onom.* IV 96 a dancer is described *inter alia* as : παντοδαπός, εὐτράπελος, εὔτρεπτος. *ibid.* VI 121 the word κοῦφος is defined as ῥᾴδιος, εὐμετάβολος, εὔτρεπτος, εὐτράπελος, κτλ.

Julian, *Or.* VII 227A ἔοικας οὖν οὐδὲ πεποιηκὼς μῦθον, ὦ ξυνετώτατε, μάτην νεανιεύεσθαι· καίτοι τοῦτο τίτθης ἔργον ἐστὶν εὐτραπέλου.[43]

Though this list of texts is incomplete,[44] we now have a collection of instances, covering more than eight centuries, which may form a solid basis for determining the meanings of the word.

Four things are clear right from the start: 1. εὐτραπελία is a *vox media*, having negative overtones nearly as often as positive ones.[45] 2. the meaning of the word has changed; but that development has not been rectilinear.[46] 3. εὐτραπελία denotes not only a characteristic of speech and words, but often one of a whole way of life, an attitude. 4. In antiquity there has often been a consciousness, it seems, of the word's etymology, so that the word could be filled time and again with the meanings of its etymological components εὖ and τρέπω.[47]

---

[41] "So versatile and so adaptable a thing is its nature."

[42] "In political matters the Athenians were extremely fickle and above all inclined to changes."

[43] "It seems then that you did not invent your myth, my very clever friend, and that yours was an idle boast. Though in fact the thing is done by any nurse with an inventive turn."

[44] Some other instances may be found in H. STEPHANUS, *Thesaurus Graecae Linguae* (edd. C. B. HASE - G. DINDORF - L. DINDORF) III, Paris 1835, *s.vv.*

[45] In the translations we find the following substantives and adjectives rendering εὐτραπελία and εὐτράπελος: adaptable, complaisance, cunning, dexterous, fickle, flexibility, graceful badinage, inventive, jesting, nimble, perfidious, pleasantry, ready wit, urbane/urbanity, versatility, witty/wittiness.

[46] So, it is not correct when R. C. TRENCH writes (*Synonyms of the New Testament* 123): "εὐτραπελία, thus gradually sinking from a better meaning to a worse, has a history closely resembling that of *urbanitas*."

[47] Needless to say this does not involve our falling into the trap of etymologizing interpretation that James BARR has warned of so strongly (*Semantics of Biblical Language*, London 1962²). The difference is that in this case the Greeks themselves give evidence of their etymological consciousness; it is not we who try to explain εὐτραπελία in terms of its etymological constituents. One may compare, besides the examples quoted above (esp. Aristotle, *Eth. Nic.* IV 7, 1128a10), John Chrysostom, *Hom. in Eph.* XVII 3 (*PG* 62, 119) εὐτράπελος λέγεται ὁ ποικίλος, ὁ παντοδαπός, ὁ ἄστατος, ὁ εὔκολος, ὁ πάντα γινόμενος... Ταχέως τρέπεται ὁ τοιοῦτος καὶ μεθίσταται.

Dirlmeier rightly compares εὐτραπελία with πολύτροπος, which was also a *vox media*, meaning "much turned, turning many ways, various, manifold, shifty, versatile, wily, fickle, etc."[48] Indeed, as may be seen from the texts quoted, the positive meaning defined by Aristotle does not set the tone for the use of the word in the rest of Greek literature; not even in Aristotle's own writings.[49] For, whereas in his definitions the positive meaning is predominant, even he has to admit that καὶ οἱ βωμολόχοι εὐτράπελοι προσαγορεύονται (*Eth. Nic.* IV 8, 1128a14-15), so he is aware of negative connotations as well.[50] Significant too is that in *Rhet.* II 12, 1389b10-12 Aristotle mentions εὐτραπελία among the excesses of youth, which fits in with Plato's remark on the old man spasmodically imitating the εὐτραπελία of the young people (*Resp.* VIII 563a).[51] It is, therefore, only with difficulty and by straining its meaning that Aristotle can list εὐτραπελία among the virtues, since a real virtue cannot be essentially confined to a certain period of life.[52] Of the two instances in Isocrates, one has a negative meaning (*Areop.* 49) and the other a positive one (*Antid.* 296), a fact which is very illustrative in itself. Moreover, Isocrates points out in the former instance that, much to his regret, the meaning of the word has changed from negative to positive due to a slackening of morals.[53] From the fifth century B.C. onwards (cf. Thucydides and

---

This etymology is, of course, also found in the great Byzantine etymologica, e.g. *Etym. Magn.*, *s.v.* εὐτράπελος· ὁ κοῦφος καὶ μωρὸς καὶ ἀπαίδευτος. ὥσπερ γὰρ παρὰ τὸ εἴκω, τὸ ὁμοιῶ, γίνεται εἴκελος, οὕτως καὶ ἀπὸ τοῦ τρέπω, οὗ ὁ δεύτερος ἀόριστος ἔτραπον, γίνεται τράπελος καὶ εὐτράπελος. ... παρὰ τὸ εὖ τρέπεσθαι τὸν λόγον εἴρηται. Cf. also *Anecd. Bekk.* 92 ἐπὶ τοῦ εὖ τρεπομένου πρὸς πάντα καὶ ἐπὶ τοῦ εὐστρόφου (quoted from W. Pape-M. Sengebusch, *Griechisch-Deutsches Handwörterbuch*, Braunschweig 1888, 1103).

[48] F. Dirlmeier, *Aristoteles. Nikomachische Ethik*, Berlin 1956, 392 "εὐτραπελία war im gemein-griechischen Sprachgebrauch nicht festgelegt auf die positive Bedeutung, die Arist. zur Bezeichnung der Mitte brauchte. Die "Wendigkeit" ist so wenig eindeutig wie bei Odysseus, dem πολύτροπος, worüber die Homererklärer viel nachgedacht haben."

[49] The short study of O. Lück, Die Eutrapelia des Aristoteles, *Pharus* 24 (1933), 85-87, is without any value for the present investigation.

[50] Abbot, *Ephesians* 149, who has rightly observed this, explains: "as in many other cases, the extreme usurps the name of the near." From modern usage one might give as an example the use of the word "democracy".

[51] Dirlmeier, *o.c.*, 392 "bei den Älteren wirkt sie kindisch."

[52] Cf. F. Dirlmeier, *Aristoteles. Magna Moralia*, Berlin 1958, 307 "die zeitliche Einschränkung (sc. to the period of youth) ... verträgt sich nicht mit dem Begriff der Tugend als ἕξις." See also Dirlmeier, *Aristoteles. Eudemische Ethik*, Berlin 1962, 354 where D. proves that according to Aristotle's own views he should actually regard εὐτραπελία as a πάθος, but that there were some reasons why he tried not to do so.

[53] R. A. Gauthier-J. Y. Jolif, *L'Ethique à Nicomaque* II, Louvain-Paris 1959, 316

Aristophanes) we find the positive and negative meanings side by side. And, whereas the positive sense seems gradually to get prevalence after Aristotle, the negative sense has never entirely disappeared.[54] For instance, in Plutarch, *Quom. adul. ab am. internosc.* 7, 52E Alcibiades, the opportunist flatterer, is described as μετ᾽ εὐτραπελίας ζῶν, in *Quaest. Rom.* 40, 274D it is judged as a sign of having become effeminate that the Greeks try to become εὐτράπελοι καὶ παλαιστρῖται καλοί, and in *Virt. Mor.* 2, 441B Chrysippus is censured for listing εὐτραπελία among the virtues. And in Dio Chrys. 66, 19 εὐτραπελία seems to have the connotation of mordent sharpness.

That is to say that, when εὐτραπελία is used as a qualification of speech or conversation, it need not be a positive one but may quite well be meant *in sensu malo*. It may be buffoonery or some kind of inhumane or degrading jesting. No clear indication has been found that εὐτραπελία lies in the sphere of dirty jokes, as several translations of Eph. v 4 suggest. Moreover, from the twenty jokes of an εὐτράπελος which are told on the ancient book of jests *Philogelos* (with jokes from the second to the fifth century A.D.), not a single one is really obscene.[55] Nevertheless, since the context of Eph. v 4 more or less seems to suggest this interpretation, one may consider whether a hint

---

"les mœurs devenant plus indulgentes, le mot n'allait pas tarder à perdre cette nuance péjorative et à s'appliquer non plus aux mauvais plaisants, mais aux gens d'esprits. Isocrate ... nous est le témoin, d'ailleurs mécontent, de cette évolution."

[54] GAUTHIER - JOLIF, *o.c.*, 317.

[55] Some examples may suffice. The German translation given is that by A. THIER-FELDER, *Philogelos, der Lachfreund, von Hierokles und Philagrios*, München 1968: 140 εὐτράπελος ἰδὼν γραμματοδιδάσκαλον ἀφυῆ διδάσκοντα προσελθὼν ἠρώτα, διὰ τί κιθαρίζειν οὐ διδάσκει. τοῦ δὲ εἰπόντος· Ὅτι οὐκ ἐπίσταμαι — εἶπε· Πῶς οὖν γράμματα διδάσκεις οὐκ ἐπιστάμενος; (Ein Witzbold sah, wie ein unfähiger Lehrer Lesen und Schreiben lehrte, trat hinzu und fragte: "Warum lehrst du nicht Zither-spielen?" Er erwiderte: "Weil ich es nicht verstehe." Und der andere: "Warum lehrst du also Lesen und Schreiben, ohne es zu verstehen?"). 141 εὐτράπελος κυβερνήτης ἐρωτηθείς, τί φυσᾷ, εἶπε· Φάβα καὶ κρόμμυα. (Ein witziger Steuermann wurde gefragt, was für Wind weht (Doppelsinn: was "Wind" macht), und er antwortete: "Bohnen und Zwiebeln".). 146 εὐτράπελος χοῖρον κλέψας ἔφευγεν. ἐπεὶ δὲ κατελαμβάνετο, θεὶς αὐτὸν ἔτυπτε λέγων· Ἄλλων ὄρυγε καὶ μὴ τὰ ἐμά. (Ein Witzbold hatte ein Schwein gestohlen und lief damit weg. Als (die Verfolger) ihn einholten, setzte er es auf die Erde, prügelte es und sagte: "Anderer Leute Land zerwühle und nicht meines!"). 148 εὐτράπελος φλυάρου κουρέως ἐρωτήσαντος· Πῶς σε κείρω; — Σιωπῶν, ἔφη (Ein Witzbold, der von einem geschwätzigen Barbier gefragt wurde: "Wie soll ich dich scheren?" erwiderte. "Schweigend."). 151b εὐτράπελος ἰδὼν ἰατρὸν κόρην ὑπαλεί-φοντα ἔφη· Ὅρα, νεανίσκε, μὴ τὴν ὄψιν θεραπεύων τὴν κόρην διαφθείρῃς (Ein Witzbold sah, wie ein Arzt einem hübschen Mädchen die Augen mit Salbe einrieb. Er sagte: "Gib acht, junger Mann, dasz du nicht, wenn du die Augen behandelst, die Pupille zerstörst (Doppelsinn: das Mädchen verführst).").

in this direction might be found in Aristotle's remark in *Eth. Nic.*
IV 8, 1128a23-24. Here he illustrates the difference between a buffoon
and an εὐτράπελος by referring to the difference between old and
modern comedies : the earlier dramatists found their fun in obscenities
(αἰσχρολογία), the moderns prefer innuendo (ὑπόνοια). If that means
that the wittiness of the εὐτράπελος is characterized by its oblique
insinuations in the direction of shameful things, then that might justify
the nice translation "suggestive language", proposed in the *Translator's
New Testament*.[56]

Another negative aspect of the wittiness of an εὐτράπελος is that it
is often at somebody else's expense. This is very clear from the two
passages in Josephus (which for that reason have been very extensively
quoted); and also from some of the εὐτράπελος-jokes in the *Philogelos*
(more or less also from Philo and Dio Chrys. 66, 19). It is the sharp-
wittedness of the debunker. The un-christian element therein is obvious.

In several texts εὐτραπελία is not said of any kind of speech but
simply denotes great adaptability and adroitness, and also changeable-
ness. Several times it is mentioned in connection with ἐπιδεξιότης
(dexterity),[57] and sometimes with derivatives of μεταβάλλειν (change).
Though not necessarily negative in itself, one may surmise that this
quality will not have appealed to the author of Ephesians. Someone
who εὖ τρέπεται, who easily turns himself in different directions, who
is εὐμετάβολος,[58] is not one to be cited as an example to Christians.

From some texts it is clear that εὐτραπελία was regarded as typical
of the way of life of urbane high-society persons, the cultivated, no
doubt well-to-do young men, who could afford the life of a gentleman.
"It forms part of the relaxation of life, ἀναπαύσεως ἐν τῷ βίῳ,
which includes διαγωγῆς μετὰ παιδιᾶς, all the lighter occupations of
which amusement or relaxation is the object and accompaniment,
opposed to the serious business of life, and corresponds exactly to the
French *passe-temps*".[59] It needs no argument that this "virtue" could

---

[56] London 1973. In the note on p. 501 it is said that the author clearly has in
mind here "innocent-seeming words with underlying meanings." It is significant that
the Modern Greek New Testament has substituted βωμολοχία (dirty joking) for
εὐτραπελία in Eph. v 4.

[57] See on this word DIRLMEIER, *Aristoteles. Nikomachische Ethik*, Berlin 1956, 393.

[58] Often close to being opportunistic and fickle; cf. the quotation from John
Chrysostom above (n. 47), and also Suidas *s.v.* εὐτράπελος who quotes a sentence
οὕτω δ᾽ ἦν εὐτράπελος τὴν φύσιν, ὥστε παρ᾽ Ἀθηναίοις Ἀθηναῖος ἦν ἄκρος, καὶ
Λάκων Λακεδαιμονίοις, καὶ Θηβαίοις Θηβαῖος. (In a positive sense, however, Paul
is also a εὐτράπελος in view of 1 Cor. ix 19-23).

[59] E. M. COPE - J. E. SANDYS, *The Rhetoric of Aristotle* II, Cambridge 1877 (repr.

not recommend itself to the early Christian communities, which in most cases will have consisted of "not many wise, nor many mighty, nor many of nobility" (1 Cor. i 26).

Of course, the previous remarks are far from being an exhaustive analysis of every semantic aspect of εὐτραπελία. We have been content to indicate some aspects that must have been conceived *in malo sensu* by the early Christians. Whichever one of the several meanings outlined above actually did move the author of Ephesians to formulate his warning, it cannot now be discerned exactly; but it is clear that the word εὐτραπελία has aspects which made it sometimes unattractive to the Greeks and still more aspects which made it impossible to be posited as a Christian virtue. At any rate the warning in Eph. v 4 need not be read as a denouncement of humour and wittiness in the church.[60]

Hildesheim, 1970), 150. One may cite here Aristotle, *Eth. Nic.* VIII 6, 1158a30ff., *Rhet.* II 12, 1389b2ff.; Polybius IX 23, 3; Plutarch, *Quom. adul. etc.* 7, 52E.

[60] Cf. J. GNILKA, *Der Epheserbrief*, Freiburg 1971, 247. Gnilka remarks in passing "Der gute Witz scheint bestimmte soziologische Strukturen zur Voraussetzung zu haben", thereby probably indicating that, if εὐτραπελία does indeed mean "wittiness" in Eph. v 4, the verse may be explained from a sociological point of view. This cannot be worked out here, the more so since the sociology of humour is still in its infancy; see e.g. A. C. ZIJDERVELD, *Sociologie van de zotheid. De humor als sociaal verschijnsel*, Meppel 1971. One must admit that humour is not recommended in the N.T. From all the words meaning "humour, wit, joke, jest, laugh, etc." dealt with by SCHMIDT, *Synonymik* III 447ff. only two occur in the N.T. (παίζειν in 1 Cor. ix 7 and γέλως in James iv 9), and that in a negative sense. Cf. K. H. RENGSTORF, γελάω, *ThWNT* I (1932), 657f. and G. BERTRAM, παίζω, *ThWNT* V (1954), 625-629.

EPH. V 28 — VERSUCH EINER ÜBERSETZUNG

G. BOUWMAN

Die Stelle Eph. v 28 gehört zu den vieldiskutierten Versen des Neuen Testaments.[1] Trotzdem ist, soweit ich sehe, nie eine Einzeluntersuchung dieser schwierigen Stelle gewidmet worden. In Kommentaren fehlt meistens der Raum für eine eingehende Untersuchung. Die hier gebotene Lösung wird den Kollegen zum Gedankenaustausch als Anregung zu weiterer Erörterung des Problems vorgelegt, wie das bei den Sitzungen des "Convents" üblich ist.

1. *Die Übersetzung : wie ihre Leiber/als ihre Leiber*

Das Problem wird von Heinrich SCHLIER wie folgt formuliert : "V. 28a beginnt einen neuen Gedanken, der im Zusammenhang einer Exegese von Gen 2, 24 auftaucht... Das οὕτως bezieht sich nicht auf bisher Gesagtes, sondern gehört mit dem folgenden ὡς zusammen, das infolgedessen doch mit 'wie' und nicht mit 'als' zu übersetzen ist. Der neue Gedanke soll die Mahnung des Apostels an die Ehemänner, ihre Frauen zu lieben, von neuem motivieren: So liebt sie, wie ihr ja doch den eigenen Leib liebt".[2] Das griechische ὡς und sein hellenistisches Äquivalent καθώς können bekanntlich wie das hebräische *ki* nicht nur vergleichenden sondern auch begründenden Sinn haben, wie z.B. in Mt. vi 10, wo die Parallelstelle Lk. xi 4 ein γάρ hat.[3] Man könnte deshalb auch übersetzen: "So müssen auch die Männer ihre Frauen lieben, weil sie ja ihre eigenen Leiber sind".[4] Damit fällt dann mehr

---

[1] Vgl. J. GNILKA, *Der Epheserbrief* (HTC), Freiburg, u.s.w. 1971, 283.

[2] H. SCHLIER, *Der Brief an die Epheser*, Düsseldorf 1957, 260. Ähnlich übersetzen noch : GNILKA (*a.a.O.*); EWALD (KNT); G. DELLING, *Paulus' Stellung zu Frau und Ehe*, Stuttgart 1931, 126. GNILKA (*o.c.*, 284, Anm. 1) nennt weiter noch ABBOTT, wohl zu Unrecht, denn dieser übersetzt : "as being their own bodies". Übrigens sind die meisten Übersetzungen zweideutig, weil das lateinische *ut*, das englische *as* und das französische *comme* beide Bedeutungen zulassen.

[3] BLASS-DEBRUNNER, 453, 2; K. ROMANIUK, De usu particulae καθώς in epistulis Paulinis, *VD* 43 (1965), 71-82 (75f.). Vgl. Eph. iv 32; v 2.

[4] Als Vertreter dieser Auffassung nennt SCHLIER (*o.c.*, 260, Anm. 2) : DISPING, BECK, VON SODEN, WESTCOTT, KNABENBAUER, ROBINSON, HUBY, DIBELIUS. Ein energischer Verteidiger ist M. BARTH (*Anchor Bible*, New York 1974), der übersetzt : "for they are their bodies". Er sagt, dass die Übersetzung der Mehrheit der älteren und jüngeren Kommentare widerspricht, nennt aber (629, Anm. 78): H. OLSHAUSEN (New York 1858), HAUPT, ABBOTT, DIBELIUS und einige Monographien. Hinzuzufügen wären noch BEARE und MASSON.

oder weniger die Korrespondenz mit dem bevorstehenden οὕτως weg
und muss dies auf das bisher Gesagte bezogen werden. Die beiden
Möglichkeiten werden von A. FEUILLET klar herausgestellt : "Le *hôs*
du verset 28 a une valeur comparative, et non pas argumentative
(en tant que), car il est en rapport avec le *houtôs* du début de la phrase :
les maris doivent aimer leurs femmes *de la même façon que* leurs
propres corps".[5]

Die Frage lautet also : sollen die Männer nach Eph. v 28 ihre
Frauen lieben in ähnlicher Weise wie sie ihre eigenen Leiber lieben,
oder weil die Frauen ihre Leiber sind? Die letzte Aussage wird allgemein als den Frauen unwürdig abgewiesen. Man fragt sich aber, ob
der Vergleich, an sich betrachtet, nicht genau so unwürdig anmutet.[6]
Deshalb beziehen die Verteidiger der letzten Übersetzung fast immer
was in den VV. 25-27 über Christus und die Kirche gesagt wurde in
den Vergleich mit hinein, auch wenn sie mit V. 28 einen neuen
Gedanken beginnen lassen. So z.B. FEUILLET, der in Nachfolge von
SCHLIER mit V. 28 "un troisième développement" beginnen lässt, aber
trotzdem den Vergleich ausdehnt auf Christus und die Kirche : "tout
comme le Christ a aimé l'Église qui est son Corps".[7] Damit wird aber
zugegeben, dass mit V. 28 eigentlich kein neuer Abschnitt beginnt,
sondern der Gedanke aus VV. 25-27 fortgesetzt wird und dass οὕτως
nicht nur mit dem folgenden ὡς sondern wenigstens auch mit καθώς
aus V. 25 zu verbinden ist. Ähnlich urteilt GNILKA : "Obwohl die Rede
vom Leib bereits auf das Genesiswort in V. 31 Rücksicht nimmt und
V. 28 somit nach vorn orientiert ist und einen gedanklichen Fortschritt
bezeichnet, ist das, was über Christus und die Kirche in den VV. 25-27
gesagt wurde, in den Vergleich miteinzuschliessen".[8]

Wenn aber auch bei einer bloss vergleichenden Übersetzung das
Christus-Ekklesia-Verhältnis miteinbezogen werden muss, gibt es keinen Grund mehr den begründenden Sinn als der Frau unwürdig
auszuschliessen. Das eigentliche Motiv für die Ehemänner ihre Frauen
zu lieben ist dann das Beispiel Christi und der ὡς-Satz enthält nicht
eine neue Aufforderung sondern eine Feststellung.[9] Und auch diese

---

[5] A. FEUILLET, La dignité et le rôle de la femme d'après quelques textes pauliniens,
NTS 21 (1974/75), 157-191 (173f.).

[6] Die Übersetzung "als" kann schliesslich auch nur bildlich gemeint sein : "als
wären sie ihre Leiber"; vgl. DIBELIUS (94); EWALD (238).

[7] *A.a.O.* (Anm. 5).

[8] GNILKA, *o.c.*, 283; ähnlich : ABBOTT (171); BARTH, *o.c.*, 630; EWALD (238); u.s.w.

[9] SCHLIER, *o.c.* 260.

Feststellung wird in V. 29c wieder christlich gedeutet. Tatsächlich schwingt die begründende Nuance in einem paränetischen Text fast immer etwas mit. Wenn man nämlich ein Beispiel erwähnt, hält man es auch als Motiv vor.[10] So auch hier, denn der Verfasser fährt fort : "Wer seine Frau liebt, liebt sich selbst".[11] Damit will er doch wohl mit einer vielleicht sprichwörtlichen Redensart das eben Gesagte bestätigen.[12] Der begründende Sinn kann bloss ausgeschlossen werden, wenn bewiesen ist, dass es hier nicht um die Liebe überhaupt, sondern um die Art und Weise des Liebens geht. In dieser Weise deutet EWALD das καθώς in V. 25, weil dort beschrieben wird, *wie* der Christus die Kirche geliebt hat, nämlich indem er sie heiligte und reinigte.[13] Aber gerade in dieser Hinsicht hinkt der Vergleich, denn kein Ehemann ist dazu imstande.

Ich glaube übrigens wohl, dass SCHLIER recht hat, wenn er in V. 28 den Schwerpunkt auf den vergleichenden Sinn legt. Das geht erstens aus einem Vergleich mit V. 33 hervor (οὕτως...ὡς) und weiter meine ich mit SAMPLEY, dass V. 28 (wie auch V. 33) eine deutliche Anspielung enthält auf das vielzitierte Liebesgebot (Lev. xix 8; vgl. Mt. xix 19; xxii 39; Mk. xii 31. 33; Lk. x 27; Röm. xiii 9; Gal. v 14; Jak. ii 8).[14] Der begründende Sinn ist höchstens sekundär. Man wird etwa umschreiben müssen : "So müssen auch die Männer ihre Frauen lieben wie ihre eigenen Leiber. (Das sind sie eigentlich auch, denn so heisst es doch :) Wer seine Frau liebt, liebt sich selbst".

2. *V. 25b : Vordersatz oder Nachsatz?*

Es ist klar, dass diese Argumentation, wer seine Frau liebt, liebt sich selbst, deutlich nicht-christlich ist. Schon von einer ausserehelichen Verbindung sagt Paulus : "Wisst ihr nicht, dass wer an einer Dirne hängt, eines Leibes ist?" (1 Kor. vi 16). Und das alttestamentliche Verbot einer Verbindung zwischen Blutsverwandten, z.B. zwischen dem Sohn und seiner Mutter, wird begründet mit "sie ist deines Vaters

---

[10] A. SCHULZ, *Nachfolgen und Nachahmen*, München 1962, redet hier von "Vorbildparänese". Vgl. R. A. BATEY, *New Testament Nuptial Imagery*, Leiden 1971, 30f. : der Mann soll seine Frau lieben *wie* sich selbst, *weil* (as being) sie sein Leib ist.

[11] NESTLE erwähnt eine Konjektur von P. SCHMIEDEL, der diesen Halbsatz (V. 28b) streichen möchte. Eine solche Konjektur, die von keiner Handschrift gestützt wird, ist im Grunde ein *testimonium paupertatis* des Verfassers.

[12] SCHLIER, *o.c.*, 260; EWALD (238).

[13] EWALD (235); vgl. W. SCHRAGE, Zur Ethik der neutestamentlichen Haustafeln, *NTS* 21 (1974/75), 1-22 (18, Anm. 4).

[14] J. P. SAMPLEY, *"And the Two Shall Become One Flesh"*, Cambridge 1971, 141.

Fleisch" (Lev. xviii 8). Sir xxv 26 sagt von einer schlechten Frau : "Geht sie nicht an deiner Seite, trenn sie ab von deinem Leibe". Will man also den christlichen Charakter dieser Aufforderung sicherstellen, dann ist man gezwungen den in V. 28 angestellten Vergleich nicht als auf sich beruhend zu betrachten sondern ihn in Zusammenhang zu sehen mit dem was in den VV. 25-27 über die Kirche als Leib Christi gesagt wurde. Die Lehre vom Leib Christi steht ja zentral im Epheserbrief und wird im unmittelbaren Zusammenhang erwähnt (V. 23). Das kann der Verfasser nicht auf einmal vergessen haben.[15] Nicht umsonst sagt er, dass die Männer ihre Frauen lieben sollen wie ihre *Leiber* und nicht "wie sich selbst", wie es am Schluss des Verses und in V. 33 lautet.

Rein grammatikalisch betrachtet könnte das οὕτως ohne Beziehung aufs Vorige direkt mit dem folgenden ὡς verbunden werden, obwohl sich die asyndetische Verbindung schwer rechtfertigen lässt.[16] In diesem Falle würde aber der ὡς-Satz parallel stehen zu καθώς in V. 25a und die Motivierung würde im Vergleich zum ersten Satz seltsam kurz und profan erscheinen.[17] In der ganzen Mahnung ist immer die Beziehung zwischen Christus und der Kirche Prototyp für das Verhältnis zwischen Mann und Frau (V. 23 und 24). Dasselbe Schema wird deshalb auch hier vorliegen.[18] Charakteristisch für die christlichen Haustafeln ist eben, dass die Christuswirklichkeit und nicht der irdische Tatbestand zur Illustration der religiösen Wirklichkeit dient.[19] Richtig wird deshalb von EWALD der ganze Satz auf das Vorangehende bezogen : "Wie Christus die Gemeinde als seinen Leib ansah und ihr seine Liebe erwies, so sollen auch die Männer die zu ihnen gehörenden Frauen als die zu ihnen gehörenden Leiber ansehen".[20] D.h. also : ὡς hat grammatikalisch mit dem vorhergehenden οὕτως nichts zu tun, sondern gehört als Komplement zu αγαπᾶν. Ein analoger Fall findet sich in 1 Kor. iv 1. Auch dort fasst οὕτως das Vorhergehende zusammen und ist ὡς als Komplement zu λογίζεσθαι zu betrachten.[21]

---

[15] GNILKA, *o.c.*, 283.

[16] So übersetzen ESTIUS und ALFORD (ABBOTT 170).

[17] "Only if *kai* were placed before *sōmata*, would this verse clearly affirm that husbands must love their wives as (or because) they 'love also their bodies'" (BARTH, *o.c.*, 630).

[18] E. D. ROELS, *God's Mission : The Epistle to the Ephesians in Mission Perspective*, Franeker 1962, 143.

[19] K. WEIDINGER, *Die Haustafeln*, Leipzig 1928, 60.

[20] EWALD (238).

[21] H. CONZELMANN, *Der erste Brief an die Korinther* (KEK), Göttingen 1969, 101 Anm. 1. Vgl. 2Kor. x 2.

Unsere vorläufige Schlussfolgerung lautet : οὕτως in Eph. v 28a ist auf keinen Fall mit dem folgenden ὡς zu verbinden. Entweder steht es asyndetisch als Schlussfolgerung zu VV. 25-27, oder es korrespondiert mit καθώς in V. 25b. Die letzte Möglichkeit ist, soweit ich sehe, bis jetzt von keinem Übersetzer benutzt worden.[22] Das ist um so merkwürdiger, weil die meisten Kommentare das οὕτως inhaltlich wenigstens auch auf die vorhergehenden Verse beziehen.[23] In meinem Kommentar zum Epheserbrief habe ich erstmals diese Lösung vorgeschlagen.[24] Ich war damals nicht in der Lage die neue Übersetzung ausführlich zu verantworten. Dieser Versäumnis soll hier abgeholfen werden.

Man wird zugeben müssen, dass die vorgeschlagene Verbindung zumindest theoretisch möglich ist. Es entsteht in dieser Weise sogar ein schönes symmetrisches Satzgefüge : ὡς-οὕτως : καθώς-οὕτως. Inhaltlich sind so die Mahnungen an Frauen und Männer gleichfalls symmetrisch gebaut, wie es BALTENSWEILER gezeigt hat :

1. Die Aufforderung (V. 22 und 25a).
2. Die christologische Begründung (V. 23 und 25b-27).
3. Die Folgerung (V. 24 und 28a).[25]

Die einzige Schwierigkeit bildet V. 25a; der Satz ist in diesem Fall wie eine Art Überschrift über die nachfolgenden Ermahnungen zu denken. Bedenkt man, dass die Haustafel des Epheserbriefes die des Kolosserbriefes sehr wahrscheinlich als Vorlage benutzt hat, und dass der betreffende Satzteil exakt mit Kol. iii 19 übereinstimmt, dann lässt sich diese Schwierigkeit leicht beseitigen. In ähnlicher Weise fängt der Verfasser in vi 2 mit einem neuen Satz an, nachdem er in V. 1 Kol. iii 20 fast wörtlich übernommen hat.[26] Man soll dabei bedenken, dass die VV. 25b-27 stark liturgisch geprägt sind.[27] Zumal das παρέδω-

---

[22] Der Einzige, der m.W. οὕτως als Apodosis zu καθώς betrachtet, ist CAMBIER; vgl. J. CAMBIER, Le grand mystère concernant le Christ et son Église, Éphésiens 5, 22-33, Bib 47 (1966), 43-90; 223-242 (60f.). Er arbeitet den Gedanken aber nicht weiter aus. KAHLEFELD setzt einen Gedankenstrich hinter V. 25a, aber hat trotzdem einen Punkt hinter V. 27; vgl. H. KAHLEFELD, Wie wird in der Perikope Eph. 5, 22-33 über das eheliche Leben gesprochen, KatBl 91 (1966), 185-192 (190).

[23] Vgl. Anm. 7f.; weiter : ABBOTT (170); HUBY (241); KNABENBAUER (156); SCHLIER, o.c., 260; u.s.w.

[24] G. BOUWMAN, De brief aan de Efeziërs, Bussum 1974, 141f.

[25] H. BALTENSWEILER, Die Ehe im Neuen Testament, Zürich/Stuttgart 1967, 220.

[26] Auch v 21 ist als allgemein einleitendes Gebot der Ermahnung vorangestellt; vgl. E. KAMLAH, Ὑποτάσσεσθαι in den neutestamentlichen "Haustafeln", in : Verborum Veritas (Festschrift für G. Stählin), Wuppertal 1970, 237-243 (237).

[27] BALTENSWEILER, o.c., 226.

κεν weist auf eine liturgische Vorlage hin.[28] Markus BARTH meint
sogar, dass die VV. 25b-27 ein Zitat sind und καθὼς καὶ als Einleitungs-
formel zu betrachten sei (just as [we confess]).[29] Soweit möchte ich
nicht gehen, denn es gibt m.W. kein einziges Beispiel eines Zitats, das
eingeleitet wird mit καθώς ohne γέγραπται oder Ähnliches. Ausserdem
würde man dann eher διὸ λέγει erwarten wie in iv 8 und v 14. Ein
implizites Zitat wie in ii 17; iv 25 und v 2 könnte allerdings wohl vorliegen. Tatsächlich finden sich hier Ausdrücke, denen man sonst nir-
gendwo begegnet : nur hier wird gesagt, dass der Christus die Ekklesia
geliebt hat. Weitere hapax legomena sind : Bad des Wassers; Flecken
noch Runzel. Zuzugeben ist auch, dass der Gedanke, obwohl in sich
geschlossen, nicht ganz in den Zusammenhang passt. In den VV. 22-
24 und 28-32 erscheint die Kirche als Ehefrau, hier aber als Braut
Christi.[30] Möglich ist ein vorchristliches Brautlied zu einem "Hieros
Gamos" christlich umgeprägt und hier vom Verfasser übernommen
worden.[31] Das würde dann auch das καί nach καθώς in V. 25b aus-
reichend erklären. Man könnte dann etwa wie folgt umschreiben :
"Wie ja auch bekanntlich der Christus..." (vgl. 1 Kor. xiv 34). Jedenfalls besagt dieses καί nicht notwendig, dass V. 25b ein Nachsatz ist.
Es kann nämlich auch in beiden Gliedern einer Vergleichung stehen
wie z.B. in Röm. i 13; Kol. iii 13 und 1 Thess. ii 14.[32] Es hat in diesem
Falle emphatische Bedeutung.[33] Wir können also die beiden Möglichkeiten unbevorurteilt untersuchen : V. 25b (καθὼς καὶ...) ist entweder
Nachsatz zu 25a oder Vordersatz zu V. 28.

3. Textkritische Frage : das καί in V. 28

Nach GNILKA wäre der Bezug von οὕτως auf VV. 25-27 sicherer, wenn
das textlich umstrittene καί zum Text gehörte.[34] Für ABBOTT ist dieser
Bezug sogar der einzig mögliche, wenn καί gelesen wird.[35] Zuerst wäre

---

[28] N. PERRIN, The Use of (παρα)διδόναι in Connection with the Passion of Jesus
in the New Testament, in: Der Ruf Jesu und die Antwort der Gemeinde (Festschrift
J. Jeremias), Göttingen 1970, 204-212 (212); K. WENGST, Christologische Formeln und
Lieder des Urchristentums, Gütersloh 1972, 58.

[29] M. BARTH, o.c. II, 607.622.

[30] F. J. STEINMETZ, Protologische Heils-Zuversicht: Die Strukturen des soteriolog-
ischen und christologischen Denkens im Kolosser- und Epheserbrief, Frankfurt am Main,
1969, 92.

[31] N. A. DAHL, Das Volk Gottes, Darmstadt ²1963, 260. Jedenfalls muss das
Thema den Lesern vertraut gewesen sein, denn es wird nicht als Lehrstück geboten.

[32] BLASS-DEBRUNNER 453,1; BAUER (s.v. II, 3).

[33] SAMPLEY, o.c., 127.

[34] GNILKA, o.c., 283, Anm. 5.

[35] ABBOTT (170).

also hier die textkritische Frage zu untersuchen. Das καί fehlt im
Sinaiticus, in der *Koine*-Text und in der Peschitta. Es wird von NESTLE
und VOGELS in eckigen Klammern eingeschlossen.[36] Grund dessen ist
wohl, dass TISCHENDORF hier wie immer dem von ihm entdeckten
Codex Sinaiticus den Vorrang verleiht. Zwar sind die Textzeugen die
das καί haben unter einander uneinig über dessen Stellung. Entweder
liest man mit P[46], B und 33 οὕτως ὀφείλουσιν καί u.s.w., oder mit
ADG lat und Clem. Alex. οὕτως καί οἱ ἄνδρες u.s.w. Die letzte Lesart
ist wohl als Korrektur zu betrachten: Verb und Infinitiv werden
zusammengerückt. Diese Lesung könnte auch von der Exegese beein-
flusst sein, wie später zu zeigen ist. Man hat m.E. die Lesart mit καί,
die von weithin den meisten Handschriften bezeugt wird, als die beste
zu betrachten. Sie wird ohne weiteres bevorzugt von ALAND, BLACK,
METZGER und WIKGREN in *The Greek New Testament* und wird deshalb
auch wohl von ALAND in seiner 26. Auflage aufgenommen werden.[37]

Wie wenig konsequent die Wahl der Herausgeber in ähnlichen
Fällen ist, möge aus einigen Beispielen hervorgehen. In Mt. xxiv 39
wählt NESTLE (οὕτως)...καί obwohl das καί fehlt in BD it syr[sp] und
von WESTCOTT/HORT nicht aufgenommen worden ist, angeblich, weil
für sie der Vaticanus massgebend ist. Hier verwendet *GNT* eckige
Klammern, NESTLE aber nicht. In Lk. xxiv fehlt (καθὼς) καί in P[75] BD
lat syr und wird wiederum von WESTCOTT/HORT weggelassen. Hier
haben sowohl *GNT* als NESTLE/ALAND (26. Aufl.) das καί beibehalten.[38]
In Röm. v 15 schliesslich wird (οὕτως) καί von NESTLE eingeklammert,
weil es von WEISS weggelassen wird, während TISCHENDORF es (mit
der Rezension des Hesychius, Koine DG pl) beibehält.

Wir betrachten die Lesart mit καί und zwar nach ὀφείλουσιν also
als gesichert. Die Stellung ist nicht unwichtig. Ein absolut gebrauchtes
οὕτως καί am Anfang, das sich inhaltlich auf das Vorhergehende
bezieht, grammatikalisch aber selbständig ist, findet sich öfters im
N.T. Aber καί steht in diesem Fall, soweit ich sehe, immer unmittelbar
hinter οὕτως; z.B. Mt. xviii 35; xxiii 15; xxiv 33; Mk. vii 18; xiii 29;

---

[36] Vgl. die NBG-Übersetzung: "Zo zijn [ook] de mannen...".

[37] So u.A. ABBOTT, BARTH, GROSHEIDE; die Herausgeber BOVER, MERK, WEISS.
Viele Autoren erwähnen die Variante nicht einmal. Nach EWALD (237, Anm. 4) ist die
omissio wahrscheinlich ursprünglich. GNILKA hält es für wahrscheinlich, dass καί ge-
strichen wurde um den Gedanken zu vermeiden, dass Christus der Kirche Liebe
schulde.

[38] Vgl. den Überblick bei K. ALAND, Der heutige Text des griechischen Neuen
Testaments, in: *Studien zur Überlieferung des N.T. und seines Textes*, Berlin 1967,
58-80 (68). WESTCOTT/HORT folgt hier wiederum Kodex B.

Lk. xvii 10; xxi 31; Röm. vi 11; xi 5; 1 Kor. ix 14; xiv 9.12; xv 42.[39] Wenn dagegen οὕτως auf einem vorhergehenden καθώς, ὥσπερ, ὡς oder καθάπερ folgt, werden οὕτως und καί öfters vom Verb getrennt; z.B. Mt. xxiv 39 (s. oben); Lk. xi 30; xvii 26; Röm. v 15 (s. oben); 2 Kor. i 5.

4. Stilistische Untersuchung

Betrachten wir jetzt den Gebrauch von καθώς an sich, so lässt sich das folgende Gesetz feststellen: enthält der Satz einen Imperativ oder eine ähnliche Aufforderung (imperativischen Infinitiv; Umschreibung mit ἵνα u.s.w.), dann steht der kausal-komparative Satz mit καθώς (resp. ὥσπερ, ὡς) als Nachsatz. Beispiele sind: Mt. v 48; vi 10; xviii 33; Lk. vi 36; xi 1; Joh. xiii 34; xv 12; xvii 11.21.22; Röm. xv 7; 1Kor. v 7; x 6.7.8.9.33; xi 1; xiv 34; 2Kor. i 14; Eph. iv 17.32; v 1.2; v 25 (?); Kol. i 7; Hebr. v 4; Jak. ii 12.[40] Ausnahmen sind, soweit ich sehe: Joh. xiii 15; 1Kor. vii 17; Kol. iii 13; Hebr. v 3; 1Joh. ii 6.27. Dabei sind Joh. xiii 15; 1Kor. vii 17; Hebr. v 3; 1Joh. ii 6.27 nur scheinbare Ausnahmen, weil der καθώς-Satz proleptisch konstruiert ist. So lautet Joh. xiii 15 eigentlich: ἵνα (καὶ ὑμεῖς ποιῆτε), καθὼς κτλ.[41] Kol. iii 13 ist für uns ein sehr interessanter Fall. SCHULZ rechnet diesen Vers zum normalen Schema, wobei der (implizite) Imperativ χαριζόμενοι vorangeht.[42] Die Ellipse οὕτως καὶ ὑμεῖς ist dann als selbständiger Satz zu betrachten. So interpretierte der Verfasser des Epheserbriefes (vgl. Eph. iv 32) und die Wiederholung des Verbs χαρίζεσθαι ist eine Hinweisung in dieselbe Richtung.[43] Übersetzer und Herausgeber verbinden aber mit Recht καθώς mit οὕτως. Wir begegnen hier also einer Parallele mit Eph. v 25-28, wo allerdings die Übersetzer für ein selbständiges οὕτως wählen.

SCHULZ erwähnt ausserdem noch als Ausnahmen: Joh. xiii 14; 1Joh. iii 16; iv 11. Hier geht ein Konditionalsatz voraus (in 1Joh. iii

---

[39] Die Vertreter der Lesart von ADG u.s.w. haben wahrscheinlich das οὕτως als absolut betrachtet.

[40] SCHULZ, o.c., 303. Der Verf. beschränkt sich auf die Vorbildparänese. So erwähnt er Eph. iv 17 nicht, weil dort nicht vom vorbildlichen Tun Gottes oder Christi die Rede ist. Andrerseits rechnet er Sätze, wie 1 Joh. iii 3.7; iv 17 zur Vorbildparänese.

[41] Hierzu ist auch die mit κατά konstruierte Vorbildparänese 1 Petr. i 15, die SCHULZ als Ausnahme betrachtet, zu rechnen.

[42] Zur Verwendung des Partizips in imperativischer Bedeutung, vgl. BLASS-DEBRUNNER, 468, 2; W. D. DAVIES, *Paul and Rabbinic Judaism*, London ³1970, 328; E. LOHSE, Paränese und Kerygma im 1. Petrusbrief, *ZNW* 45 (1954), 68-89 (75) = *Die Einheit des NT*, Göttingen 1973, 307-328 (314).

[43] S. unten. Übrigens wäre natürlich die Ellipse mit demselben Wort zu ergänzen.

16 implizite), der einem begründenden "da" sehr nahe kommt,[44] und stets wird dabei das für Johannes eigentümliche ὀφείλομεν verwendet. Die vergleichende Bedeutung tritt in diesen Bedingungssätzen nicht hervor. Vielleicht dürfen wir daraus eine vorsichtige Schlussfolgerung ziehen. Wenn in paränetischen Sätzen der Nebensatz mit καθώς u.s.w. nach vorn gerückt wird, so geschieht das, um die begründende Bedeutung hervorzuhcben.[45] Überwiegt dagegen der Beispielcharakter des Satzes, wie z.B. in Joh. xvii 22, dann wird der Vergleich nachgestellt. Meistens wird dabei der vergleichende Nebensatz dem Hauptsatz nach Form und Inhalt nachgebildet, wie z.B. in Eph. iv 17.32. Zu diesen Beispielen würde sich nun auch Eph. v 25 gesellen, wenn wir die herkömmliche Interpretation übernehmen. Der Satz könnte sogar als klassisches Beispiel gelten : ein Imperativ wird gefolgt von einem komparativ-kausalen καθώς-Satz, der genau parallel aufgebaut ist.[46] In der von uns vorgeschlagenen Exegese dagegen würde Eph. v 25b-28 zu den Ausnahmen gehören, weil der imperativische Satz (ὀφείλουσιν) nachsteht.

Dabei ist aber zu bedenken, dass von einem wirklichen Vergleich nicht die Rede sein kann. Kein Mann kann behaupten, dass er seine Braut geheiligt und gereinigt hat.[47] Dazu kommt noch, wie schon gesagt, dass der Vergleich nicht stimmt, weil hier von einem Brautsverhältnis die Rede ist. Also muss der begründende Sinn überwiegend sein, und in diesem Fall kann, wie wir sahen der καθώς-Satz vorweggenommen werden. Zudem ist V. 28a kein eigentlicher Imperativ. Die Männer werden nicht angeredet wie in V. 25a. Der Satz ist eher eine Feststellung, zu vergleichen mit Joh. iii 14 oder Apg. xxiii 11, wo in ähnlicher Weise δεῖ verwendet wird. Von einer Ausnahme kann also kaum die Rede sein. Wohl kann man feststellen, dass die herkömmliche Exegese exakt mit der Regel übereinstimmt, nicht aber, dass unser Vorschlag gegen sie sündigt.

---

[44] BLASS-DEBRUNNER, 372, 1.

[45] In seinem *Johannine Grammar* (London 1906, No 2122) nennt ABBOTT diesen καθώς-Satz "suspensiv", die umgekehrte Stellung nennt er "explikativ" oder "supplementär".

[46] A. VAN ROON, *Een onderzoek naar de authenticiteit van de brief aan de Epheziërs*, Delft 1969, 100 gibt gerade Eph. v 25 als klassisches Beispiel.

[47] Vgl. K. BARTH, *K.D.* III/4. 195 : "Das Urbild der Liebe, in der Jesus Christus seine Gemeinde geliebt hat und noch liebt, wie es V. 25-27 beschrieben wird ..., ist einmalig, einzigartig, unwiederholbar, unnachahmbar".

Andererseits lässt sich die hier vorgeschlagene Lösung durch viele Beispiele belegen. Untersucht man nämlich mit Hilfe einer Konkordanz die Verbindung καθώς (ὥσπερ, ὡς) ... οὕτως, so stellt sich heraus, dass dabei der καθώς-Satz fast immer vorangeht. In der Konkordanz von MOULTON/GEDEN sind diese Verbindungen unter dem Stichwort οὕτως mit einem (3) vermerkt.[48] Von den 56 von mir gezählten Beispielen, wobei Eph. v 25-28 nicht mitgezählt wurde, wohl aber v 28, gibt es nur 13 Stellen, wo οὕτως vorangeht: Mk. iv 26; Lk. xxiv 24; Joh. vii 46; Apg. i 11; 1Kor. iii 15; iv 1; ix 26(bis); 2Kor. ix 5; Eph. v 28.33; Phil. iii 17; Jak. ii 12. BAUER erwähnt noch Röm. xi 26, aber dort bezieht sich οὕτως nicht auf das folgende καθώς, sondern weist zurück auf das Vorhergehende, während das übliche καθὼς γέγραπται das Ganze abschliesst.[49] Weiter nennt er noch Joh. iii 16 und Apg. xiv 1, wo aber ὥστε als konsekutiver Partikel zu betrachten ist (derart dass). Von den oben genannten 13 Stellen scheiden 1Kor. iv 1 und Eph. v 28 ohne weiteres aus, weil das ὡς wie oben gezeigt wurde, dort nicht auf οὕτως zurückweist, sondern unmittelbar mit dem Verb zu verbinden ist. Auch Phil iii 17, sowohl von BAUER als von MOULTON/GEDEN erwähnt, ist wohl zu streichen, weil οὕτω das folgende Partizip bestimmt.[50] Von den restlichen zehn Stellen ist Folgendes zu sagen. In Mk iv 26 ist οὕτως prädikativ gebraucht.[51] In allen übrigen Fällen wird οὕτως unmittelbar mit ὡς verbunden (Lk xiv 24; 1Kor iii 15; 2Kor ix 5) oder durch bloss *ein* Wort (meistens ein Verb) davon getrennt, wie z.B. in Eph v 33. In diesem Fall hat οὕτως nur emphatische Bedeutung. Die Übersetzungen schwanken denn auch zwischen 'ebenso wie', 'so wie' oder einfach 'wie'. Man

---

[48] Zusätzlich nennt BAUER noch Joh. vii 46; Hebr. ix 27f (καθ'ὅσον); sowie Apg. i 11 und 2Tim. iii 8 (ὃν τρόπον).

[49] Vgl. P. STUHLMACHER, Zur Interpretation von Römer xi 25-32, in: *Probleme biblischer Theologie* (Festschrift für G. von Rad), München 1971, 555-570 (560). Der Verf. behauptet mit Recht, dass Röm. xi 26 eine heilsgeschichtliche Ordnung feststellt. Aber damit ist noch nicht gesagt, dass καθώς mit οὕτως korrespondiere. Οὕτως hat hier temporalen Sinn (und dann) wie in Apg. xvii 33; xx 11. Vgl. E. KÄSEMANN, *An die Römer*, Tübingen 1974, 303. Dasselbe gilt mutatis mutandis von Röm. xv 20f.

[50] Vgl. G. BOUWMAN, *De brief van Paulus aan de Filippiërs*, Roermond/Maaseik 1965, 89. Wenn οὕτω mit καθώς korrespondierte, würde man ἔχουσι statt ἔχετε erwarten. Das οὕτω bezieht sich nicht auf das Beispiel des Paulus sondern auf V. 16. So GNILKA, *Der Philipperbrief*, Freiburg, u.s.w. 1968, 203 mit Hinweis auf BEARE, DIBELIUS, und H. D. BETZ, *Nachfolge und Nachahmung Jesu Christi im NT*, Tübingen 1967, 151. Anders: H. LJUNGVIK, Zum Gebrauch einiger Adverbien im NT, *Eranos* 62 (1964), 26-39 (35f.).

[51] Vgl. BLASS-DEBRUNNER 434, 1; Joh. vi 58; Phlm. 9.

kann also sagen, dass bei der Verbindung der Nebensatz praktisch immer vorangeht. Damit ist zwar die Richtigkeit unserer Hypothese nicht bewiesen, aber ihr Möglichkeit doch reichlich gesichert.

Es wäre jetzt eigentlich noch zu untersuchen, warum bei der Verbindung mit οὕτως der καθώς-Satz fast immer vorangeht. Ein Schriftzitat, eingeleitet mit καθώς geht z.B. immer nach (vgl. Joh xii 14). Der Grund ist vielleicht darin zu suchen, dass die christliche Gemeinde die Prophezeiung erst entdeckt, *nachdem* sie erfüllt ist. Sobald aber ein οὕτως dazu kommt, wird dieses Gesetz aufgehoben und geht die Weissagung voran: 'Sowie Moses in der Wüste die Schlange erhöhte, so (οὕτως) muss der Menschensohn erhöht werden' (Joh iii 14; vgl. Mt xii 40; Lk xi 30; xvii 26; u.s.w.). Wahrscheinlich wird hier die oben geäusserte Vermutung bestätigt: Wenn der Verfasser sagen will, dass etwas so geschehen musste, *weil* es vorhergesagt wurde und der begründende Sinn also überwiegend ist, so geht der καθώς-Satz voran. Wenn dagegen das Schriftzitat nur sagen will, weshalb es so und nicht anders geschehen sollte und die vergleichende Bedeutung stärker ist, folgt der Nebensatz mit καθώς. Vielleicht könnte eine strukturelle Untersuchung, wie sie etwa DINECHIN für das johanneische Schrifttum angestellt hat, hier mehr Klarheit bringen,[52] aber dafür fehlt der Raum. Für unseren Zweck, nämlich eine alternative Übersetzung von Eph v 28, dürfte eine grammatikalische Analyse, wie wir sie oben versucht haben, ausreichen.

Schlussfolgerung

Ziehen wir also das Fazit! Die traditionelle Übersetzung, die Eph v 25b als Nachsatz betrachtet und mit οὕτως in V. 28 einen neuen Satz beginnen lässt, kann sich auf einem Gesetz stützen, das kaum Ausnahmen kennt: Bei einem imperativischen Satz steht der Nebensatz mit καθώς an zweiter Stelle. Die von uns vorgeschlagene Übersetzung, wobei V. 25b Vordersatz zu V. 28 ist, stützt sich aber auf einem Gesetz, das genau so ausnahmslos und weithin besser belegt ist: bei der Verbindung mit οὕτως geht der καθώς-Satz voran. Die philologischen Argumente halten einander also mehr oder weniger im Gleichgewicht. In diesem Fall wird die Exegese entscheiden müssen. Wir haben gesehen, dass die Mehrheit der Exegete zwar mit V. 28 einen neuen Gedanken beginnen lässt, aber diesen Vers trotzdem

---

[52] O. DE DINECHIN, ΚΑΘΩΣ : La similitude dans l'évangile selon saint Jean, *RSR* 58 (1970), 195-236 (197).

gedanklich mit dem vorhergehenden verbindet, weil sich nur so sagen lässt, dass die Männer ihre Frauen lieben müssen wie ihre eigenen Leiber. "Aus dem Beispiel der Liebe Christi, der sich für die Kirche in den Tod hingegeben und sie im Taufbad geheiligt hat, sollen die Männer lernen ihre Frauen als ihre eigenen Leiber (σῶμα!) zu lieben".[53] Wenn es aber möglich ist die Übersetzung mit dieser Exegese in Einklang zu bringen, soll man m.E. eine solche Übersetzung bevorzugen. Ich glaube in dieser kurzen Notiz genügend Materialien herangetragen zu haben, um die Übersetzer in der Zukunft zu einer neuen Untersuchung einzuladen. Damit wäre dann zugleich die vielumstrittene Frage, ob ὡς in v. 28 vergleichenden oder begründenden Sinn hat, wenn nicht entgültig gelöst, doch wenigstens zu einer unbedeutenden Nebenfrage herabgesetzt.

---

[53] F. MUSSNER, *Christus, das All und die Kirche, Studien zur Theologie des Epheserbriefes*, Trier [2]1968, 154.

DIE ZAHL DES TIERES, DIE ZAHL EINES MENSCHEN

Apokalypse xiii 18

L. VAN HARTINGSVELD

"Die Geheimschrift, die der eine erfindet, kann der andere entziffern." Die Geschichte der Exegese der Stelle Apok. xiii 18. zeigt aber, dass diese Aussage von SHERLOCK HOLMES [1] nicht immer zutrifft. Schon IRENÄUS wusste nicht mehr, wer mit der Zahl 666 gemeint war. Ausserdem habe Johannes auch nicht die Absicht gehabt, den Namen des Antichrist zu offenbaren. [2]

Man könnte der Auffassung sein, dass es nicht wichtig sei, wer oder was hinter dieser Zahl versteckt sei und erklären, dass nur weniges verloren wäre, wenn das Geheimnis verborgen bliebe. [3] Dennoch liegt hier ein neutestamentliches Problem vor. Die Lösung würde allerhand sinnlose Auslegungen entkräften. Katholiken dachten bei 666 an Martin Luther, Protestanten an den Papst. Im zweiten Weltkrieg suchte man so lange, bis man Hitler oder Churchill herausgelesen hatte. Sogar die Gegner der vorgeschriebenen Kuhpockenimpfung haben sich auf die Zahl des Tieres berufen, zum Beleg dafür, dass dieses Gesetz teuflischen Ursprungs sei. [4]

Es handelt sich in Apok. xiii 17.18. um den Namen des Tieres. Da im Hebräischen und Griechischen die Buchstaben einen bestimmten Zahlenwert haben (A = 1, B = 2, C = 3 u.s.w., א = 1, ב = 2, ג = 3 u.s.w.), [5] kann man diesen Namen durch seine Zahl ersetzen. Diese sogenannte Gematrie war ein beliebtes Rätselspiel. Nun ist es leicht die Summe eines Namens zu berechnen, schwer ist es aber, aus der Summe auf den Namen zu schliessen. Ein bekanntes Beispiel ist die

---

[1] "Het geheimschrift, dat de een uitvindt, kan de ander ontcijferen". Angeführt aus dem sehr lesenswerten Aufsatz eines nicht genannten Autors "Het geheim der geheimschriften", *Op den Uitkijk* (christ. cult. maandblad) no. 1, Oct. 1955, 32.

[2] Eduard SCHWARTZ, *Eusebius Kirchengeschichte*, Kleine Ausgabe Leipzig [4]1932: v 8, 6.

[3] "Little would be lost, if the cipher were insoluble". M. KIDDLE, *The Revelation of St John* (MNTC), London 1940, 261.

[4] Die Summe der numerischen Werte der griechischen Buchstaben des fingierten Wortes κουποκς (20 + 70 + 400 + 80 + 70 + 20 + 6) ergibt gerade 666. M. H. A. VAN DER VALK, *666*, Schoonhoven 1925, 25.

[5] Eine Liste kann man in den Sprachlehren finden.

Inschrift auf einer pompejischen Mauer: φιλω ἧς ἀριθμος φμε.[6] Ich
liebe (die Frau), deren Zahl 500 + 40 + 5 = 545 ist. Mehrere Namen
weisen die gleiche Zahl auf, und das ist eben die Schwierigkeit. Deshalb
ist "Verstand" vonnöten, den richtigen Namen zu erraten.

In Apok. xiii 17.18. ist die Zahl des Tieres die Zahl eines Menschen.
Die Aufgabe ist zu erforschen, welche Person mit 666 (oder 616) be-
zeichnet worden ist. Damit ist uns ein Massstab an die Hand gegeben
Lösungen zu prüfen. Was etwas anderes als einen Menschen von
Fleisch und Blut ergibt, ist auszuscheiden. Folgende Vorschläge können
vor der Kritik nicht bestehen:

H. GUNKEL hebt in seiner religionsgeschichtlichen Untersuchung von
Genesis i und Apokalypse xii besonders hervor, dass am Ende der
Anfang wiederkehrt: die Schöpfung, das Paradies, die Schlange, das
Gericht. Die letzten Dinge entsprechen den ersten Dingen. Auch das
Chaos erscheint wieder. Folglich ist die Zahl 666 Tiamat, das Meerunge-
heuer aus der Urzeit תְּהוֹם קַדְמוֹנִיָה[7] (400+5+6+40) + (100+4+40+
6 + 50 + 10 + 5) = 666.

A. DEISSMANN sieht einen Zusammenhang mit dem Anspruch des
römischen Kaisers auf göttliche Ehre. Zweifelsohne ist das Haupt-
thema der Apokalypse der Konflikt zwischen Kirche und Staat. Der
Satz καισαρ θεος[8] = (20+1+10+200+1+100) + (9+5+70+
200) = 616 passt ausgezeichnet zu der Anmassung des Kaisers, stimmt
aber nicht zu der Bedingung, dass 666 (616) die Zahl eines Menschen
sein soll.

E. B. ALLO geht von der Formel aus, dass 6 = 7—1. Sieben ist die
heilige Zahl, die die Vollkommenheit darstellt. Das Tier habe zwar
eine grosse Macht, nicht aber die Allmacht, die Gott sich selbst
vorbehalten habe.[9] In gleichen Sinne denkt auch S. GREIJDANUS. Gott
schuf die Welt in sechs Tagen. Am siebenten Tage ruhte er von seinem
Werke. Die Zahl 666 (drei Mal die Ziffer 6 hintereinander) sei das
Symbol für die Ganzheit der Welt in ihrer höchsten Entwicklung,
vollständiger Zusammenarbeit und letzter Kraftanstrengung.[10] K. H.

---

[6] O. RÜHLE, ἀριθμέω, ἀριθμός, *TWNT* I, Stuttgart 1933, 462.
[7] H. GUNKEL, *Schöpfung und Chaos in Urzeit und Endzeit*, Göttingen 1895, 368
Anm. 1.
[8] A. DEISSMANN, *Licht vom Osten*, Tübingen ⁴1923, 238.
[9] E. B. ALLO, *St. Jean, l'Apocalypse* (Et. B), Paris 1921, 194 "La Bête sera un
pouvoir incomplet".
[10] S. GREIJDANUS, *De Openbaring des Heeren aan Johannes*, (CNT(K)), Amsterdam
1925, 285.

MISKOTTE vertritt dieselbe Ansicht, wenn er schreibt, dass die zusammengeballte Energie der Völker es gerade nicht schafft.[11]

G. A. VAN DEN BERGH VAN EIJSINGA zählt die Ziffern 1 bis 36 zusammen und das ergibt eben 666 (1 + 2 + 3 + 4 + 5 + 6 + ... 36 = 666). Die Zahl 36 ist aber wiederum die Summe der Ziffern 1 bis 8 (1 + 2 + 3 + 4 + ... 8 = 36). Daraus sei zu folgern : 666 = 36 = 8. Acht sei die heilige Ogdoas, die Sophia der Valentinianer.[12] E. LOHMEIJER und G. BRAUMANN haben sich dieser Meinung angeschlossen.[13] Man braucht zwar Weisheit, die Weisheit selber ist aber nicht die konkrete Person, die die Apokalypse im Auge hat.

IRENÄUS, der, wie schon bemerkt, nicht mehr wusste, auf wen 666 zu beziehen war, nennt dennoch drei Namen : Τειταν Λατεινος Ευανθας.[14] Wie kommt er darauf? Interessant ist, was R. H. CHARLES über die Vermutung seines Freundes J. A. SMITH, eines Puzzle-Experten, erzählt. Die Zahl 666 könne theoretisch sehr viele Namen enthalten. Dies mache das Problem unlösbar. Es sei aber mit einem Vorbehalt zu rechnen. Lege man die Zahl in Hundertern, Zehnern und Einern auseinander und setzte man diese in drei Spalten nebeneinander, dann gebe es eine Einschränkung der Möglichkeiten und sei die Chiffre zu enträtseln.[15] Wenn wir dieses Verfahren anwenden, resultiert folgendes :

Τειταν

$$\tau = 300 \qquad \nu = 50 \qquad \varepsilon = 5$$
$$\frac{\tau = 300}{600} \qquad \frac{\iota = 10}{60} \qquad \frac{\alpha = 1}{6}$$

Λατεινος

$$\tau = 300 \qquad \nu = 50 \qquad \varepsilon = 5$$
$$\sigma = 200 \qquad \iota = 10 \qquad \alpha = 1$$
$$\frac{\lambda + o = 100}{600} \qquad \frac{}{60} \qquad \frac{}{6}$$

Ευανθας

$$\sigma = 200 \qquad \nu = 50 \qquad \varepsilon = 5$$
$$\frac{\upsilon = 400}{600} \qquad \frac{\theta + \alpha = 10}{60} \qquad \frac{\alpha = 1}{6}$$

[11] K. H. MISKOTTE, *Hoofdsom der Historie*, Nijkerk (1945), 325.

[12] G. A. VAN DEN BERGH VAN EIJSINGA, Die in der Apokalypse bekämpfte Gnosis, *ZNW* 13 (1912), 293-306.

[13] E. LOHMEIJER, *Die Offenbarung des Johannes* (HNT) Tübingen 1926. BRAUMANN, *KThW*, IX 603.

[14] IRENAUS, *Adversus Haereses*, V 30, 2.

[15] R. H. CHARLES, *The Revelation of St. John* (ICC), Edinburgh 1920, I 366.

Wie aufschlussreich diese Methode sein mag[16] — abgesehen von einigen wenigen Unstimmigkeiten! —,[17] können wir dennoch mit den von IRENÄUS genannten Namen nichts anfangen. Wer war Ευανθας? Für Kaiser Titus ist Τειταν doch wohl eine sonderbare Schreibung. Und Λατεινος ist kein Eigenname. Somit ist die Bedingung, dass 666 (616) die Zahl eines Menschen sein soll, nicht erfüllt.

Die meisten Kommentatoren sind darin einig, dass die Zahl 666 (616) auf die Legende des aus dem Totenreich wiederkehrenden Kaisers Nero anspielt. Auf hebräisch geschrieben ergibt נרון קסר (50 + 200 + 6 + 50) + (100 + 60 + 200) = 666. CHARLES wendet auch hier das "Drei-Spalten-Verfahren" an :

נרון קסר

נ + נ = 100		ס = 60		ו = 6
ר = 200				
ר = 200				
ק = 100				
600		60		6[18]

Da Nero(n) mit oder ohne n buchstabiert werden kann, wäre dies eine Erklärung der verschiedenen Lesarten 666 und 616. Das hebräische נ hat eben den Zahlenwert 50.

Gegen diese Lösung sind zwei Bedenken zu erheben.[19] Erstens ist in den beiden Wörtern das י ausgelassen. Bei M. JASTROW findet sich sowohl קֵיסָר als auch קֵסָר, aber nur נֵירוֹן.[20] DALMAN gibt die beiden Wörter nur mit י.[21] Zweitens ist es fraglich, ob die Legende des

---

[16] Diese Methode ist auch anwendbar zur Lösung der Frage, wer in den sibyllinischen Orakeln I 328 mit der Zahl 888 gemeint ist.

Ιησουσ

σ = 200	o = 70		η = 8
σ = 200	ι = 10		
υ = 400			
800	80		8

[17] λ + o in der ersten Spalte des Wortes Λατεινος. θ + α in der zweiten Spalte des Wortes Ευανθας.

[18] R. H. CHARLES, o.c., 367. Auch hier eine Unstimmigkeit : נ + נ aus der ersten Spalte gehört in die zweite, aber dann ist die Parallele 600 60 6 verschwunden.

[19] RÜHLE, o.c., 463.

[20] M. JASTROW, A Dictionary of the Targumin, the Talmud Babli and Yerushalmi and the Midrashic Literature, New York 1950.

[21] G. DALMAN, Aramäisches-Neuhebräisches Handwörterbuch zu Targum, Talmud und Midrasch, Frankfurt a.M. ²1922.

"Nero redivivus"[22] in den Tagen der Apokalypse schon bekannt war.

J. DE ZWAAN setzt voraus, dass die Zahl des Menschen den Kaiser Domitianus bezeichnet. Den Nachweis führt er wie folgt. Er transskribiert den vollständigen Namen des Kaisers Titus Flavius Domitianus Augustus auf hebräisch und dies ergibt als Zahlenwert: 94 + 192 + 179 + 151 = 616.[23] Leider ist nicht die hebräische Transskription gedruckt worden.[24] Diese kann, weil auch die einzelnen Additionen stimmen, wohl nicht anders lauten als

Titvs	טיטוס	$9 + 10 + 9 + 6 + 60 =$	94
Plavivs	פלויוס	$80 + 30 + 6 + 10 + 6 + 10 + 60 =$	192
Dmtinvs	דמטינוס	$4 + 40 + 9 + 10 + 50 + 6 + 60 =$	179
Avgvstvs	אוגוסטוס	$1 + 6 + 3 + 6 + 60 + 9 + 6 + 60 =$	151
			616

Dies alles stimmt aber doch nicht ganz. Bei einer Nachprüfung konnten wir uns dem Eindruck nicht entziehen, dass die von DE ZWAAN gebildete Transskription eine eigene Erfindung des Verfassers sei. Titus טי טוס ist zwar richtig. Flavius פלויוס konnten wir nicht belegen. Domitianus wird anders transskribiert, nämlich דומיטינוס[25] (Zahlenwert 195). Den Kaisertitel Augustus schreibt man אוגוסטוס (Zahlenwert 145) oder אגושטוס.[26] So ergibt sich die Summe 94 + 192 + 195 + 145 = 626.

RÜHLE stellt fest, dass von allen vorgeschlagenen Lösungsversuchen keiner ganz befriedigt. Es fragt sich, ob man gut daran tut, diesen Versuchen weitere anzureihen. Sie können ja doch nur den Charakter des Experimentierens tragen. Vielleicht werde die Stelle rein eschatologisch zu fassen sein, in dem Sinne, dass die Gläubigen erst am Ende der Tage das Geheimnis unmittelbar schauen werden.[27] Viele andere äusserten sich ebenfalls mehr oder weniger skeptisch.[28]

Wie dem auch sei, wir möchten doch noch auf eine Möglichkeit zur Lösung des Rätsels hinweisen. Aus Biographien der römischen Kaiser geht hervor, dass sie sich der Geheimschrift bedienten. Dann liessen

---

[22] Friedrich DUSTERDIECK, Die Offenbarung Johannis (KEK), Göttingen ²1865, 439-444. Th. ZAHN, Offenbarung des Johannes (KNT), Leipzig Erlangen 1924/25, 490ff.

[23] J. DE ZWAAN, De Openbaring van Johannes, Haarlem ²1929, 51.

[24] J. DE ZWAAN, transskribiert wie folgt: "Titvs Plavivs Dmtinvs Avgvstvs", o.c., 51

[25] M. JASTROW, o.c., sub voce.

[26] M. JASTROW, o.c., sub voce.

[27] O. RÜHLE, o.c., 464.

[28] "Misschien vindt op dit moment, dat ik dit schrijf, iemand de duizendste methode uit". A. J. VISSER, De Openbaring van Johannes (PNT), Nijkerk 1965, 141.

sie z.B. in einem Brief die Buchstaben des Alphabetes einen oder mehrere Plätze aufrücken. Kaiser Augustus änderte A in B, B in C, u.s.w.[29] Julius Caesar machte es neugierigen Leuten noch schwieriger. Er substituierte D pro A, E pro B, u.s.w.[30]

Auch die Juden kannten dieses Verfahren. Zur Meidung des Gottesnamens ersetzte man das Tetragramm יהוה durch כוזו[31] Von Königin Helena von Adiabene erwähnt der Talmud, dass sie für den Tempel einen goldenen Tisch hatte herstellen lassen, worauf die Verse Num. v 11, 12. באלף ביח geschrieben waren. D.h. man hatte alle Buchstaben einen Platz aufgeschoben um durch dieses "Sühneanathem" die Königin, eine Proselytin, nicht öffentlich zu blamieren.[32]

Nun haben wir diese Aufschiebung der Buchstaben angewandt auf den Namen des Kaisers Domitianus in hebräischer Transskription. Dazu diene Diagramm I. Auf der ersten Zeile ist das hebräische Alphabet anfangend mit א ausgeschrieben, auf der zweiten anfangend mit ב, auf der dritten mit ג, und so weiter bis zu ת. So enstand ein "chiffre carré", in der Geheimschriftlehre eine bekannte Erscheinung.[33] In Diagramm II haben wir die hebräischen Buchstaben durch ihren Zahlenwert ersetzt. Mittels der beiden Diagramme haben wir jedesmal die Summe der Zahlen von קיסַר דּוֹמִיטִינוּס berechnet. Das Fazit zeigt die tabellarische Übersicht. Es stellte sich heraus, dass nur bei א = ק die Zahl 616 zum vorschein kam. Dies wäre kaum zufällig. Wichtig dabei ist, dass ק der erste Buchstabe des Wortes קיסַר ist. Auch dies könnte kaum ein Zufall sein. Der Schlüssel zur Entzifferung des Rätsels ist also א = ק, קיסַר ← ק.[34]

Bei dieser Lösung ist nicht 666, sondern 616 für die ursprünglichere Lesart zu halten. Bekanntlich wollte IRENÄUS davon nichts

---

[29] "Quotiens autem per notas scribit, B pro A, C pro B ac deinceps eadem ratione sequentis litteras ponit; pro X autem duplex A". SUETONIUS, De Vita Caesarum, Liber II Divus Augustus 88, 3. Wir zitieren nach der französischen Ausgabe SUETONE, Vies des douze Césars (CUFr), Texte et Traduction, Tome I, Paris ²1954; Tome II, ²1957 Tome III, ²1957.

[30] "Extant et ad Ciceronem, item ad familiares domesticis de rebus, in quibus, si qua occultius perferenda erant, per notas scripsit, id est sic structo litterarum ordine, ut nullum verbum effici posset: quae si qui investigare et persequi velit, quartam elementorum litteram, id est D pro A et perinde reliquas commutet". SUETONIUS, o.c., Liber I Divus Julius 56, 8.

[31] Franz DORNSEIFF, Das Alphabet in Mystik und Magie, Leipzig-Berlin ²1925, 71.

[32] DORNSEIFF, o.c., 70/71.

[33] Op den Uitkijk (cf. n. 1), 37.

[34] Das gleiche Verfahren haben wir angewandt auf die griechische Transskription der beiden Wörter Kaiser Domitianus, dabei kam aber weder 666 noch 616 heraus.

wissen. Seiner Ansicht nach ist unbedingt auf 666 zu bestehen.[35] Er erklärt auch, wie die Lesart 616 entstand. Sie beruhe auf einem Schreibfehler. Ξ = 60 sei versehentlich zu I = 10 "ausgedehnt" worden.[36]

Dennoch spricht mehr dafür anzunehmen, dass 616 nachher in 666 abgeändert worden ist als umgekehrt. Es fällt auf, dass 666 genau die Zahl des griechischen Wortes θηριον in hebräischer Umschreibung aufweist. תריון = 400 + 200 + 10 + 6 + 50 = 666. Auch hier erweist sich die "Drei-Spalten-Methode" als ein geeignetes Hilfsmittel.

$$
\begin{array}{lll}
ת = 400 & י = 10 & ו = 6 \\
ר = 200 & נ = 50 & \\
\hline
600 & \hline 60 & \hline 6
\end{array}
$$

Diagramm I

```
ת ש ר ק צ פ ע ס נ מ ל כ י ט ח ז ו ה ד ג ב א
א ת ש ר ק צ פ ע ס נ מ ל כ י ט ח ז ו ה ד ג ב
ב א ת ש ר ק צ פ ע ס נ מ ל כ י ט ח ז ו ה ד ג
ג ב א ת ש ר ק צ פ ע ס נ מ ל כ י ט ח ז ו ה ד
ד ג ב א ת ש ר ק צ פ ע ס נ מ ל כ י ט ח ז ו ה
ה ד ג ב א ת ש ר ק צ פ ע ס נ מ ל כ י ט ח ז ו
ו ה ד ג ב א ת ש ר ק צ פ ע ס נ מ ל כ י ט ח ז
ז ו ה ד ג ב א ת ש ר ק צ פ ע ס נ מ ל כ י ט ח
ח ז ו ה ד ג ב א ת ש ר ק צ פ ע ס נ מ ל כ י ט
ט ח ז ו ה ד ג ב א ת ש ר ק צ פ ע ס נ מ ל כ י
י ט ח ז ו ה ד ג ב א ת ש ר ק צ פ ע ס נ מ ל כ
כ י ט ח ז ו ה ד ג ב א ת ש ר ק צ פ ע ס נ מ ל
ל כ י ט ח ז ו ה ד ג ב א ת ש ר ק צ פ ע ס נ מ
מ ל כ י ט ח ז ו ה ד ג ב א ת ש ר ק צ פ ע ס נ
נ מ ל כ י ט ח ז ו ה ד ג ב א ת ש ר ק צ פ ע ס
ס נ מ ל כ י ט ח ז ו ה ד ג ב א ת ש ר ק צ פ ע
ע ס נ מ ל כ י ט ח ז ו ה ד ג ב א ת ש ר ק צ פ
פ ע ס נ מ ל כ י ט ח ז ו ה ד ג ב א ת ש ר ק צ
צ פ ע ס נ מ ל כ י ט ח ז ו ה ד ג ב א ת ש ר ק
ק צ פ ע ס נ מ ל כ י ט ח ז ו ה ד ג ב א ת ש ר
ר ק צ פ ע ס נ מ ל כ י ט ח ז ו ה ד ג ב א ת ש
ש ר ק צ פ ע ס נ מ ל כ י ט ח ז ו ה ד ג ב א ת
```

---

[35] A. F. C. TISCHENDORF, *Novum Testamentum Graece* II, Leipzig 71859, 644 "ignoro quo modo erraverunt quidam sequentes idiotismum et medium frustrantes numerum nominis, quinquaginta numeros deducentes, pro sex decadis unam decadem volentes esse".

[36] "Hoc autem arbitror scriptorum peccatum fuisse, ut solet fieri, quoniam et per litteras numeri ponuntur, facile litteram Graecam quae sexaginta enuntiat numerum, in jota Graecorum litteram expansam", TISCHENDORF, *o.c.*, 644.

Diagramm II

ת	ש	ר	ק	צ	פ	ע	ס	נ	מ	ל	כ	י	ט	ח	ז	ו	ה	ד	ג	ב	א
400	300	200	100	90	80	70	60	50	40	30	20	10	9	8	7	6	5	4	3	2	1
1	400	300	200	100	90	80	70	60	50	40	30	20	10	9	8	7	6	5	4	3	2
2	1	400	300	200	100	90	80	70	60	50	40	30	20	10	9	8	7	6	5	4	3
3	2	1	400	300	200	100	90	80	70	60	50	40	30	20	10	9	8	7	6	5	4
4	3	2	1	400	300	200	100	90	80	70	60	50	40	30	20	10	9	8	7	6	5
5	4	3	2	1	400	300	200	100	90	80	70	60	50	40	30	20	10	9	8	7	6
6	5	4	3	2	1	400	300	200	100	90	80	70	60	50	40	30	20	10	9	8	7
7	6	5	4	3	2	1	400	300	200	100	90	80	70	60	50	40	30	20	10	9	8
8	7	6	5	4	3	2	1	400	300	200	100	90	80	70	60	50	40	30	20	10	9
9	8	7	6	5	4	3	2	1	400	300	200	100	90	80	70	60	50	40	30	20	10
10	9	8	7	6	5	4	3	2	1	400	300	200	100	90	80	70	60	50	40	30	20
20	10	9	8	7	6	5	4	3	2	1	400	300	200	100	90	80	70	60	50	40	30
30	20	10	9	8	7	6	5	4	3	2	1	400	300	200	100	90	80	70	60	50	40
40	30	20	10	9	8	7	6	5	4	3	2	1	400	300	200	100	90	80	70	60	50
50	40	30	20	10	9	8	7	6	5	4	3	2	1	400	300	200	100	90	80	70	60
60	50	40	30	20	10	9	8	7	6	5	4	3	2	1	400	300	200	100	90	80	70
70	60	50	40	30	20	10	9	8	7	6	5	4	3	2	1	400	300	200	100	90	80
80	70	60	50	40	30	20	10	9	8	7	6	5	4	3	2	1	400	300	200	100	90
90	80	70	60	50	40	30	20	10	9	8	7	6	5	4	3	2	1	400	300	200	100
100	90	80	70	60	50	40	30	20	10	9	8	7	6	5	4	3	2	1	400	300	200
200	100	90	80	70	60	50	40	30	20	10	9	8	7	6	5	4	3	2	1	400	300
300	200	100	90	80	70	60	50	40	30	20	10	9	8	7	6	5	4	3	2	1	400
ת	ש	ר	ק	צ	פ	ע	ס	נ	מ	ל	כ	י	ט	ח	ז	ו	ה	ד	ג	ב	א

	א = א	א = ב	א = ג	א = ד	א = ה	א = ו	א = ז	א = ח
ק	100	200	300	400	1	2	3	4
י	10	20	30	40	50	60	70	80
ס	60	70	80	90	100	200	300	400
ר	200	300	400	1	2	3	4	5
ד	4	5	6	7	8	9	10	20
ו	6	7	8	9	10	20	30	40
מ	40	50	60	70	80	90	100	200
י	10	20	30	40	50	60	70	80
ט	9	10	20	30	40	50	60	70
י	10	20	30	40	50	60	70	80
נ	50	60	70	80	90	100	200	300
ו	6	7	8	9	10	20	30	40
ס	60	70	80	90	100	200	300	400
	565	839	1122	906	591	874	1247	1719

א = ט	א = י	א = כ	א = ל	א = מ	א = נ	א = ס	א = ע
5	6	7	8	9	10	20	30
90	100	200	300	400	1	2	3
1	2	3	4	5	6	7	8
6	7	8	9	10	20	30	40
30	40	50	60	70	80	90	100
50	60	70	80	90	100	200	300
300	400	1	2	3	4	5	6
90	100	200	300	400	1	2	3
80	90	100	200	300	400	1	2
90	100	200	300	400	1	2	3
400	1	2	3	4	5	6	7
50	60	70	80	90	100	200	300
1	2	3	4	5	6	7	8
1193	968	914	1350	1786	734	572	810

א = פ	א = צ	א = ק	א = ר	א = ש	א = ת
40	50	60	70	80	90
4	5	6	7	8	9
9	10	20	30	40	50
50	60	70	80	90	100
200	300	400	1	2	3
400	1	2	3	4	5
7	8	9	10	20	30
4	5	6	7	8	9
3	4	5	6	7	8
4	5	6	7	8	9
8	9	10	20	30	40
400	1	2	3	4	5
9	10	20	30	40	50
1138	468	616	274	341	408

Da man nicht mehr wusste, wie die Zahl 616 zustandegekommen war, ist aller Wahrscheinlichkeit nach 616 mittels θηριον → תריון durch 666 berichtigt worden. Dann ist im buchstäblichen Sinne die Zahl des Menschen (616) von der Zahl des Tieres (666) verdrängt worden.

Voraussetzung unseres Lösungversuches ist, dass das Rätsel nur durch Kenntnis des Hebräischen zu bewältigen ist. Es gibt Gelehrte, die der Auffassung sind, dass nur das Griechische in Betracht kommen kann. Trägt der Christus nicht den Hoheitstitel "das A und das O"? Und ist dies nicht der erste und letzte Buchstabe im griechischen Alphabet?[37]

Dagegen ist einzuwenden, dass R. H. CHARLES aus seiner Untersuchung des Stils der Apokalypse gefolgert hat, dass man manchmal den griechischen Text ins Hebräische zu übertragen genötigt sei, damit der eigentliche Sinn entdeckt werden könne und die richtige Übersetzung ermöglicht werde.[38]

Ausserdem verrät die Benennung Alpha und Omega gerade einen alttestamentlichen und jüdischen Hintergrund. Der Ausdruck "der Erste und der Letzte" findet sich Jes. xliv 6. Die Rabbiner haben diese Stelle spekulativ verwendet. Die Erfüllung dieses Schriftwortes sei die Wahrheit (אֱמֶת), weil es aus א, dem ersten, מ, dem mittleren, ת, dem letzten Buchstaben des Alphabetes besteht. Die Alpha und Omega-Aussage geht, entgegen dem Septuaginta-Text dieses Wortes, auf den masoretischen Text zurück.[39]

Schliesslich war eben die hebräische Sprache sehr beliebt in Kreisen derjenigen, die sich mit Magie und Geheimschrift befassten.[40] Nur Eingeweihten war diese Sprache zugänglich und verständlich. Fremdsprachige Laute erhöhten die Wirkung der Zauberformel. Und das Geheimnis der Geheimschriften wurde um so grösser als Fremdworte zur Verfügung standen.

Zusammenfassend ist zu sagen, dass das Problem, das in Apok. xiii 17, 18 vorliegt, zu lösen ist, wenn man von der hebräischen Transskription der beiden Wörter Kaiser Domitianus, also קיסר דומיטינוס ausgeht. Sodann lässt man jeden dieser Buchstaben 18 Plätze aufrücken, also סוכע תבטוהויבכ. Zum Schluss zählt man den Zahlenwert

---

[37] z. B. DÜSTERDIECK, o.c., 458/59.

[38] "The Greek text needs at times to be translated in Hebrew in order to discover its meaning and render it correctly in English." CHARLES, o.c., Introduction CXLIV.

[39] KITTEL, KThW, I, 2/3. cf. LXX Jes. 44, 6 ἐγω πρωτος και ἐγω μετα ταυτα.

[40] DORNSEIFF, o.c., gibt passim viele Beispiele.

jedes Buchstabens zusammen. Dies ergibt (60 + 6 + 20 + 70) + (400 + 2 + 9 + 6 + 5 + 6 + 10 + 2 + 20) = 616.

Beweiskräftig ist diese Lösung aus dem Grunde, dass nur wenn man sich als Schlüssel der Formel א = ק (קֵיסָר ← ק) bedient, man aus der Zahl des Tieres, aus der Zahl des Menschen den Namen des Menschen herausfinden kann.

So ist dann am Ende das Ziel, das Karl MENNINGER kurz fasste: "Verzahlung der Schrift — Verschriftung der Zahl"[41] erreicht.

---

[41] Karl MENNINGER, *Zahlwort und Ziffer* II, Göttingen ²1958, 73.

INDEX OF AUTHORS

INDEX OF SUBJECTS

INDEX OF REFERENCES

A. OLD TESTAMENT

B. APOCRYPHA AND OTHER EARLY JEWISH LITERATURE

C. NEW TESTAMENT

D. GREEK AND ROMAN LITERATURE